THIN AIR

THIN AIR

ENCOUNTERS IN THE HIMALAYAS

SECOND EDITION

GREG CHILD

THE
MOUNTAINEERS

To Doctor Peter Thexton

 Published by
The Mountaineers
1001 SW Klickitat Way, Suite 201
Seattle, WA 98134

First edition 1988, second edition 1998

Published simultaneously in Great Britain by Cordee, 3a DeMontfort Street, Leicester, England, LE1 7HD

Manufactured in the United States of America

Maps by Jennifer Shontz
All photographs by the author unless otherwise noted
Cover design by Helen Cherullo
Book design and layout by Jennifer Shontz

Cover photograph by Greg Child
Frontispiece: *Greg Child on the west summit of Gasherbrum IV*

Library of Congress Cataloging-in-Publication Data
Child, Greg.
    Thin air: encounters in the Himalayas/Greg Child.—2nd ed.
        p.   cm.
    ISBN 0-89886-588-3
    1. Mountaineering—Himalaya Mountains. 2. Himalaya Mountains—Description and travel. I. Title.
GV199.44.H55C49 1998
796.52'2'095496—dc21   98-20400
                                                    CIP

Contents

Part Three
Gasherbrum IV, Karakoram, 1986

Foreword

It was in November of 1977 that I first met Greg Child. He had been lured to Great Britain by British climbers such as Guy Lee whom he had met in California's Yosemite Valley. It was Guy who told me of Greg's prowess on the short hard rock climbs and long big wall routes of the Valley. Since those early days he has gone on to climb the huge monolith of El Cap, which dominates Yosemite, a dozen times. Today two of the most difficult ascents of that 3,000 ft big wall—'Lost in America' and 'Aurora'—were pioneered by Greg with friends Randy Leavitt and Peter Mayfield.

Greg had begun his climbing career in much the same way as British climbers of the pre-mountain school/climbing wall generation. As a thirteen-year-old Sydney school boy, he and other local pupils such as Michael Law, Kim Carrigan and Chris Peisker went out onto local crags, picking up information here and there from older climbers and from a Boy Scouts Manual on how to climb. He served a long apprenticeship learning the hard way from his own experiences and mistakes, breaking a few bones in the process. Short day visits turned into weekend excursions and long holidays away from home to the now more popular climbing grounds such as Mount Arapiles and in the Blue Mountains. His 1977 Yosemite season was his first visit abroad.

Guy, like most other climbing friends, was busy working to pay off debts accrued while climbing during the summer so he recommended that Greg join me on a lecture tour in Scotland, making it obvious that I would enjoy Greg's company, not only for the climbing, but because Greg was a good lad. He was, for his age, remarkably self-contained and sure of himself, abrasive at times but with a twinkle in his eye and a huge disarming grin. I soon took to this warm-hearted Australian and thus our paths met and have continued to do so sporadically since on trips to the mountains.

So Greg set off with me to work the night, shifting place every day, but sometimes having days and nights off in between my lectures, to climb with me on snow and ice, and me with him on rock, such as at Dunkeld on a damp, greasy, steep and overhanging crag where he pulled me up and held me by my arms with trailing legs swinging about like a tadpole's tail, still recovering from a descent on the Ogre. What a fine rock climber: rock steady on an overhanging route of which he had no information and taking each move as it came, sure and certain of his ability. An hour later he was operating the projector in the Adam Smith Theatre,

Kirkaldy, with me to one side of the screen giving the audience my version of the truth with regard to our ascent of the South West Face of Everest, hyped up with a little lecturer's license.

It is a well known fact that if twelve climbers on an expedition, for example to the South West Face of Everest, were to write an expedition book and the reader was to read all twelve accounts, it would seem that the climbers had been on twelve different expeditions, at least in parts. Truth is seen to be relative to all the previous experiences of the seeker and each writer is seen to have a unique perception based upon where he was actually standing, his mood, his current interest, his imagination, his powers of observation and much else.

The mountains are seen to be a mirror reflecting our different and unique perceptions of them and all that happens on their flanks. The Indians of Greg's adopted North America knew this and more: 'The Universe is the mirror of the people . . . and each person is a mirror to every other person.' Every statement, observation and idea which Greg writes about here will surely affect his readers in different ways. In this book there is something for everyone, particularly as Greg is a keen observer with good recall of the situations in which he found himself, the mood of the mountains and time spent with the local people. I can vouch for this as I was with him on two out of the three expeditions he writes about here. He does not sit on the fence being all things to all men in an effort to please—he is far too honest a writer for that, but this is not to say he has not been influenced by other climbers and by the writings of such as Carlos Castaneda.

I have greatly appreciated the opportunity to relive these experiences. His book has evoked from me feelings of great sadness, but sometimes I have found myself laughing out loud at some of the incidents which happened on our trips: at others I have been gripped, holding back my breath, reliving the drama, strung out on a limb as we often were, battling with the elements and ourselves up in the thin air.

He is a powerful writer, concentrating in the main upon definite events rather than trying to achieve a grand Olympian view. In short he has expressed what he has seen rather than sought to impress us with that which he has not. All of us, I am sure, will be able to identify with Greg's story, through his early Himalayan apprenticeship, his coming of age on Lobsang Spire and Broad Peak and establishing himself as one of the up and coming great Himalayan mountaineers of the world with his ascent of Gasherbrum IV.

—*Doug Scott*
Cumbria, April 1988

Preface to the Second Edition

A decade has passed since *Thin Air* was first published in Britain and the United States, and I find it interesting now to reflect on the changes to my personal climbing landscape since I typed the last sentence of this book in 1988. Though I have never stopped climbing since the Himalayan expeditions to Shivling, Lobsang Spire, Broad Peak, and Gasherbrum IV, about which this book is concerned, I know that my attitudes toward climbing have changed. I cannot quite put my finger on exactly what those changes are, but in essence I no longer embrace the culture of risk taking as being integral to the climbing experience. That is not to say that I now condemn risk taking, or that I don't take risks on the climbs I have done in recent years or that I may do in the future. Risk is inherent to climbing; the two are indivisible. Embracing risk, however, is a different matter. I was younger when I wrote this book, and I was intrigued with the notion that I was involved in a "sport" in which the consequences of a mistake, or of just standing in the wrong place at the wrong moment, could be death. Being young, I romanticized that notion; treading the mental terrain of Himalayan climbing was exciting, cultish, meaningful—it still is. I would probably not do anything differently today on the climbs I describe in this book, but I think it is important to say that I now go about the psychological side of my climbing differently. And don't mistake these words as being an apology for risk: I am glad I did things as I did, and thought as I did on those climbs of the 1980s.

Perhaps these words would do better as an epilogue, but another purpose of this preface is to provide an update on the people and the climbs described herein. In view of my comments about risk, it seems important to note that several of the men who were my companions on the ascents in this book are no longer alive. During the course of this story, which spans four climbs made from 1981 to 1986, Doctor Peter Thexton will die from pulmonary edema on Broad Peak, Georges Bettembourg will be killed in a rock avalanche while crystal hunting in the French Alps, Don Whillans will die of a heart attack in his bed after riding his motorbike home from Chamonix, Roger Baxter-Jones will be killed by avalanche while guiding above the same French mountain town, and Alan Rouse will perish in a blizzard on K2.

In the years after this story ends, the mountains will claim two more good men, with whom I climbed on Gasherbrum IV. Geoff Radford was taken by an avalanche while back-country skiing in the hills behind his home in Anchorage,

Alaska, in 1992, and Doctor Stephen Risse was swept off the Canadian ice route *Slipstream* by a torrent of snow and ice, in 1993. Their passing left great gaps in the world for those who knew them.

As for the mountains, they freeze, they thaw. Broad Peak has seen many ascents since Pete and I set out for it in 1983, but the other mountains in this book have few visitors. I find it satisfying to be able to say that the second ascent of the route on Shivling that Georges Bettembourg, Doug Scott, Rick White, and I climbed was fifteen years coming. It was made by the strong American pair of Mark Richey and John Bouchard in 1996. Our route had repelled a lot of attempts before they came along. As for Lobsang Spire, no climbers have succeeded in repeating the route that Doug Scott, Pete Thexton and I authored on it. In fact that needle-sharp summit has not been visited since we three edged our backsides onto it in 1983. Nor has the Northwest Ridge of Gasherbrum IV been repeated, though in 1997 a group of Koreans climbed a new route on the treacherous West Face to make the only other ascent to the summit since our 1986 route put Tim Macartney Snape, Tom Hargis, and me on top—twenty-eight years after Walter Bonatti and Carlo Mauri made that Karakoram pyramid's first ascent.

Climbing mountains is a very odd way to spend one's days. Describing the experience is not easy. Of all the stories I have written about climbing over the years, this book is my truest shot at getting to the heart of the matter. For resuscitating *Thin Air,* and for encouraging and publishing my other two collections, *Mixed Emotions* and *Postcards from the Ledge,* I owe many thanks to Margaret Foster of The Mountaineers Books.

— *Greg Child*
Seattle 1998

Part One

Shivling, Garwhal Himalaya, 1981

The Simple Life

'Never write anything. You'll only regret it.'
—Don Whillans, 1983

Monsoon clouds spilling onto the Gangotri Glacier before the storm. Karchakund is the peak on the right.

Right: A map of Gangotri Glacier and its surrounds.

12

Parting Clouds

'Hey—wake up. The storm's blown over,' Rick says, nudging me with his elbow at first light.

We poke our heads out of the semi-collapsed tent and look along the final 1,500 ft of the East Pillar of Shivling. Wind howls high up on the mountain, whipping a snowplume from the summit. Mounds of new snow cling to the towers and cornices around us, breaking loose in flurries of powder as gusts cut across the mountain. In the north, the billowing monsoon clouds that had engulfed us ebb back along the Gangotri Glacier, retreating into the depths of the Himalayas.

'Is this the ninth or the tenth day?' I ask.

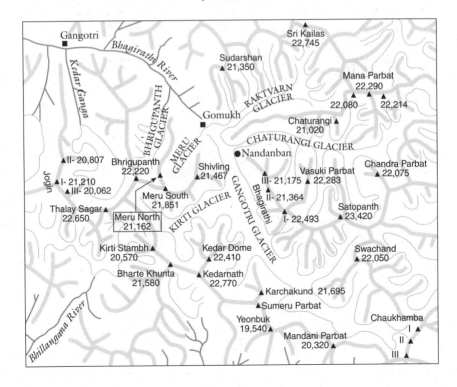

'Eleventh,' Rick replies.

For 24 hours the four of us have been pinned down by a blizzard on a knife-edged ridge crest, at 20,000 ft. Strong winds have pushed and shoved our tents on their tiny ledges, half-burying them with snow, twisting them into strange asymmetrical shapes.

Hearing our voices, Doug and Georges crawl out of their tent on a tiny ledge a few feet away. They look around at the rapidly clearing skies.

'Any food left?' calls Doug.

'Only a handful of cereal.'

'Save it. We've got a packet of soup. We'll eat them tonight.'

'So we're going on?' I ask with uncertainty.

Doug pauses. The four of us look down the 5,500 ft of cliffs, icefields, and narrow ridge crests we'd climbed up. Our food and gas are nearly gone: our supply of pitons and slings has dwindled. We probably didn't have enough supplies to go down even if we wanted to. To reverse the labyrinthine path we've followed would take days. We'd agreed the day before to press on to the summit, but we hash it out again. It's a decision not to be taken lightly.

'We've got no choice, kid,' Doug says, finally, echoing our previous analysis. 'We've got to go up and over the top. It's the only way we'll make it down.'

In front of us the final rock headwall rises to the summit. Beyond the summit lies the West Face of Shivling, down which we'll have to climb to the Meru Glacier. Questions rise in my thoughts: how many more days to reach the summit and descend? How long till we eat again? Will the weather hold, and if it doesn't, what then? I'd wanted to climb this mountain, but had I bargained for this? Had any of us? As we pack our sacks I feel the hollowness of my stomach. My throat is parched from dehydration: my fingertips numb and split from cold. My presence on the mountain feels like a dream.

In that dream, home seems far away. In its place is a single purpose: to keep moving. That's the only way back. Life has never been so simple.

On the northern skyline, the jagged peaks of Tibet sit under a clear, cold sky. As I look to the south I see a pall of dust and haze rising from the boiling Indian plains. Down there in the heat—yes, that's the real India. That's where the climb had started, where the dream had begun, in a baking city, two hundred and fifty miles away. . .

Delhi: a crazy quilt of humanity baking on the plains of northern India. The sunrise, a violet haze of smog and dust, the May air thick and steaming with the smell of compost and human sweat. Sitting on the pavement outside the airport, waiting for our transport, we watch the chaotic traffic and jostling crowds that spread for miles in every direction. Rupee sharks and beggars tug at our sleeves. A sacred cow with a garland of flowers around its neck plods along the street. Jet-lagged, bleary-eyed, and sweating, I close my eyes and picture our destination, the snow-capped mountains to the north. . . .

It's the spring of 1981, and my first Himalayan expedition. That things run altogether differently in India is already becoming apparent. I know of no restaurant

Georges Bettembourg, Don Whillans and an Indian boy at the Delhi airport. "Are you not too fat to be a climber?" asked the boy. "Perhaps," replied Whillans. "But by the time we're finished with our mountain, I'll be skinny and they'll be non-existent."

in the West where you can order a meal at three in the morning, roll out your bedsheet on the floor for the night, then crawl out from under the table at dawn and order breakfast, as we'd just done.

My daydream of mountains is interrupted as a small Indian boy seats himself between Don Whillans and me and strikes up a conversation in perfect English.

'Are you an expedition to the Himalaya?'

'Aye,' replies Whillans in his Lancashire drawl, lowering his dark glasses to the tip of his nose.

'But are you not too fat to be climbing mountains?'

'Perhaps,' returns Whillans, eyeballing the insolent kid. 'But by the time we're finished with our mountain, I'll be skinny and they'll be non-existent.'

In the weeks ahead, Don's prediction would prove clairvoyantly accurate.

We were eight climbers from different parts of the world, spanning ages from 21 to 48. I doubt we would all have ever met except for an idea to climb a mountain in the Garwhal Himalaya of India, in a cluster of steep granite peaks, called the Gangotri Region. Shivling is the name of that mountain. At 21,467 ft, it is not a big mountain. Not, at least, by Himalayan scale. But it is a beautiful mountain, as well defined as the Matterhorn.

Few westerners had visited the Gangotri since 1947, when a Swiss expedition climbed the first ascents of Satopanth and Kedarnath, two of the Gangotri's highest summits. The region was closed to foreigners by the Indian government, when the 'Inner Line', an area along the border of India and Chinese-occupied Tibet, was created after China's 1962 invasion of northern India. Since India's reopening of the Gangotri to the outside world in the late 1970s numerous expeditions had descended on the area, snatching such first ascents as Karchakund and the North Ridge of Shivling, to the Japanese; Brighupanth to an American women's expedition; and the slender Thelay Sagar to a British-American team.

I'd needed about half a second to make up my mind when the expedition's leader, the British mountaineer Doug Scott, asked me to join the team, even though his invitation mystified me. You see, I was no alpinist—in fact, I knew practically nothing about mountaineering. I was a rockclimber, accustomed to the sun-soaked cliffs of places like Yosemite Valley. My smattering of alpine experience was limited to a few moderate Scottish ice routes and a fruitless season in the Argentine stormpot of Patagonia. My ice tools were undulled and I was uneasy with tongue-tying terms like bergschrund, cwm, and couloir—words that I needed a dictionary to decipher and that I always mispronounced. Climbing a Himalayan peak was the wildest dream I could imagine, a quantum leap beyond any previous experience. Common sense told me that a Himalayan climber is the product of a long apprenticeship on smaller mountains. But a phrase of Kurt Vonnegut's, 'Strange suggestions to travel may be dancing lessons from God,' cast Doug's invitation in an irresistible light.

The team was a mixed bag. Rick White, a fellow Australian, Colin Downer, an Englishman, and Steve Sustad, an American, had climbed difficult alpine routes and big walls from Yosemite to the European Alps, but were novices to the Himalayas. Merv English, a New Zealander, was there for perhaps more complex reasons than to simply let a dream take shape. He was returning to the Himalayas after recovering from a disaster on the West Face of Amaa Dablam in Nepal, in which a massive avalanche had swept the face, killing one of his companions and seriously injuring Merv and his two surviving partners. I sensed there was much more to Merv's pilgrimage than the magnetic pull between mountains and climbers.

For Don Whillans, Doug Scott, and Georges Bettembourg this expedition was another to add to long Himalayan careers. Don, at 48, was climbing mountains before I was even born. A legendary British climber, he was best known for his first ascent of the South Face of Annapurna I with Dougal Haston in 1970, and for twice attempting Everest's Southwest Face. I'd read his biography, *Portrait of a Mountaineer*, in high school, and it had left me with an image of him as a hard-boiled and earthy individualist, blue-collar to the bone, quick-tempered, yet soft-hearted. A master of laconic wit, his philosophic gallows humor was a phenomenon of the British climbing scene and was extolled in climbers' pubs from Wales to Chamonix. It had moved Whillans' old climbing partner, Tom Patey, to write, 'Don has that rarest of gifts, the ability to condense a whole paragraph into a single, terse, uncompromising sentence. But there are also occasions when he can become almost lyrical in a macabre sort of way.' To be the brunt of a Whillans tale or joke was both painful and the greatest honour. It was like being cast in stone.

The Indian boy at the airport had made a pertinent observation in pointing out that Don was somewhat greater than thin. Once possessed of an athletic rock-gymnast's body, Don attributed his now Buddha-like physique to his wife Audrey's incomparable cooking, and perhaps a bit to his legendary capacity to put away beer. When asked why he drank so much, his fond reply was that he had 'a morbid fear of dehydration'.

Georges Bettembourg and Doug Scott were the helmsmen of the expedition, steering it on its course. Doug had been to the Himalayas fifteen times, and many of his trips were with Georges. Together they'd been to Kangchenjunga, Nuptse, Kusum Kanguru, and Makalu, all in light-weight style. Climbing mountains was a way of life for them both. They were as attuned to the tempo of mountain life as they were inured to the hazards of storm and cold and thin air.

I felt privy to a strange, slightly sinister world as I listened to their tales. My knowledge of their adventures was a measure for what I could expect on Shivling. Surely, I kept thinking, nothing on Shivling could be as horrific as their ordeal on Kangchenjunga, where, at 26,000 ft, Doug, Georges, and Pete Boardman had been perched precariously on the mountain's North Ridge when a hurricane-force wind had ripped their tiny tent to shreds around them. They had crawled down the ridge all night, fighting against the wind, pulling themselves forward with their ice axes, clawing at the snow ahead. Georges' pack had been blown off the mountain, and large rocks had flown about in the air. By the time they'd reached base camp, their faces were raw from the wind, their hands were numb from crawling down the mountain, and their minds and bodies utterly spent.

They spoke of this incident in awe. It had been terrible and terrifying, yet I gathered they wouldn't have missed it for anything. It was a shared experience, a lesson learned. Such tales evoked an image of Himalayan climbing in my mind—a picture of a person being strained through a metaphysical sieve, separating each component of the inner being, shedding all but the components essential to survival, then forcing those vital remnants to function at the limit. I'd had a taste of that singleness of purpose on the hardest freeclimbs I'd done, and on multi-day aid-climbs on the 3,000 ft walls of El Capitan. Such climbs had risk, but Himalayan climbing seemed to narrow the margin for error to the width of a tightrope.

Georges, a Frenchman, tempered this 'dark side' of his personality with an irrepressible impishness and a love of playing the clown. He moved through life the way he drove—beyond the speed limit. Appropriately, I first met Georges in his Volvo, in England, before leaving for India. We were running a last minute errand and Georges was at the wheel, speeding through the narrow streets of Nottingham, completely lost.

'My God, you're going the wrong way down a one-way street!' I screamed, seeing a head-on collision approaching.

'We're in a big 'urry, no?' he said nonchalantly, bouncing onto a footpath to dodge the oncoming car.

Boxes of expedition shopping spilled and flew weightlessly about the car as he threw the Volvo around a corner. The wind tossed Georges' dark curly hair with its occasional wisp of grey across the elegant lines of his face. He waved at a pretty girl. All I knew about Georges was that the blood of the Charlet family of mountain guides flowed in his veins, but I was about to learn more, quickly.

'What do you do for money?' he asked in his rapid-fire accent.

'I'm a sort of builder. A butcher really. Jack of all trades, master of none. And you—you're a guide—related to Georges and Armand Charlet—right?'

'*Ah, oui.* Georges—Pepe—was my grandfather; Armand *mon oncle.* I was almost a Charlet, but my mother married a Bettembourg. Too bad, eh? Charlet is a better name for a mountaineer. Yes, I make my living as a guide in Chamonix. I hunt crystals too. That's how I paid for this trip—I sold some crystals the night before I crossed the Channel. I' ave a fantasteec collection. My fluorine rose is one of the best ever found.'

Doug, on the other hand, was of a more serious nature, yet easily led into light-heartedness with comedians like Georges and Don around. Doug's fascination for the lands and people of the Himalayas ran deep. The cultures and religions of Asia attracted him as much as the mountains. Doug looked like a Himalayan climber—tall and powerful, with huge, nicotine-stained hands, scraggly shoulder-length hair, and a thick beard. Georges described him as a man 'designed to fell mountains'. Frequently introspective, Doug could sit quiet and distant for long periods, his eyes hidden behind his wire-rimmed glasses, his thoughts a mystery. Mountaineering was of great importance to him. More than a mere hobby it was a life's work, a pursuit with both a frontier and a barrier. For twenty years he had been exploring that frontier, pushing back its limits a little further each year. I wasn't sure what lay beyond that barrier except for cold, storm, and incredible physical and mental punishment. Without putting it into words, Doug assured me there was more, much more. It was one of those things that has to be experienced to be understood.

Our permit from the Indian Mountaineering Foundation was a unique one, *gratis* of peak fee, that gave us permission to climb new routes not only on Shivling, but on any of the Gangotri Region's peaks. In return for this arrangement, we were to impart our knowledge of modern climbing techniques to a group of young Indian mountaineers who were candidates for Indian expeditions to Everest and Nanda Devi. Doug had been rather vague with us about what this 'seminar' in the mountains would involve, because the IMF had been rather circumspect with him about what they wished us to do. All that really mattered to us was that we had permission to climb in the Gangotri.

Traversing the city by truck from the airport to the IMF on the outskirts of Delhi, we plunged into a swarm of bicycles, motor scooters, three-wheelers, aging Austin taxis, and Japanese pickups, all madly honking at each other. Lining the roads, rambling shanty-towns of mud-brick, cow dung, and tin, sweltered beside plush air-conditioned hotels. Families of beggars sifted through garbage within sight of Rolls-Royces and Mercedes Benz limousines. Crumbling fortresses of long dead empires stood beside billboards luridly depicting the latest in Hindi movie gore. Every gutter was stained crimson from the spit of betel nut chewers. For those of us who'd never visited the Third World the throng of beggars begging and trinket-sellers begging us to buy was an almost overwhelming mixture of color and craziness, at once beautiful and pitiful.

As we dusted ourselves off from the truck ride, outside the imposing black stone edifice of the IMF head office, an official greeted us and handed Doug a document stating the terms of the expedition. Doug read it. His face sank. He passed it to the rest of us.

The document was like a death at a birthday party. It began reasonably enough, stating that we were to climb new routes in the Gangotri and to conduct a seminar in modern climbing techniques for IMF mountaineers. But when we read that we were to split up and spend our time in India as advisors to eight Indian-led climbing teams, our jaws dropped, one incredulous face turned to another, and unprintable utterances emanated from the group. This plan bore no resemblance to any plan of ours, and the idea of leading a team of unproven Indian climbers with Everest-fever had the sound of an accident waiting to happen. It sounded even more dangerous than climbing with me. The document was my first glimpse of the devilish mechanics of third world bureaucracy, where Kafkaesque twists and turns to previously agreed-upon arrangements are the rule. While we'd been planning our own expedition among ourselves, the IMF had been designing one of their own. Suddenly, we were instructors, advisors, nursemaids. The perk that had saved us peak fees had become a Faustian pact.

'Bollocks to that,' grumbled the recalcitrant Whillans. 'That plan'll never fly.'

'What are we going to do then? I could have stayed home for this,' said Colin, a professional instructor at an outdoor education centre.

'Go home?' ventured Doug.

'No. Go see the man at the top,' corrected Whillans.

Crossing Delhi again by taxi, weaving through a sea of traffic, we sped toward the residence of Mr Sarin, the head of the IMF. At every traffic jam, outstretched palms thrust toward us. A baksheesh-demanding voice, as harsh and insistent as the caw of a crow, caught my ear. I turned to see a toothless, ragged, legless beggar coasting toward us on a trolley. Not even living in Berkeley, California had prepared me for such pitiful sights. I gave the beggar a few paise, the near-worthless coins that comprise the rupee. He scornfully tossed them away and demanded more.

'Not enough,' said the taxi driver, laughing.

At Mr Sarin's plush bungalow we sat in enormous cane chairs, sipping tea beneath a swishing ceiling fan. Beside Mr Satin sat Colonel Kholi, the famed Indian Everest climber and Sarin's fellow patriarch in the IMF. Our expedition lay in their hands. They listened to Doug explain our dilemma, accepting the blame for the misunderstanding (a vital letter must have been lost in the mail; Royal mail, that is), yet remaining adamant that we would not abide by such an arrangement. In India, an agreement's importance can be measured by the number of cups of tea it takes to settle it. In this case, many cups were drunk. Finally we reached an understanding. In the time it takes to strike out a few lines with a pencil, the terms of the expedition were modified. We'd conduct a week-long seminar, but after that we were free agents. Colonel Kholi shook our hands to clinch the deal, and told us floridly that 'All dreams will be realized'.

We were ready to set off on the 250-mile journey toward the source of the Bhagirathi River and the mountains of the Gangotri.

Moonrise over Bhagirathi III.

The Place Where the World Began

The Ganges River is a broad torrent that gouges a 1,678-mile swath through the arid plains of India, as it flows toward the Bay of Bengal. Its three tributaries—the Alakananda, the Mandakini, and the Bhagirathi—flow out of the Garwhal Himalaya. The Ganges is an unstoppable force that annually overflows its banks and perpetually devours the surrounding land. It is also a route of pilgrimage for hundreds of thousands of Hindus and many Buddhists. Hindus believe that by visiting the headwaters of the Ganges' tributaries, which are said to be the fonts of creation, and bathing in the waters that pour from the glaciers of the Himalaya, they will cleanse themselves of sin, in preparation for the next life.

On 9 May we set out by bus from Delhi, rumbling along beside the Ganges, and then the Bhagirathi River. We share the road with dozens of buses packed with pilgrims making their way toward the holy village of Gangotri, near the source of the Bhagirathi River. Along the way we pass through towns and villages, where we are channeled through narrow cobbled streets into snarls of crawling vehicles, market-shoppers, and bicycles. In these places, the hum of bartering fills bazaars cluttered with wares and choked with carts piled high with exotic fruits. Snippets of the daily life of India play out as we pass: Sari-clad women haggling with a shopkeeper over the price of his silk; a cart driver waggling a cucumber threateningly at a thieving monkey as it bounds away with a mango.

A character with the look of an extra from a Bogart movie leans against a three-wheeler taxi and watches our bus full of western faces creep through the bazaar. He wears a sweat-stained safari suit and curls his greasy moustache with his fingers. He slips over to our bus. 'Psst . . . You want sell?'

'Sell what?' I ask.

'Cigarettes, whisky, American dollars . . .'

'No. Sorry.'

He leans forward, his leer revealing his blackened, betel nut stained teeth, 'Then you want buy?'

On the outskirts of Dehra Dun we pass a team of elephants dragging logs for the building of a bridge, climb into the foothills of the Himalayas, and leave the dusty plains behind. The air becomes laced with wisps of cloud and the smell of rain, and the landscape alternates between terraced rice fields and wooded hillsides.

We drive all night on winding roads until, near dawn on 11 May, with the roar of the Bhagirathi in our ears once again, we arrive at the town of Uttarkashi—eighteen hours after setting out from Delhi. Despite the hour, busloads of pilgrims fill the muddy streets. People and baggage move on and off buses, some travellers having completed their pilgrimages, others just beginning. Kerosene lamps and street vendors' stoves cast an amber glow over the crowd. Whillans cracks open an eye, looks out the window, makes a pun about arriving in Utter Chaos, then goes back to sleep. As the sun rises, our bus pulls in to the Nehru Institute of Mountaineering.

Colonel Balwant Sandhu, the expedition's Liaison Officer and the Principal of the Institute, welcomes us to Uttarkashi. Balwant, accustomed to giving orders from his days as a commanding officer in the Sixth Indian Paratroop Battalion, snaps a command to his staff and cold bottles of Hindi Cola are brought to us. Balwant and Doug are old friends from the 1974 Anglo-Indian Changabang expedition. The plan is for Balwant and twenty Indian mountaineers to meet us in the mountains in a few days' time.

During our day spent in Uttarkashi we find that the town is surrounded by dense fields of marijuana. Doug enquires of Balwant if it is permissible to harvest some of the abundant crop, for the herb, suggests Doug, is reputed to help acclimatization. Balwant, formal, dignified, and pukka to the hilt, bristles.

'Come now, Doug,' he says politely. 'Are you aware that you are asking a colonel in the Indian Army to help you procure Ganja?'

On 13 May we jostle and shove our way onto another bus for the final sixty miles to the holy town of Gangotri. Pilgrims struggle with a desperate urgency to get on the bus. The fervour reminds me of that grim newsreel of the last helicopter to leave the American Embassy in Saigon. The driver gauges the capacity of the bus not by counting the passengers, but by weight: when the vehicle's springs are bottomed out, he closes the doors and guns the engine. As the bus lurches forward a woman thrusts two infants through the window, onto Georges' and my laps. We glance at one another and at the startled children, wondering if this is adoption, Indian style, and hope that the mother is among those limpeted to the outside of the bus.

'Have you and your wife any children?' asks Georges.

'No. We've been married only a few months. We've yet to cross that bridge. Do you have any children?'

'No. I am divorced. Expeditions did my marriage in.' He shrugs. 'But it's water under the bridge now.'

Georges googles French lullabies to the children until their mother takes them from us at a village stop a few miles down the road.

The road ahead is blasted into the side of the Bhagirathi River Gorge and is so narrow that when we pass other buses our wheels skim the rim of the gorge, knocking stones into the abyss. Mountaineering is about taking calculated risks, but the bus ride to Gangotri casts our fates completely to the whim of chance. It comes as no surprise to hear from a passenger that occasional bus loads of pilgrims meet untimely ends in the river below.

The first section of road ends at Harsil, a village of temples on a tongue of rugged forest cut with granite gorges, through which the river channels into a foaming jet. We hire local porters to carry our loads the few miles along foot trails and narrow bridges to Bhaironaghati, where, almost magically, the road begins again and other buses await.

Being part of an expedition to climb a mountain is a strange way to see the world. Most of the reading I'd done before landing in India concerned matters of who had climbed what in the Gangotri, rather than aspects of culture, leaving me unprepared for the sights surrounding the Bhagirathi arm of the Ganges. The sense of the ancient gains intensity with each mile along the river. For centuries pilgrims from every part of India and of every class and caste have padded along these trails, heading, like us, to Gomukh, at the snout of the Gangoth Glacier, twelve miles beyond Gangoth. Even the old and sick, carried in wicker chairs slung over the backs of hired porters, make the journey to bathe in the holy waters one last time before 'embracing the mystery'.

But it is the lean, wraith-like yogis that we see wandering the trail that capture our imaginations. Each time one of these mystics passes a tingling sensation rushes to my head. To them, the twentieth century is merely a rumour. Detached from the realities of cold, hunger, and material possessions, they have abandoned everything of their past lives, sometimes even name and identity. The yogis wear little more than loincloths. Wild eyed, with thick mops of curls on their heads and strange symbols daubed in paint on their brows, they wander the banks of the river, meditating and worshipping ancient deities. Some carry heavy iron tridents, identifying them as devotees of Shiva, the god of destruction and transformation. The points of the trident symbolize the three worlds of Shiva's reign: earth, heaven, and the underworld.

The first night out of Uttarkashi we camp beside the road, a few miles from Gangotri. As we sit by a fire, an old pilgrim dressed in faded orange robes approaches. He holds a brass pot of Ganges water in one hand and a stout walking stick in the other. Watching our cook prepare dinner he begins to giggle and shuffle about excitedly, till finally, his entire body quivering with bemusement, he erupts into a fountain of laughter, points to the pot of dahl, and declares 'Baba wants!'

Doug suggests to Baba that he might make himself useful by gathering an armful of firewood, in return for a meal. Baba shakes his head: he is not interested in working for a living, for tradition in India dictates that the holy wanderer, or saddhu, should be supported by those with wealth. By giving alms and sustenance to the saddhu, the man of means attains spiritual merit, for he, like the saddhu, is a traveller on the endless cycle of birth and death intrinsic to Hinduism. Both have the same goal: to attain enlightenment and escape the wheel of life—the holy by ascetic practices, the wealthy by doing good works. On a more temporal level, the system reminds us of England's dole, or of America's welfare system. Baba has paid into his system with years of prayer, and now he wants his plate of dahl. In a land where millions starve, Baba's system seems a good way of distributing the wealth, so we let him eat his fill without making him fetch wood.

The tease of fleas touring my sleeping bag wakes me early next morning. Doug is already up, sitting beside Baba on a log. Baba watches intently as Doug rummages through his bag of tapes, then plugs one into his cassette deck. The whining voice of Bob Dylan shatters the misty silence, closely followed by Baba's knee-slapping laughter. He'd probably never seen a tape deck, and certainly had never heard Dylan.

Roused by the music, Georges' head emerges from his sleeping bag. 'Ah. I see Doug 'as another guru. We 'ad one with us in Nepal last year, at Makalu base camp,' he says.

'Really? What did you learn from him?' I ask.

'Oh, nothing special. I wasn't interested in anything flashy, like levitating cross valleys. I just asked him if he could 'elp me from sinking through soft snow.'

A final bus ride and we reach Gangotri, a village of tin-walled shops and stone temples, flanked by steep orange cliffs that frame the three peaks of the Bhagirathi group, twenty miles distant. The streets of Gangotri teem with yogis, saddhus, sannyasins, gurus, pilgrims, yatras, and charlatans of every description. By night, the town resounds to chanting and the blare of copper horns from Hindu and Buddhist temples. By day, on the river-polished granite flats beside the thundering waterfall, yogis contort their bodies into rigorous yoga positions.

On 15 May we hire 45 Garwhali porters to carry our 2,700 lb of food and equipment into the mountains and leave Gangotri on foot, bound for Gomukh. The journey is short: one day to Gomukh, a second to base camp, but we hike slowly as we ascend from 11,000 ft to over 14,000 ft. The roar of the river fills the valley and the air is scented with wildflowers, herbs, and juniper trees. Above the

East meets West: Don Whillans, umbrella around his neck, and Colin Downer encounter a yogi along the pilgrim trail to Gangotri.

trail massive walls of glacier-carved granite flank the river. Some, like the over-hanging south face of Manda, stand sheer for 4,000 ft.

Whillans strolls along the trail, shielding himself occasionally from the beating sun with a red umbrella. As he rounds a bend on the path he confronts a gaunt, ash-covered yogi. It is a meeting of the worlds. They stare at each other for a moment, then the yogi raises his open palm for Whillans to drop a coin into. 'Hmm,' Whillans says. 'Are you on some sort of sponsored walk?' Whillans then grasps the yogi's hand firmly and shakes it, utterly confounding the Indian.

By evening we reach Gomukh where, according to Hindu legend, all life originated. Gomukh means 'the mouth of the cow', and refers to the ice-cave at the snout of the Gangotri Glacier from which gushes the swirling Bhagirathi. All round this holy place prayer flags flutter in the wind given off from the rushing river, and needles of stacked stones, constructed by pilgrims to symbolize Shiva, poke up from glacial debris. Towering above the rim of the glacier stand the Bhagiraure Peaks, their walls golden-brown in the afternoon light. Facing them stands Shivling, frozen blue after a passing spring storm. We set up camp, then hurry before dark to bathe in the river and thus complete our pilgrimage.

Doug stands up to his ankles in the frigid waters of Gomukh, naked. Colin and I sit waiting, ready to fling off our clothes and bathe in the sin-cleansing waters, but only after Doug has immersed himself, to prove it can be done. We'd decided to observe Hindu custom and reach base camp with a clean slate by washing away our sins. It seemed a logical move before facing the perils of a Himalayan climb, but, at over 12,000 ft, the water is cold and uninviting. Not bold enough to bathe, we paddle, dabbing the holy water behind our ears as if it is expensive cologne. Determined to do as the Hindus do, Doug clenches his teeth, crouches, splashes a handful of water across his back, then leaps out. It seems a poor show for someone who'd spent a night in 1975 sitting out near the summit of Everest.

I look upriver and see an old pilgrim calmly dipping himself up to his neck, motioning for us to do likewise. I kneel before the murky water and thrust my head into the river. The expiation leaves me with a splitting headache.

For India, the Ganges is not merely a river, but a symbol of creation and fertility, for without it, the plains would be a dusty, lifeless desert. The ancient people who first worshipped the Ganges were a mixture of indigenous tribes and the Aryan invaders who swept down from the passes of the Hindu Kush 3,200 years ago. To these ancestors of the modern India, reality was inextricably entwined with legend. Rivers, trees, and mountains were personified as celestial beings who created the world. The gods lived in the Himalayas, and the Ganges was their gift to man. The Ganges brought life-giving waters from the mountains, took away the ashes of the dead, and conferred spiritual immortality on its devotees by re-moving earthly sins. So coveted was Ganges water that vessels of it were traded throughout the land.

According to ancient legend, the Ganges was a celestial river encircling Mount Meru at the centre of the universe. The tale of the Ganges' descent to earth begins with the mythical King Sagara's wish for an heir. Sagara and his two wives lived below Mount Kailasa, a peak in Tibet, where they practised austerity and prayed for a son. Finally, their prayers were answered by Bhrigu, a great sage who dwelt in the mountain, and Sagara's wives bore many sons.

Thus Sagara's empire grew. To spread his greatness, Sagara undertook a ceremony of horse sacrifice, whereby a horse was turned loose to wander over the land and was then slaughtered at the year's end. All the territory over which the horse wandered would then become Sagara's. But the gods, fearing Sagara's empire would reach heaven, stole the horse. Sagara bid two of his sons to find it. They searched from the jungles to the underworld until, in an ashram by the sea, they found the horse with the sage Rishi Kapili. The sons abused the sage, and called him a thief. Rishi Kapili, disturbed from his meditations, became so enraged that he scorched the sons to ashes with his eyes, and decreed they would not attain heaven until the Ganges was brought down to purify their ashes. Upon hearing this, Sagara begged the river to descend, but he died without his wish being fulfilled, leaving the task to his heirs. When Bhagiratha became king he made his home in the Himalaya and began many years of penance and ascetic practice. This pleased the gods, who finally granted Sagara's wish.

The god Lord Shiva agreed to catch the river in his hair as it fell from heaven, lest its thunderous descent destroy the earth. Shiva, standing on top of a mountain, commanded the river to descend. The river-goddess Ganga grew angry with

Shivling from Tapovan Base Camp.
1. E Pillar (British/French/Australian, 1981).
2. NE Face (Italian, 1986).
3. N Ridge (Japanese, 1980).

Shiva and planned to sweep him away, but Shiva caught her in his densely matted hair and released the river into Lake Manasrovar in Tibet. The Ganges then flowed into seven streams. One of them, the Alakananda, followed King Bhagiratha across the plains and jungles of India to Rishi Kapili's ashram, where the river then graced the ashes of Sagara's sons, and lifted them to paradise. . .

On 17 May, two days out of Gangotri, the expedition crossed the Gangotri Glacier and reached Tapovan, a boulder studded meadow at 14,775 ft that would be our base camp for the next month. Above Tapovan, the precipitous flanks of Shivling rose to a conical summit, while the East Pillar and the South Ridge embraced Tapovan like two rocky arms. Between them stood the triangular South Face, as sheer as if a scalpel had cleaved through Shivling's ice and granite. Chiselling slowly away at it all, millenium by millenium, flowed the Gangotri Glacier, inching imperceptibly toward Gomukh.

Two days later Balwant arrived, leading a caravan of twenty Indian mountaineers, mostly students and public servants in their mid twenties; a doctor; the doctor's (missing) batman; Ratan Singh, the chief instructor at the Nehru Institute; several porters; and a menagerie of goats and chickens. No sooner did the caravan arrive than we set off for two days, combing the glacier and probing crevasses for the doctor's young batman, who had got lost on the Gangotri Glacier. No one, least of all the doctor, seemed bothered by this loss. Perhaps there is truth in the cliché that life is cheap in the Third World. But just as we wrote the boy off as dead, he appeared in base camp, looking very confused after wandering into a French expedition's base camp ten miles away, mistaking it for ours. The doctor, who'd had to rough it without his servant for two days, gave the boy a thorough tongue-lashing.

'Expedition doctors are either good doctors and lousy climbers, or lousy doctors and good climbers. This bloke is neither,' decreed Whillans.

We began the prescribed seminar by instructing the Indians in the rudiments of climbing, making use of the crags around Tapovan. We then divided into three groups, each with several Indian students, and set off up different glaciers for reconnaissance and acclimatization. Steve, Merv, Colin, and Balwant went up the Meru Glacier to reconnoitre the original route on the West Face of Shivling, first climbed by Indians in 1961; Doug, Don, and Georges headed along the Gangotri Glacier, towards Kedarnath Peak, to look at Shivling from the north and east; Rick and I, with Ratan, crossed the Gangotri to the meadow Nandanban and followed the Chaturangi Glacier toward Satopanth, where views of the South Face and East Pillar of Shivling would be best.

From Nandanban the landscape bristles with mountains. Almost every surrounding peak is named after some figure of Hindu mythology: Shivling, named for Shiva; Meru, the celestial mountain-temple; Bhrigupanth, named for the sage Bhrtigu; Kedarnath, a legendary place beside the Ganges; Sudarshan Parbat, the weapon of Lord Krishna; the Bhagirathi Peaks, named after the king whose devotion brought the Ganges down from heaven; and Vasuki Parbat, the name of a serpent of the underworld.

But the East Pillar of Shivling, a steeply angled granite prow rising to a summit 7,000 ft above Tapovan, dominated the panorama around us. The pillar appeared to incorporate every type of alpine climbing, with rock walls, narrow ridgecrests, and ice smears plastering the final headwall. It was a magnificent sight, hard to stop staring at and hard to imagine in terms of difficulty. The scale was as if Yosemite Valley's El Capitan had been stacked upon itself twice, dumped on top of Northwest USA's Mt Rainier, then crowned with an icy cone.

Clouds rolled along the Gangotri Glacier behind us as Rick, Ratan, six Indian mountaineers, and I hiked up the Chaturangi Glacier to a campsite at 17,000 ft, beneath Bhagirathi II. None of us were yet adjusted to the altitude, and we felt it pressing at our foreheads and squeezing our lungs. Even so, the Indian mountaineers insisted on carrying enormous packs laden with massive steel frypans, bundles of firewood, and blunt ice axes not even fit for gardening. Indian mountaineering was still light years from lightweight alpinism.

By nightfall they were exhausted, but at dawn Rick and I awakened to the jangling of equipment. When we peeked out of the tent Ratan and his team announced their plan to march to the 21,365 ft summit of Bhagirathi II. Sleepy and confused, Rick and I observed their preparations, wondering when this premature plan had been hatched, and how we'd missed hearing about it.

As one of the Indians lashed an antiquated set of crampons to his feet with string, Ratan held up a very old and unsafe looking length of rope and declared, 'We go alpine-style!' With only a few days of low altitude acclimatization, none of us were physically prepared to go high. It was clear that if they went onto the icy East Face of Bhagirathi II they would never return. Since neither Rick nor I had ever been to a Himalayan summit, and Ratan had climbed 25,645 ft Nanda Devi, with the Japanese, dissuading him from his plan was not easy. Yet we convinced the Indians of their folly and they gave up their plan. Ratan, his pride bruised, sat facing a boulder, sulking.

By late May, and after several acclimatization forays to 18,000 ft, it came time to think seriously about climbing a mountain. With three to four weeks before the monsoon, we began to look at our options. Acclimatization rates divided us into two groups, as each of us adapted to the restraints of altitude a little differently.

Accordingly, Doug, Georges, Rick, and I grouped together and looked to the impeccable granite of Shivling. Before us stood three possibilities: the unclimbed East Pillar, the South Face, also unclimbed, and the Japanese South Ridge. Other possibilities existed on the north side, where Shivling was visible as a twin-summited peak, but none were more attractive or more accessible than the three above Tapovan. Finally, we chose the East Pillar as our route, ruling out the South Face because of danger from collapsing seracs that frequently peel off the summit and sweep the face, and also rejecting the route of the Japanese, because it had already been climbed.

No climbers had ever set foot on the East Pillar. It was a complete unknown. For days we studied it through binoculars, trying to estimate distances between bivouac sites, and whether ledges were Cadillac-sized or mere foot ledges. From our observations, the pillar fell into five distinct stages. The first began at 16,500 ft, with a knife-edged, horizontal ridge some 2,000 ft long. The second stage was short—a 300 ft vertical wall leading to a helmet-shaped dome where, at about 18,100 ft, a good bivouac looked likely. The third stage was the longest: a sweep of granite nearly 2,000 ft long, vertical in places, broken by no obvious ledges. From Tapovan, it was difficult to tell whether the climbing on this section would be fast and friendly jam-cracks or slow and troublesome aid climbing. Whatever the case, it appeared unlikely we'd be able to cover such a long stretch of technical climbing in any time less than two days. The fourth stage, another intricate and jagged horizontal knife-edge at 19,800 ft, studded with rock towers and corniced throughout, was the most foreboding. The intimidating feature of this stage was not only technical difficulty, but that once beyond it and into the final stage of the climb, retreat would be awkward in the event of storm or accident. The fifth and final stage began at 20,250 ft and took the 1,200 ft headwall to the summit ice cone. This section also had a daunting appearance, smeared with licks and runnels of ice that would demand steep mixed climbing.

The climb up would be difficult and committing: descent from the summit almost as problematic. To get down we had two options: rappel the route we climbed, or traverse Shivling and descend the original route on the West Face. The second alternative seemed more feasible, not only because we knew it to be an easier route, climbed by Indian and Japanese expeditions, but because Don, Steve, Merv, and Colin had elected to climb it, and their tracks would probably mark the way. Timewise, the sum of all these pieces added to an estimated ten days.

The 'big wall' element to the route would necessitate masses of equipment and heavy loads. Pitons, Friends, chocks, fifty carabiners, and many slings would be needed for the rock; ice tools, crampons, and ice screws for the mixed ground. We would also carry two two-man tents, down sleeping bags and jackets, Gore-Tex suits, two stoves, fifteen gas cylinders, and ten days' food. As the weight began to add up it became clear that to climb Shivling would be a major exercise in logistics. The problem with long rock climbs in the Himalayas is that the weight of the equipment and the slow nature of technical climbing at high altitude forces the climber into the vicious circle of load hauling. The longer and more difficult the route, the more provisions are needed—but the more one takes, the slower is the pace.

So, to economize on weight, we chose to take the bare minimum to do the job, trimming personal gear wherever possible, leaving behind anything that might conceivably be termed unessential. Even so, we found we had six loads, each weighing fifty pounds! To cope with the logistics of four climbers shuttling six loads up the 7,000 ft from base camp to the summit, we took five ropes—enough to enable constant forward progress while two of us led, yet still allow the other two to carry loads to the high point.

'Zis is looking very 'eavy for alpine style,' said Georges, shaking his head at the mound of gear. His climbs in the Himalayas had been much lighter, even though some of the mountains were 5,000 ft taller. Yet there was little comparison between the terrain on an 8,000 metre peak and the East Pillar of Shivling. The usual routes on the 8,000ers are snow and ice climbs of moderate difficulty, on which one needs only ice axes and a few ice-screws and pitons. The main difficulty on big peaks is high altitude and distance, so one carries as little as possible. To climb the steep rock of Shivling, we had no choice but to take heavy loads.

The thought of what we were about to embark on loomed in my mind. I had no idea if I was capable of acclimatizing to high elevations, or of my endurance for the dozens of pitches we would encounter. Rick sat massaging his ankle, perhaps feeling the same concerns. He had the added worry of a recently healed broken leg, caused by a rockclimbing fall in Australia. It was still weak and had given out on the trail a couple of times already, but if it concerned him he didn't admit it. Stoicism was in Rick's nature.

As I fiddled, adjusting my crampons to my boots, I told myself that my knowledge of alpine climbing could fit on the head of a pin. Compared to Doug and Georges, I was only impersonating an alpinist. Rick kept telling me not to worry. As a businessman he was accustomed to taking gambles, to getting into situations over his head. A few years before, he'd started a part-time business selling climbing equipment from out of his garage. Now he operated sports stores in every major city in Australia and ran a manufacturing plant in Brisbane. Risks, for Rick, had always paid off. But that was of little consolation to me. Tropical Queensland is better known for raising pineapples than alpinists, and ice is something they use in his hometown to chill beer. The first time he'd seen snow, during a spring snowstorm on El Capitan, with Doug, Rick had thought it was pollen. How we managed to team up with two of the most experienced Himalayan climbers of the day is a mystery I'll never fathom.

The cook's assistant brought us tea as evening gathered. The summit ice cliffs of Shivling took on a diamond brightness. As we took turns using the last spoon in the kitchen to stir our tea, Rick tapped a tea-drop off against the rim of his cup. Like so many before it, it broke and plopped into the tea.

'Oh, spoon!' moaned the cook's assistant, throwing his hands to the sky. Lachi, the cook, dashed out of the kitchen tent looking as if there'd been a death in his family.

'Spooon, spooon,' went up the cry. A crippling laughter beset us as, having broken twenty spoons in two weeks, we realized we were spoonless before the mountain. The Indian-made utensils couldn't take the pace of our eating, often snapping inside our mouths or collapsing under the weight of a load of porridge.

'Jerry-built garbage,' muttered Rick, waving the remains in front of Lachi's eyes, as if Lachi were responsible. 'How's a man supposed to eat around here now?'

Eating on this expedition was a major problem for Rick. Raised on a western fare of steak and potatoes, he found the staples of India—dahl and chapati—totally inedible. Lachi was Rick's gastronomic nemesis and the scapegoat for everything that went wrong. Rick was the scourge of the kitchen, skulking about and casting aspersions at Lachi's efforts to fry eggs, cook porridge, or make a stew. It was true that Lachi's eggs tasted like deep fried leather, his porridge like glue, and his stews were volcanicly spiced, but, to the Indian, that is good cooking.

'I need white man's food! Not this slop!' Rick vented his frustration by kicking the expedition chicken as Lachi delivered a pot of dahl and a foot-high plate of

Rick White contemplates the East Pillar of Shivling while trekking across Nandanban meadow.

chapatis. Don, meanwhile, sat staring contemplatively up at Shivling. He balanced a cigarette on his lips and lit it.

'What, exactly, does Shivling mean?' he asked Balwant.

'It's a fertility symbol. It refers to Lord Shiva's phallus—his "linga", or organ of generation.'

'Is that so? Well, let's hope his lordship doesn't get brewer's droop and fall down on us during the night,' replied Don.

Scorched Eyebrows

The 1979 Japanese route on the South Ridge of Shivling had been climbed over a 47-day siege, using 7,000 ft of fixed rope, and involving many climbers. On the neighbouring East Pillar, we planned to make a climb of similar difficulty, but instead of laying siege to the mountain like the Japanese, we hoped to climb Shivling by alpine-style tactics, the four of us climbing from the ground to the summit in a single self-contained push.

Siege climbing has been the traditional tactic of many ascents throughout the Himalayas. It is a long war of attrition against a mountain. At its worst, the siege can be a monstrous operation. For instance, in 1974 an Italian expedition repeated the original route on Everest using 2,000 porters to base camp and a hundred Sherpas and 64 climbers on the mountain. Involvement in operations of such scale is like living on a battleship, where the crew fore never meet the crew aft. The justification of siege climbing is that safety lies in numbers; with alpine style safety lies in speed. On a heavyweight siege a climber might have to carry loads back and forth beneath a hazardous serac or across a treacherous slope many times. On the other hand, on a carefully planned alpine-style ascent, the climber crosses such sections once on the ascent, and perhaps once on the descent.

Reinhold Messner's three-day alpine-style solo ascent of Everest's North Ridge, climbed without supplementary oxygen during the monsoon of 1980, is one of the pivotal events of climbing history. In the mountaineering psyche nothing could be more pure than to climb Everest alone. Doug's own involvement with huge sieges like Everest's South West Face, and his subsequent lightweight expeditions to 8,000 metre peaks, had led him to conclusions similar to Messner's: that to climb by 'fair means' (as Messner described lightweight alpine-style climbing) was the natural way to climb a mountain. The peaks of the Gangotri Range, being between 21–23,000 ft high, were the perfect size for alpine-style ascents.

On 29 May Doug, Georges, Rick and I set off toward the East Pillar. To get our six loads to the foot of the climb, two porters accompany us. Before leaving, we split a coconut, a ceremony, according to Doug, performed before leaving on long sea voyages. The coconut is rotten. We joke about that being an omen.

From base camp we walk across easy snowfields to the foot of the ridge. All the way, Doug and the two Garwhali porters chain-smoke *bidis,* the native cigarette, and cough at the thinning air. At 16,500 ft we camp, and the porters scurry back to base camp as the sun drops behind the mountain tops.

Next morning we climb a few hundred feet higher and gain our first view along the horizontal ridge. For 2,000 ft it remains knife-edged, corniced, and problematic, with few bivouac sites—a deflating start to the climb. Rising from the end of the knife-edge is the East Pillar itself, adorned with turrets and pinnacles like a medieval fortress. Higher, the twin summits of Shivling seem a hellish distance away.

A sudden ripping sound a thousand feet above makes us look up. Out of nowhere appear a pair of whirlwinds. Caused by the straining of wind through the turrets of the pillar, they tear at the ice and rock, scouring and feeding on the mountain like a living organism. They reach a frenetic pitch, then subside as suddenly as they appeared, dropping lumps of ice tinkling down the walls. I'd seen a tornado in Wyoming once, but a twister on a Himalayan peak is something entirely unexpected. Rick looks at me with eyes that seem to say 'What the hell have we got ourselves into?' Contemplating what would happen if we were caught in one, I remember the Whillans euphemism for catastrophic events: 'End of story,' he'd say.

We climb along the knife-edge for three pitches, fixing ropes behind us, but seeing the approach of storm clouds, we dump our loads on a flat spot and return to the start of the ridge to bivouac in a notch between two fangs of rock. At dawn it's snowing heavily. We lie in our tents, reprieved from the climb until some sign of clearing comes. By late afternoon the storm has passed, but another storm front is blowing in fast.

'Let's get out of here and give the ridge a couple of days to clear,' calls Doug from his and Georges' tent.

Moving for the first time in twenty hours we gear up for the descent. Rick flops about weakly, fumbling with boot laces and the zippers of his windsuit.

'Bloody boots,' he mutters in a slurred voice. His expression is puzzled, as if he is unsure of where he is or what he is doing. Though I'd been laying beside him all day, it is only then that I realize the effects of altitude are responsible for his quietness and lethargy. I tie his laces and help him out of the tent. He sways like a drunk.

'Rick is pretty spaced out,' I call to Doug, who is already starting down. 'Keep an eye on him.'

We follow Doug's and Georges' tracks down the steep slope, then take off on our backsides, sliding like otters in the snow, racing each other and laughing. The four of us funnel into one chute, bunch up together like a human train, and accelerate toward Tapovan. Rick is still groggy but seems to have the hang of falling down the mountain well under control. We descend to base camp in two hours. Looking back towards our tents on the ridge, we see Shivling wearing a heavy layer of storm. Rick staggers into his tent and collapses, watched by Whillans.

'That lad is going to suffer,' he says to Doug. It's another of those Whillans pronouncements that I take as prophecy.

The West Face team had fared no better than we had. Penned up in the huge cul-de-sac of the Meru Glacier, with reflective walls of smooth granite and ice all

Day 1 on Shivling's East Pillar: Doug Scott carries a load along the knife-edge ridge. The summit is more than 50 pitches away.

around them, temperatures had been intolerably hot, turning the falling snow into rain. Colin had been plagued by debilitating headaches, triggered by the altitude. But weather and acclimatization had not been their only problem.

Colin, Merv, and Steve sat talking with Doug about the difficulty of communicating with Ratan, who, along with Balwant, had joined them. Because of Ratan's rudimentary English, in order to tell him anything it must go through Balwant for translation. Even ordering Ratan out of the way of falling rocks requires this roundabout procedure.

'And old Don—he won't carry a load,' says Merv. 'He fills his bloody pack with his sleeping bag. If you ask him to carry something he says "It's not the weight—it's where to put it".'

'Well, Don's getting on in years. He had trouble with his knees,' counters Doug in defence of his canny old friend. Don had long ago decided that his seniority excused him from carrying heavy loads.

'And he wouldn't brew you a cup of tea if your life depended on it. He expects us to do all the bloody cooking,' snarls Colin, fiddling with a Rubik's Cube. He grows frustrated with the thing and tosses it on the ground. Colin revelled in his fiery impatience to achieve results quickly. Whether trying to achieve a full body tan or to acclimatize as fast as the rest of us the results were always of the same order: sunburnt genitals or headaches.

Doug smiles at Colin's complaint.

'Ah, well I warned you about Don and cooking before we left. It's his generation, his upbringing. There are certain things he simply won't do, and cooking is one of them. He thinks it's women's work, or something like that. On Everest in '72 I spent a week in a tent with him, cooking all his meals. I finally told him "Don, I'm not your mother." He just sat there and said "You're not one of those types that moans about a bit of cookin', are you?".'

But if Don's idiosyncracies flustered his team mates, his humour galvanizes us all. At midnight a yell from his tent rouses the camp.

'Hey! Wake up! I just realized it's me fiftieth bloody birthday!'

As a full moon rose over the Bhagirathis, we gather about in the cold, passing round a bottle of Irish whisky. It wasn't really his fiftieth birthday—it was his forty-eighth—but he liked the well rounded half century figure and claimed it as his own. Soon Don's tales begin to flow. There was the tale from the Everest Expedition of 1972, where a member of the German contingent, on hearing that Germany had beaten Britain at soccer in the world cup, proclaimed to Don, 'Ha, it seems ve haft beaten you at your national game.'

'Aye,' replied Don, 'and we've beaten you at your national game—twice.'

The night wears on, the bottle grows empty, and the stars above began to sway. Don harks back to Annapurna I:

'After we came down from the summit, somewhere on the way out, we had a victory celebration. I don't remember how many bottles of whisky we polished off, but it was quite a few. The Sherpas watched us get wilder and wilder. Dougal disappeared for a while—he'd fallen in a latrine and couldn't get out. One by one we passed out. By morning we were sick as dogs—a terrible sight. The Sherpas loaded us onto a tarpaulin, dragged the entire expedition to the river, and dumped us in it. As I woke up I remember one of the Sherpas shaking his head at me in disgust, saying "Sahibs like buffalo".'

In the days awaiting the storm to clear the mountains we spent our time exploring the boulders and lakes of the meadow and visiting the hermits who lived in cave-dwellings burrowed into the moraine about Tapovan. On a windy afternoon, we found the most reclusive of the old hermits sitting crosslegged outside his hobbit-like dwelling, reading a thick tome of Buddhist scriptures. Seeing us, he struck a studious pose, motioned for us to sit with him, and began to chant a blessing for us.

'He looks like a Tibetan monk. I bet he could tell a few tales,' said Doug. We sat as the monk chanted.

Though Tibet lies only thirty kilometres away, the monk's presence at Tapovan was hardly by choice; some 100,000 Tibetans live in exile in communities in India and Nepal, driven out by the Chinese invasion of 1950. We could only speculate how the old man had come to live in Tapovan. Whatever his story, it was but a small part of the tragedy of Tibet. Between 1950 and 1973 an estimated one million Tibetans died as a result of the Chinese Cultural Revolution, and famine due to natural disasters and internal conflict. Tibetan Buddhism and society all but disappeared without any nation lifting a finger to stop its destruction.

Few countries recognized Tibet as an autonomous nation, although it had existed for 2,000 years and had developed a sophisticated culture and government based on Buddhism. Aloof on a plateau at 15,000 ft, Tibet felt shielded by the natural defences of the Himalayas to the south, and deserts, gorges, and dense forests in the north. It was a feudal society of peasants, nomads, traders, and aristocrats; of ancient trade routes, and towering monasteries where a populous priesthood studied religion, philosophy, and science. And ruling it all was the god-king, the Dalai Lama.

Tibet's history encouraged its isolation—Genghis Khan's hordes had invaded Tibet in the eleventh century; the Nepalese and the Gurkhas in the sixteenth; China's Manchu dynasty in the early twentieth. Even the British had entered the capital of Lhasa under arms, in 1904, to secure a trade treaty to block Russian expansion near India. But the death-knell to the isolated kingdom came in 1950, from communist China.

As civil war and communist infiltration eroded the government in Lhasa, comets, earthquake, and other omens warned Tibet's State Oracle and the high lamas that war was imminent. In 1950 Radio Peking broadcast China's claims over Tibet. Soon after, China's massive army and air force crushed Tibet's army of 8,500 men defending the Sino-Tibetan border. Lhasa's pleas to the United Nations got little response. Fearful of Chinese aggression, India only gave sanctuary to Tibetan refugees; America supplied aid to Tibetan freedom fighters, but would not intervene directly.

From 1950 to 1959 Chinese occupation forces within Tibet swelled. Under the Chinese, the Buddhist clergy was dismantled, property and labour were collectivized, and the land colonized with Han Chinese settlers. Tibetan guerilla resistance was relentless, yet ultimately futile. Thousands of Tibetan refugees poured across the high passes of the Himalaya into Nepal and India. Even the Dalai Lama fled to India in 1959, to form a government in exile. Cold, sickness, starvation and months of strafing by Chinese troops and aircraft decimated the ranks of refugees. Groups that set out 4,000 strong would arrive in Nepal and India with a few hundred survivors.

The final blow to Tibetan society began in 1966, with the Chinese Cultural Revolution. Mao's plan to rapidly communize China by using class warfare to level society to a proletarian whole reached Lhasa. Tibet's ancient ways were seen as counterrevolutionary and the destruction of everything Tibetan began.

Religion was outlawed. Tibet's 6,524 monasteries were gutted, many were dynamited. Chinese government teams looted temples, melting down gold artifacts and selling priceless artworks on the Hong Kong antique market. Mobs of Chinese and Tibetan Red Guards burned ancient scriptures and smashed religious statues. Tibetan artworks were painted over and prayer flags replaced with revolutionary banners. Even the Tibetan language was banned, replaced with a patois of Chinese and Tibetan. Out of 600,000 monks and 4,000 incarnate lamas only 7,000 monks and a few hundred lamas escaped the purge. Those who did not flee were defrocked, imprisoned, or executed. Everywhere in Tibet, public executions and torture were used to pacify the population. In the countryside, the nomads and farmers were forcibly collectivized. Despite a famine throughout Tibet, grain produced by communes was stockpiled by the Chinese army in preparation for the war China felt was imminent with India. When Lhasa resisted these atrocities the city became a battlefield.

We would never know what had brought the old monk to Tapovan. I thought again of what a strangely monomanic way climbing was to see the world. As the monk finished chanting he pointed toward Shivling.

'Yes,' said Georges, 'we try again tomorrow.'

On the morning of 3 June we are back on the East Pillar, at 17,000 ft. The thud of our double-boots against snow-covered granite fills the clear, calm air. Doug and Georges lead, securing ropes, while Rick and I shuttle the loads in two stages, bringing the ropes up behind us. An avalanche of powder sloughs off the summit of Shivling, rumbles down the North Face, then dissipates in a mist-like cloud. Though Doug and Georges are vastly more experienced mountaineers than Rick or I, we share one thing in common: the ability to totally under-estimate the difficulty and time the 2,000 ft ridge will take to climb. Our estimate from Tapovan gave us a day and a half to climb the ridge, but for two days we climb over and around pinnacles, sidle blade-like crests, and chop down cornices blocking our path. And, as evening approaches on the second day, we are still hundreds of feet away from the pillar. We scrabble about before the afternoon snowstorm, trying to fashion a bivouac platform on the narrow ridge crest but there is room to accommodate only two-thirds of each tent. One of us sleeps part-on, part-off the ledge, suspended over a void by the fabric of the tent. So airy is our position, that we sleep in our climbing harnesses, clipped to a piton by a length of rope.

The remains of the tent the morning after our clumsiness with the stove.

As Rick and I flop about exhausted in our tent we hear the patter of snowflakes on the roof. I scoop up a pot-full of snow to melt to water, light the Bluet gas stove, and settle back in my sleeping bag.

'Damn. The stove has gone out,' I say to Rick. I light it again, but it fizzles after a spurt of flame.

'The cartridge must be empty,' says Rick, unscrewing the old cartridge and replacing it with another. A brief hiss of gas escapes. We open the tent door to vent the gas out, then I light the stove.

Wumph!

A fireball fills the tent, hanging above our heads like a sun. Rick buries his face against the floor. I toss the blazing stove out the door, feel the lick of fire against my face, scream, then dive out of the tent onto the ridge. The stove sizzles in the snow and a smell of burned nylon and hair rises from the tent. Our eyebrows are cauterized from our faces. Snowflakes dropping in the quiet night sky are caught by the beams of Doug's and Georges' headlamps, as they peer toward us.

'What the hell is going on?' calls Doug.

'The tent! The tent!' I yell back.

'What about the tent?'

'Is it insured?'

The tent is a disaster. Its interior looks like the burned out cockpit of a crashed plane. The entire upper section of the inner tent is vaporized, leaving only the stitched seams suspended from the poles, and the reflective aluminium-coated fly-sheet, which deflected the fireball. Our mistake is a bad one, but remarkably, the tent is salvageable. As Doug and Georges survey the damage they look at each other, dumbfounded, yet not entirely unamused.

We set out again on the third morning, anticipating another full day on the crest of the ridge before reaching the foot of the pillar. By then the knife-edge ridge will have cost us a tent and three days' food—a far higher price than we expected.

A Taste of Monsoon

As the morning sun hits the tent an icicle of frozen condensation dangling from a tendril of scorched nylon melts and begins to drip onto my forehead. Rick lays beside me, snoring cacophonously. At first I think I'm dreaming but the tingling of my burned face reminds me that, in fact, I'm in the precariously perched, shell-shot tent, and this is our fourth day on Shivling. The realization is sobering, like waking in hospital or jail after some awful event of the night before.

A light breeze lifts open the tent door. My eyes scan the sunlit ice flutings of Shivling's South Face, then rest on Tapovan, 3,000 ft below. The meadow is splashed yellow and mauve from an overnight bloom of wildflowers. Figures, small as ants, emerge from the tents at base camp, roused by sunlight creeping over the mountain tops. Lachi walks from tent to tent, delivering bed-tea to the sahibs. He lingers at the entrance to Whillans' tent to cadge his morning belt of whisky. An arm extends. Lachi takes the bottle, tips it back, returns it to its keeper, and trots back to the kitchen tent, satisfied. I'm watching them, but who is watching us?

Ahead, the knife-edged ridge butts into the second stage of the climb—a 300 ft wall leading to a helmet-shaped dome. Though it's only our fourth day on the mountain, our bodies feel spent. In a fit of pessimistic thought, it seems that we have a snowball's chance in hell of reaching the summit. Even so, as we rise no one mentions the previous night's defeatist suggestion—to retreat down the South Face at first light. Instead, we pack up and set off into a perfect day.

Rick and I take the lead. For the first time in three days we make vertical progress, climbing a sheet of granite split by cracks. I lead up for 150 ft, pull onto a ledge, hammer in two pitons, and clip the rope to them. Rick ascends the rope on jumars, takes the rack of gear, then heads into a shattered jumble of snow-covered, rocky spikes, while Doug and Georges haul the loads. Loose rocks zip through the air, dislodged as Rick inches up. He anchors the rope and his call to ascend drifts down. We jumar up to the top of the helmet, a snow-covered lump of rubble and ice at 18,100 ft. Doug hauls up the loads as sunset tints the clouds pink. Icicles of frozen sweat encrust his beard. He stares at the horizon, puffing. Georges joins him.

'*Merde!* This is too slow! All day to climb and haul just two pitches,' he mutters. It's true. The loads are like leg-irons around our ankles, snagging on every flake, sapping our energy, stealing precious time from us. By the time we chop out two tent platforms it's already dark.

The fifth day dawns clear, hot and windless. Across the Gangotri Glacier rise the vertical yellow walls and triangular white crowns of the Bhagirathi Peaks. At their feet, the glacier snakes northward like a white river, past the white massifs of Kedarnath and Karchakund.

The pillar above—the third stage of the climb—is a golden sheet, seemingly devoid of ledges, rising for hundreds of feet to a prominent tower. Because the wall above offers no sleeping spots, we decide to use the helmet bivouac as a base, climb as high on the pillar as we can in one day, then secure our ropes and return to the helmet for the night. The following day, the sixth, we'll haul everything up the ropes and continue.

Doug and Rick rest at the bivouac while Georges and I descend a notch, some 50 ft deep, separating the helmet from the pillar, then begin climbing up the other side. Georges aid-climbs up a thin seam by whacking pitons into the crack while standing in slings. When the cracks become wide enough to freeclimb we put our rock shoes on to speed things up. After 300 ft we reach a 5-inch-wide crack choked with ice.

'Bon,' says Georges. 'You lead. It will cheer you up.'

Perhaps he senses from my staring at the distant summit that my uncertainty is growing. We seem too slow and too small to make any impression on Shivling. To reach our position at 18,300 ft we have climbed 26 ropelengths of 150 ft in five days—approximately the length and duration of a route on El Capitan. But above lies twice that amount of climbing. It doesn't seem possible to keep up the pace or that the weather will hold for that long.

I sling the rack of gear over my shoulder, wedge my hip inside the wide crack and shimmy up it. After 30 ft the crack becomes smooth-faced, bulging, and choked with water-ice. I chop hand-holds into the ice with the pick of my alpine hammer and wedge my boots across the slick crack. The rope dangles from my waist, with no protection, until after 50 ft the crack narrows enough to cam a Friend into it. As I reach the end of the pitch a huge black crow, a chuff, lands on a ledge a few feet away and looks across at my flushed, gasping face. Georges leads another pitch, secures our last rope, then we rappel 600 ft back to the helmet for the night.

Day six dawns cloudless, but, as with every day so far, the weather deteriorates by three o'clock and thick clouds encircle us. We haul the loads up the pillar and continue up slabs covered in a foot of snow. Prospects for a bivouac are bleak where we stand at 18,700 ft but look worse in the jumble of cliffs and spires above. Doug and Georges plod toward the cliffs to search for a better place to spend the night They disappear in a waft of cloud, followed by two chuffs riding an updraft. Meanwhile Rick and I eke out a miserable tent site in case there are no ledges

Georges Bettembourg and Greg Child climbing perfect granite on the steep pillar above the knife-edge ridge.

above. The snow is shallow and we bottom out on rock. Perfectly formed snow crystals begin to float down and settle on our coats. Wind and snow grow more forceful, and with them, our sense of trepidation. The clouds are like walls closing in around us. The weather seems sure to break. Then Doug calls out of the gloom: 'Come on up—we found a ledge—a big ledge!'

Relief. Rick breathes a 'Thank Christ' at the chance to escape this inhospitable place. We shoulder our loads and jumar the ropes up the steep cliffs climbed by Doug and Georges just as snow begins to pour out of the sky.

Day gives way to night too soon as always. We arrive by headlamp at the ledge. Sparks fly and metal rings as Doug hacks into solid ice and frozen rubble to fashion a bivouac.

Zing!

'Bloody hell!'

Doug's alpine hammer snaps at the pick and the sheared blade tinkles down the mountain. By midnight we've thrown off enough rubble to accommodate both tents. It's continuing to snow heavily. I make a mental note before sleep: '6 days; 19,000 ft; 32 pitches.'

By morning, the clouds that had filled the night recede in a boiling mass over the Chaukhamba Peaks into the valley of the Saraswati River, thirty miles to the east. A dusting of snow covers the tents and our tangled piles of gear. The bivouac looks like a hobo's crash pad, and we look more like bag men each day. Daylight shows that the ledge sits below a rock spire bearing an odd resemblance to a grinning crocodile. Just as at the helmet bivouac, we decide to fix ropes on the

On the pillar at 18,600 ft: Georges Bettembourg in the foreground, Doug Scott and Rick White above.

ledgeless wall above for a day, then spend another night beneath the crocodile, before moving forward.

Around us, everything is shadowed and frozen. Loose flakes are glued to the mountain by ice: the insides of cracks are coated with verglas; hand and foot holds are covered by snow. Cold seeps into our bones as I pay out the rope and Doug leads into the afternoon storm. After 450 ft of progress we anchor the last rope then descend through a mire of cloud to the crocodile. Grimacing at the needling pain in our fingertips, we move down without a word.

In the tents, cold limbs are rubbed warm. Our fingers sting as blood surges back through shrunken capillaries. Rick has prepared a banquet of sardines, mashed potatoes, and soup. We sit huddled in one tent, talking late into the night. During the day, conversation is monosyllabic, utilitarian. At night, we remember how to speak.

'Ah, it's a crazy business this mountain climbing, no?' reflects Georges, laying back and lowering a sardine into his open mouth, suddenly resembling Nero in repose, popping grapes. 'Years ago, Grandfather Charlet was walking down a valley in Chamonix after climbing the Aiguille Verte. A tourist came up to him, pointed up the mountain, and said "Look, here is 100 francs. Now tell me the truth: You didn't go up there, did you?"

'"No," said Grandfather, taking the money. "How could anyone live up there?" The tourist winked and said, "I thought so. Here's another 100 francs".'

When it comes time for Rick and I to return to our tent it's hard to believe we're at 19,000 ft, halfway up Shivling.

'Think you can make it home all right, kid?' asks Doug.

'Hmm . . . Better call us a taxi. I'm not sure of the neighbourhood,' I reply.

There seems no end to the pillar. The eighth day takes us further up the ice encrusted wall, toward the tip of the gothic tower at 19,800 ft: 40 ft from the top of the tower, the crack that Rick is leading up blanks out. There is a moment of concern as to how we will get past this section, then Rick sees a slot on our left. He climbs to the crack's end, slides a wired stopper into it, clips a carabiner to the stopper, then clips his rope through the carabiner. 'Lower me 30 ft,' he calls, 'I'm going to pendulum into the slot to our left.'

Doug lowers him. Rick swings back and forth across the wall, gaining momentum with each swing, then lunges at an ice-mushroom in the slot with the pick of his alpine-hammer. An explosion of ice spatters the air as his pick fails to bite, and he hurtles back across the face.

'I need a longer swing. Lower me another 10 ft.' On his second swing his pick bites solid ground and he disappears into the icy slot. The rope inches out, the hours pass.

'On belay,' he calls from 150 ft above.

I jumar up and find Rick huddled in an icy alcove, shivering and nursing his frozen hands. Sweating after jumaring up the rope, I hand him my gloves and wear his frozen ones to thaw them out. Doug leads the last few feet up the slot, tunneling into a mass of overhanging, unconsolidated snow that funnels down the

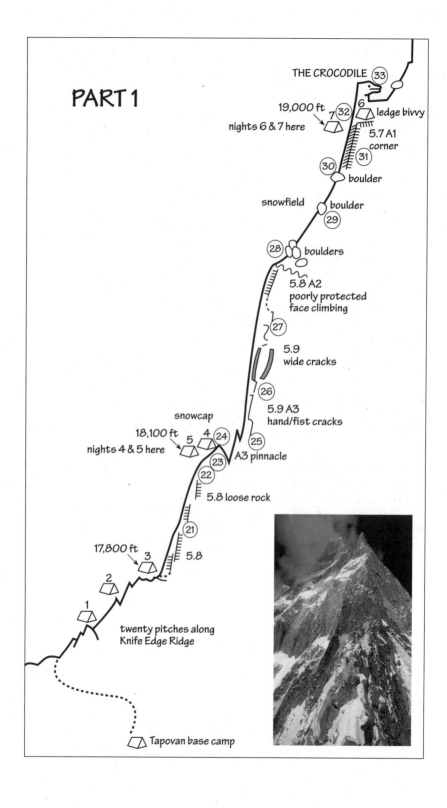

PART 1

THE CROCODILE (33)

19,000 ft (7)(32) (6)
nights 6 & 7 here ⛺ ledge bivvy

5.7 A1
corner
(31)

(30) ⬟ boulder

snowfield ⬭ boulder
(29)

(28) ⬭⬭ boulders

5.8 A2
poorly protected
face climbing

(27)

5.9
wide cracks

(26)

5.9 A3
hand/fist cracks

snowcap

18,100 ft (5) (4)(24)
nights 4 & 5 here ⛺⛺ (25)
(23) A3 pinnacle
(22)

5.8 loose rock

(21)

17,800 ft (3)
⛺ 5.8
(2)
⛺

1
⛺ twenty pitches along
Knife Edge Ridge

⛺ Tapovan base camp

The wildly exposed bivvy where Rick White and Greg Child holed up for two days on Shivling. (Photo by Doug Scott)

chimney onto the rest of us, pounding the hoods of our Gore-Tex windsuits and creeping coldly down our backs. Doug calls that the ropes are secure and a bivouac possible. We follow up into an inky sky.

By dark we are in our tents, each chopped into a mushroom of snow. Steam rises from our bodies as we shed our boots and peel off damp layers of Gore-Tex, fiberpile, and polypropylene underwear. The tent takes on the odour of a kennel and fills with more steam as the stove melts snow. Our thirst is so huge that we guzzle our water the moment the snow melts. Despite the frozen surroundings, we are as dehydrated as if we were in a desert.

From Doug and Georges' tent we hear a 'bloody hell' as their stove topples over, spilling scalding water across the floor and soaking their bags. We are all growing clumsy from being constantly on the move.

'Rick—fill the pot with more snow. We must drink more,' I say.

'Snow? What snow?' he says, half asleep.

'What the hell do you mean "what snow?" We're in snow up to our frigging necks!' My temper, like everyone's, rises closer to the surface with each exhausting day. Fatigue is wearing us down. Rick ignores me and drifts off to sleep. I dream of water that night.

Daylight on the ninth morning reveals the full insanity of our bivouac site. Chopped into an undercut blob of snow crowning the top of the tower, only luck adheres us to the mountain. We dismantle the tents and pack slowly. One day of food and two days of gas are all that remains. We've either got to speed up, or retreat now, for ahead of us lies the horizontal knife-edge of the fourth stage. Beyond this, retreat will be infinitely more difficult. To reduce the loads to four and speed our progress, Georges packs a red haulbag with a rope, extra clothing, the rock shoes, and the other haulbag, then commends it to the ice-chutes of the South Face, like a burial at sea. It shoots off like a bullet, straight toward Tapovan. Anyone watching at base camp would presume it to be one of us.

All morning an eerie mist cripples the sun, casting a half-light over our surroundings and immersing us in a waking dream. We leave the tower behind and with it the chance of an easy retreat. Our commitment to reach the summit and traverse the mountain is effectively sealed. Doug leads, straddling the razor-backed ridge, using his ice axe to smash down cornices perched along its crest. We move along on the ropes behind him, one leg dangling over the north face, the other over the south, numb to the wild exposure on the back of the abominable beast. After traversing some 700 ft we chop into the ridge for a bivouac, midway along the knife-edge. Rick and I place our tent atop a surreal snow mushroom. The snow is insecure, so we lash the tent to pitons, in case the mushroom crumbles during the night. We watch enviously as Doug and Georges pitch their tent beneath a cozy overhang.

'Doug—one question,' I ask.

'Sure, kid.'

'Why do you guys always get the good bivvy spot and we get the bad one?'

'Simple. You've already wrecked your tent, so a good site won't make any difference to it, right?'

I submit to a greater wisdom.

Inspired by the clearing afternoon mists, Rick and I fix two more ropelengths ahead of us. As I climb to the top of a tower on the ridge, the clouds suddenly dissipate. The pyramidal summit of Kamet in the northeast pierces through a sea of low cloud, dammed by the walls of the Bhagirathis. Satopanth's vast icefields reflect the evening sun. Then, the summit headwall of Shivling clears. Success seems attainable at last.

Georges Bettembourg and Rick White straddling a narrow fin at 19,950 ft. Nights 9 and 10 were spent near here snowbound in a bivvy. The ridge in the background provided insane exposure as we shuffled along it.

'The top looks really close. Two days away!' I shout excitedly.

The moment is scintillating. For the first time I fathom Doug's addiction to the nomadic beauty of exploring mountains, of setting down each night in a different place, of living for the moment. Looking to base camp below, I think back to Tapovan, to the day before we set off, to something one of the yogis there had said about our adventure: 'First travel; then struggle; finally, calm.' We don't know it yet, but the struggle is only beginning.

Struggle and Calm

As we sleep that ninth night the clouds lapping the flanks of Kamet and the Bhagirathi Peaks grow angry with storm and spill into the valley of the Gangotri Glacier, engulfing Shivling in fierce, cold tempest. Strong winds batter the flimsy tents, blowing spindrift under the outer-skin of the tent shared by Rick and me, and in through the hole left by the exploding stove, covering us with snow. By morning the storm still rages. Visibility is zero—I cannot even see Doug and Georges' tent 20 ft away.

'Looks like it's a rest day,' calls Doug at six am.

That much, at least, is good news.

'Let's hope the monsoon hasn't reached us early,' he continues, adding the bad news.

In Delhi, a month before, the newspapers had predicted an early monsoon. If this was it, then the storm could blow unabated for days. The thought fills us with a funk. We spend the day lying in our clammy sleeping bags, drifting in and out of sleep, brooding about the possibility of retreating in storm down the 43 pitches we had climbed.

During the day, occasional peeks out of the tent door show little improvement in the weather. Twice, the clouds around us thin enough for us to see each other's tents. During these insincere spells of clearing, we see torrents of snow cascading down the headwall of Shivling. The chuffs that have been following us up the mountain and scavenging our scraps appear out of the storm, hovering hopefully, like vultures. They roost beside Doug and Georges' tent. The birds don't seem perturbed by the weather, or the altitude of 20,000 ft.

What little food we have left we ration. Breakfast is a handful of cereal in sugar-less tea. We sleep through lunch until afternoon, then eat the same mush for dinner.

'This reminds me of when I was on the dole,' I say to Rick.

Afternoon comes. The sky is filled with blowing snow.

'It doesn't look good, does it?' Rick calls to the other tent.

'No. But we'll have to move tomorrow, up or down, no matter how bad the weather. We'll be out of food and gas soon,' Doug replies with grim finality.

'How many pitons 'ave we left?' asks Georges, raising the issue of descent.

We tally up what remains of our rack. Of the thirty pitons and twenty nuts that we had started out with, less than half that amount left remains. We'd broken our ten lightweight titanium pitons when hammering them out, had left several other pitons and nuts along the horizontal knife-edges, and had dropped a few as well. Even with the addition of our eight Friends, three ice screws, and ten slings, the mathematics of having enough gear to rappel over 5,500 ft didn't work out. We bat about the possibilities of different ways down, the amount of gear left, and the time a retreat would take. Doug interrupts the discussion.

'The answer is clear,' he says. 'We're committed to the summit. We have to reach it and descend the West Face. Anyway, we'd probably never make it down our route, and the South Face will be roaring with avalanches.'

We all fall silent as the situation sinks into us. Up till that point, the idea of climbing a mountain was, to me, a concept rooted in 'fun', and reaching a summit was something I'd imagined was a take-it-or-leave-it goal. But the summit now takes on a very practical application—it is the way down. After assimilating the anxieties of the moment a sort of calm settles over us. We now understand exactly what we must do the next morning, storm or not.

'Hey, Greg, what does Don Juan have to say?' says Doug.

The sole luxury we'd carried on the mountain was Doug's paperback copy of Carlos Castaneda's *Teachings of Don Juan,* the classic tale of strange journeys, and a suitable companion for our climb. I dust the spindrift off it, open it at random, and read the first passage I find. The words are strangely appropriate. 'He says to find a path with heart and follow it to the end,' I reply.

'Does our path have heart?' queries Doug.

I think for a moment.

'It's the only one we've got.'

After another starvation ration, we drop off to sleep to the patter of snowflakes beating on the tent.

On the eleventh morning our path can be clearly seen, plastered in fresh snow, gleaming under a clearing sky. Storm clouds loom on the horizon, as if waiting to pounce. We move again, climbing horizontally along the final 500 ft of towers, ice runnels, and cornices toward the base of the headwall. The cornice is undercut beneath and looks as delicate as a roll of whipped cream decorating a cake. We walk gingerly along it, as if crossing a rotten log spanning a gorge. Following Georges' tracks across the cornice, my boot punches through the cornice to the other side. As I extract my foot I get a dizzying port-hole view of the South Face. I swallow hard as a shiver runs up my spine.

At midday we reach the final barrier to the summit, the headwall at 20,150 ft. Smears of rime-ice cling to the rock and make freeclimbing impossible, but the cracks are good and Doug and I aid climb 300 ft, to the start of a long smear of ice that we reach as darkness sets in. Around us, there isn't even a footledge to stand on, let alone a place for a tent. We call to the others to find a bivouac below, then we fix two ropes in place and descend by headlamp to a scene of chopping and hacking. We dig into the only possible place on the wall—a triangular ledge just big enough to cram one 4 x 6 ft tent. We all crowd into it, laying head-to-toe.

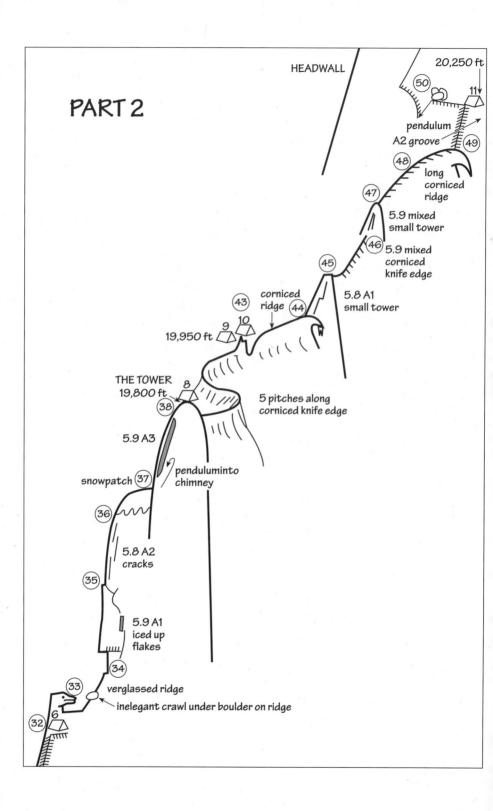

PART 2

HEADWALL

20,250 ft

50

11

pendulum
A2 groove

49

48

long
corniced
ridge

47

5.9 mixed
small tower

46

5.9 mixed
corniced
knife edge

45

44

corniced
ridge

43

5.8 A1
small tower

19,950 ft

9 10

THE TOWER
19,800 ft

8

38

5 pitches along
corniced knife edge

5.9 A3

snowpatch 37

pendulum into
chimney

36

5.8 A2
cracks

35

5.9 A1
iced up
flakes

34

33

verglassed ridge

inelegant crawl under boulder on ridge

32 6

There isn't an inch to spare, but it's warm. Georges balances a stove on his stomach, tosses the cereal and a packet of mushroom soup into a pot of water and we eat the last of our food. We sleep well, our heads full of dreams.

The next morning is cold, windy, yet clear. Gusts full of spindrift orbit the mountain while suspicious-looking clouds continue to bubble in the southwest. I buckle the belt of my climbing-harness a notch tighter around my narrowing waist and mutter semi-coherently about starving. 'Well, you'll never find enlightenment on a full stomach,' Doug tells me.

Greg Child shivering on belay high on Shivling. (Photo by Doug Scott)

Rick and Georges head off up the ropes. From below I see the silhouette of Georges leading up a sheet of ice, chinking away at the translucent wall with his crampons and ice tools. Doug and I follow, hauling the packs, first over the ice patch, then up rock. The wind increases in velocity and tosses lumps of snow, broken from cornices, about the air. Doug takes the lead at the last pitch of rock to the summit ridge. It's three in the afternoon, and we are very close to the summit—350 ft away. As we huddle from the wind on the prow dividing the South Face from the North, Doug begins to babble about voices.

'Bloody hell! I can hear someone shouting my name.'

'*Merde!* What is he saying? Has he gone crazy?' scoffs Georges.

For the moment it seems that Doug is suffering some sort of hallucination, but then we hear it too—a faint voice to our left, almost lost in the wind, calling from the col between the main summit and the subsummit of Shivling. It's been so long since we'd thought of anything except our own situation that we'd forgotten that Don, Merv, Steve, and Colin are somewhere on the mountain as well. Doug spots four figures standing on the col. He relays their words to us:

'The way down is easy. There are tracks to follow, and ropes are fixed down the harder sections of the West Face,' he shouts. We are jubilant. The end of our odyssey seems at hand.

At five o'clock we step off the rocks of the East Pillar and onto an ice rib leading to the summit. Georges leads the way, ploughing a trough through a dangerous snow-slab for 300 ft. As he kicks through the crust to reach the ice below, debris showers down, smothering us in a deluge of snow. Georges' efforts are enormous, but time slips away again. By sunset we stand on a large, flat snow ledge at 21,350 ft, just below the summit. Beside us a bleached strand of rope marks the end of the Japanese North Ridge. But the mountain has us for a twelfth night. We pitch our tents, too weary to be frustrated, and certain that we'll be on the summit the next day.

In the tent, the last of our gas fizzles out after giving us a pot of water. The meagre amount does little to sate our thirst. I massage Rick's numb feet for an hour. He hasn't felt them all day, and when I remove his socks we discover that his toenails are black, a touch of frostbite. 'That'll be a novelty back home,' he muses. Our lack of calories has us shivering all night. Tomorrow. All we think about is tomorrow.

Tomorrow comes—clear, cold, and howling. To cut down on weight we ditch anything we don't need—the wrecked tent, ragged gloves, a threadbare rope—into a crevasse. From here on, to the summit and down, the route is on snow or ice. As we sort through our ice tools for suitable ice axes to aid the descent, we find that of the eight tools we began with, only five are unbroken. What remains is a pile of short-handled alpine hammers, with picks blunt from chopping out bivouac ledges. They are too short to use as walking sticks, but they are all that we have. We each salvage a tool and set off on wobbly legs up the final snowslope to the summit of Shivling. Thirty minutes later, at seven o'clock, we surmount a cornice and step onto the bald, wind-thrashed dome of ice that is the summit. It is our thirteenth day out of base camp, our fifty-eighth pitch.

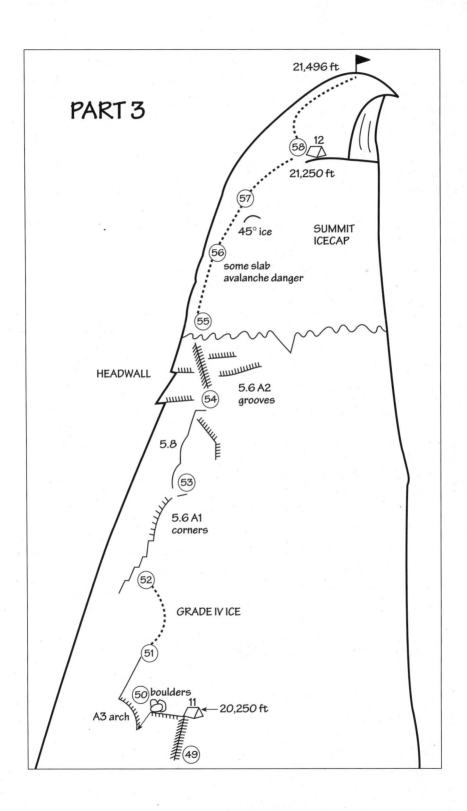

PART 3

21,496 ft

58
12

21,250 ft

SUMMIT
ICECAP

57

45° ice

56

some slab
avalanche danger

55

HEADWALL

5.6 A2
grooves

54

5.8

53

5.6 A1
corners

52

GRADE IV ICE

51

50 boulders

11 ← 20,250 ft

A3 arch

49

Doug and Georges dance around on the summit, arm-in-arm, laughing, then absorb Rick and I into their jig. As we hop about I see Rick smiling happily. We two had tried many ambitious climbs together but this is our first success. His heartfelt handshake is a warm feeling on this cold summit, yet although the relief that our long ordeal is over is enormous, our arrival is neither climactic nor anticlimactic. It is merely halfway home.

Around us the granite walls and summits of the Gangotri pierce the sky like serrated teeth. But in the south, clouds are brewing. We spend ten minutes on the summit, then prepare for the descent, roping up into two pairs—Rick and I on one rope, Doug and Georges on the other.

'We'll all be weak from lack of food, so watch your step,' warns Doug, starting down the icy slope of the West Face, toward a col 600 ft below. Rick and I follow. As the ice steepens, we face into the slope, climbing down using the front-points of our crampons and swinging the blunt picks of our ice tools at the steel-hard ice. On each roped pair, one person climbs down, belayed by the other who is anchored to an alpine hammer driven into the ice. When the rope runs out, the lower climber swings the pick of his ice tool into the slope, anchors the rope to it, then the upper climber carefully reverses toward him. Should the upper climber fall the length of the rope, there is little hope that the lower climber will be able to hold him. The belay is psychological, the rule 'don't fall'. We descend this way for 600 ft to the flat col between the main and subsidiary summits of Shivling, where just yesterday our companions had stood shouting.

Then signs of life appear. A line of tracks left by Don and the others descends a 45-degree wall of snow, ice and rock, some 800 ft high, then stretches across a flat bowl. Doug and Georges continue down, while Rick and I climb tiredly behind, placing our feet in the slots already kicked into the snow.

'How about untying?' suggests Rick, as I climb down ahead of him.

'OK. In a few minutes,' I reply, seeing a suitable place to unrope below me.

Rick starts down, 150 ft above me. I stop to wait for him.

On the flat bowl 800 ft below, Doug mentions to Georges what a good effort Rick and I have put in for our first Himalayan climb. He is cut short by Georges' scream of *'Merde!'* as he sees the horrible happen.

Rick, now 100 ft above me, places his foot in a step and something goes wrong. Perhaps it is the step crumbling beneath him, or perhaps his weak ankle gives out, but suddenly he is sliding, raking feverishly at the sugary snow with his alpine hammer. The pick fails to arrest him. He gains speed. I see this as a split second blur out of the corner of my eye.

'Here I come!' Rick yells. It is the understatement of our lives.

Fired by a surge of adrenalin, a flood of possibilities enters my mind. Plunge the shaft of my alpine hammer into the snow to hold Rick's fall—no chance it'll stop him; catch him as he slides past—he's out of reach; cut the rope to save myself—no time; untie—less time; climb down the slope—impossible; jump off—suicide.

Find a path with heart and follow it to the end. . .

The coil of rope beside me whips out as he slides past, looking like a harpooned

Greg Child and Rick White descending bullet-proof ice from the summit of Shivling. The fall occurred near the bottom of the photo.

whale plunging into the deep to drag the ship down with it. The chances for survival diminish as I watch the rope flick into the air. My mind casts out an apology to my wife Salley as I realize the folly of this final act, then in futility I plunge the shaft of my alpine hammer into the slope. The rope stretches against my waist, then propels me into the air. I suffer a final thought: 'This is it.'

We bounce down the slope, tumbling for 700 ft, legs and arms flailing like rag dolls. I land on my back, feel the wind knocked out of me, bounce again, then feel razor sharp crystals of snow grind against my cheek as I slide face-first down the slope. We hurtle over a gaping bergschrund, then slowly come to a stop in the bowl.

It's windless in the bowl, noiseless. The hiss of disturbed snow sliding down behind me sets my mind back into gear. I return from black silence as blood trickles out of my nose and onto my lips. I twitch my limbs—nothing broken—then get to my feet. Rick is lying ten feet away, feeling his ribs. He thinks a few are cracked, but otherwise we're unscathed.

Doug and Georges appear, running toward us. They are speechless when the corpses they expect to find are walking about.

'Well, Doug,' quips Rick, 'looks like we found the fast way down the mountain.' I untie the rope and toss it on the snow.

Georges walks beside me as we head down the bowl.

'You guys are so lucky. I 'ad some friends who were descending a peak in Alaska when something almost identical happened. Except they fell all the way down the mountain, and were never seen again. One of them 'ad a weak ankle, like Rick. Perhaps it gave out and . . . well, you know the rest.'

'Your friends—what were their names?' I ask, my memory suddenly jolted.

Georges tells me.

'Strange, Salley knew them both. In fact, Rick's bad ankle worried her so much that she made me promise not to rope with Rick. I broke the promise.'

We think for a moment, walking in silence. That it was a small world seems an odd thought after the past thirteen days, when all the world had seemed so big. Georges breaks the silence.

'You 'ave to watch out for yourself in the mountains. They are very beautiful, but,' he says, grabbing my neck, making me jump in shock, 'sometimes they sneak up from behind and—*chop*—you get it in the back of the neck.'

We look at each other and smile. Even after all we'd been through the bugger still looks handsome. He should have been in movies.

As we descend the final slopes of the West Face, we see a figure waiting below, perched on a rock at the foot of the mountain. As we grow closer the figure takes on a familiar form—Whillans!

Whillans the phrase-maker, the clairvoyant, the sage—the bringer of food!

Thoughts of what he might have brought—chocolate, biscuits, sardines—squeeze a last burst of energy from our legs. I hallucinate the sweet aroma of tea wafting through the air. By the time I reach him Doug has told him the tale of our thirteen-day climb, including an account of the exploding tent and our tumble down the mountain. Whillans sits calmly, like the all-knowing Buddha, and transfixes me with the same piercing glare he'd cast over the Indian boy at Delhi airport a month before. The merest hint of a smile cracks his parched lips.

'Well done, lads. You made it back,' he says. Then, satisfied that all is well, he trots off down the Meru Glacier, beginning the four-mile hike back to Tapovan.

'Did he bring anything to eat?' I ask.

'Yeah. But he got hungry while he was waiting and ate it,' Rick replies. But it's the thought that counts.

Back at base camp that evening we sit about the kitchen tent, gorging ourselves on plate after plate of eggs and fried potatoes. Rick gobbles down every leathery bit of Lachi's cuisine without a complaint, while the doctor bathes Rick's black-tinged toes in antiseptic. We look and feel shrunken from the gauntlet of Shivling. Rick's face and mine look aged, as burned skin flakes from our cheeks and brows.

There are a dozen stories to tell, as many to digest. For us, there is the deep satisfaction of success; for the West Face team, turned back by the wind the day we'd heard them calling, there is the rankling emptiness of a missed summit. But one piece of news tempers our euphoria. Nirmal Sah and Praturiam Singh, who'd been with Rick and me on the Chaturangi Glacier and who were so ambitious to climb Bhagirathi II, had died on that mountain, tumbling down a slope much the same as Rick and I had. We were just luckier. The Indians' bodies had been cremated at Tapovan, in Hindu tradition, and their ashes, in rime, would flow into the Ganges.

Steve sits with his eyes bandaged, chomping codeine, snowblind after losing his sunglasses on his attempt to reach the summit of Shivling. Balwant switches on the radio and tunes in to Radio Moscow. A torrent of words and static tells us that the Pope has been shot in an assassination attempt.

Shivling stands framed by the doorway of the tent. Were we really up there, or was it a dream? Already the experience seems to fall toward the past, like an old, fond memory. The bad times of the climb will soon be forgotten and only the elusive, intoxicating moments will remain to draw us back. Colin hands me a pile of a dozen letters from home. I shuffle them about, but cannot decide which one to open first. Doug, similarly involved in a pile of mail, looks across the tent at me.

'It's simpler up there, isn't it?' he says.

'Simple,' I reply, 'but harsh.'

Part Two

Lobsang Spire and Broad Peak, Karakoram, 1983

The Third Bird

'I lay down on the ground and gazed upon the scene, muttering to myself deep thankfulness that to me it had been given to see such glory. Here was no disappointment—no trace of disillusionment. What I had so ardently longed to see was now spread out before me. Where I had reached no white man had ever reached before. And there before me were peaks of 26,000 ft and in one case 28,000 ft, in height, rising above a valley bottom only 12,000 ft above sea level. For mountain majesty and sheer sublimity that scene could hardly be excelled. And austere though it was it did not repel—it just enthralled me. This world was more wonderful by far than I had ever known before. And I seemed to grow greater myself from the mere fact of having seen it. Having once seen that, how could I ever be little again.'

—Sir Francis Younghusband on seeing the
Baltoro Karakoram in 1887

Great Trango Tower (left) and Nameless Tower framed by an ibex skull, viewed from the Dunge Glacier.

Ice-cold in Islamabad

Sitting on lawn-chairs beside the pool at the British Embassy Club in Islamabad, shaded by a large umbrella, the members of our expedition pour ice-cold Muree beers down their throats. The pool steams under the beating May sun's impact and seems to chlorinate the air around it. As I examine the label on the beer bottle I notice a contradiction: Muree beer is brewed in Pakistan.

'Isn't there prohibition in Pakistan?' I ask Whillans.

'Aye, there is. You won't find a pub to save your life outside these embassy grounds. If a Pakistani is caught boozing it's sixty lashes. So sup up while you can.'

'Yes, but this beer is brewed here . . .'

'Aye. The mysteries of Asia.'

Our waiter, a tall, poker-faced Pakistani dressed in white, steps over and around the tanning and peeling bodies of Sahibs and Mem-Sahibs, weaving a path through the satanic bikinis and immodest undress of Englishmen out-in-the-midday-sun. He moves with the unseeing eyes of a harem eunuch, and delivers a round of drinks to a table of embassy staff. Beside him, even the most tanned mem-sahib appears pale and cloud-nurtured. His boss, the club manager, also a Pakistani, sits with one ear glued to the radio, listening to a cricket match, while the other ear attends the lament of a regular customer bemoaning the loss of his cook, just processed for immigration to Britain.

'Damn fine cook,' reflects the regular, pensively.

'He'll hate the rain,' consoles the manager.

The manager's voice bespeaks everything beautiful about the English language, even though he isn't English. Overhearing a remark at our table about his incongruous accent, he drifts over to tell us, very toffily, that when we are in the mountains we may hear his 'dulcet tones' broadcast at four every afternoon as he reads the weather forecast.

It is the eve of our departure for the mountains of the Karakoram, a rugged range of the Himalayas where the earth's tectonic plates collide, buckle, and thrust up peaks up to 8,000 metres high. The old Tibetan traders had named the place well, their words *Kara* meaning black, and *koram* meaning covered in earth. Even the sound of the word had a sharpness to it, like the broken rubble riding atop the snapping and crackling Baltoro Glacier, our destination in the Karakoram.

We sit talking, drinking, passing around photographs of our three climbing objectives, and sizing each other up. Among the team are some of the hardest players in Himalayan climbing: Doug Scott, Roger Baxter Jones, Alan Rouse, Peter Thexton, Andy Parkin, Jean Afanasieff, Don Whillans; and, with less experience, Stephen Sustad and me.

The team had gelled as much as a 'business venture' as anything else. Not that there is a profit to be made from our plan to climb alpine-style ascents of a succession of peaks, beginning with the unclimbed 18,742 ft high Lobsang Spire and ending with Broad Peak and K2—the twelfth and second highest mountains in the world. On the contrary. The expedition has put us up to our neck in debt. It's more that, like hiring on to a corporation, each member of the expedition offers some skill to invest in the strength of the enterprise.

The expedition is the brainchild of Doug, Roger, and Alex Macintyre who climbed Shishapangma together in 1982, an 8,000 metre peak in Tibet. Their ascent of a new route on the south face of the mountain, climbed in pure alpine style, is the inspiration for this expedition. But tragically, late in 1982, Alex was killed while climbing Annapurna I in Nepal, struck by a solitary stone bouncing down the South Face. The gap widened when the fourth architect of the expedition, Georges Bettembourg, dropped out with plans to marry in the summer of '83. Doug filled the gaps left by Georges and Alex with the additions of the Britons Alan Rouse, who'd climbed Nepal's Jannu and Nuptse, as well as Kongur in China; and Alan's climbing partners, Andy Parkin and Doctor Peter Thexton. Andy, a weasel-lean lad with a temperament so well-balanced that he made Ghandi look like Attila the Hun, had recently soloed the Grandes Jorasses in Chamonix during winter. As for Peter, a similarly composed man, he'd climbed the first ascent of Thelay Sagar in the Gangotri Region, and had attempted Everest during the winter of 1980, with Alan. Three from the 1981 Shivling expedition, Don Whillans, American Steve Sustad, and I, also joined the team. With the addition of Jean Afanasieff, the first Frenchman to climb Everest, the climbers total nine. Jean, I find, is so well known in France that there even exists a snakes-and-ladders board game of his Everest climb. Michelle Stamos and Beth Acres, Jean's and Pete's girlfriends, bring the total to eleven.

I listen to the tales of climbing floating about the table. The ascent of Shivling and an ascent of a hard new route on the 2,500 ft overhanging East Face of El Capitan that same year had broadened my confidence and ambitions, yet I felt, once again, that I was treading in very deep water. Particularly when I listen to Jean's tale of near misses, luck, and tragedy on Nanga Parbat's Rupal Buttress, which he'd attempted the year before.

'It was a shooting gallery up there. Serac fall and avalanche swept the route nearly every day. Sheikh Ali, our high altitude porter, slipped from a fixed rope and died. Then Yannick Seigneur and I were narrowly missed by a windslab avalanche that tore out hundreds of metres of fixed rope. Finally, a massive ice avalanche hit the four of us as we made our way to the summit. Yannick took an ice-block in the chest. He had twelve broken ribs and a fractured pelvis. But we were lucky. A few minutes either way and we'd have been in the thick of the avalanche and, *finis.*'

'Wasn't Rheinhard Karl planning to go with you on that expedition?' asked Alan.

'He was, but he dropped out because of Nanga Parbat's dangerous reputation,' said Jean. 'Over forty have died for ten successful ascents. Instead, he went to Cho Oyu in Nepal. He thought it would be straightforward, safe . . . A bergschrund collapsed on him as he slept, and crushed him,' Jean shrugs.

Michelle and Beth look stony at Jean's frankness about death. I wonder if, after enough expeditions, I too will see it so objectively. Silently, we sip our beers, trying to think into the weeks ahead. Meanwhile, Doug shuffles a sheaf of papers after spending the morning finalizing the details of the expedition at the Ministry of Tourism.

'Everything is done then—helicopter rescue bond taken care of, money exchanged for a sackful of rupees, porters insured, the truck rented,' he says with relief.

'We've packed the last load, so we're ready to go tomorrow,' adds Pete. 'How does this Captain Malik seem?' queries Don of our Liaison Officer.

'Hard to say. He was a bit annoyed with us at first. The poor bugger didn't realize he was in for a hike up the Baltoro until last week. It seems he was notified at the last minute. He keeps complaining about leaving his missus, but I think he's got a sense of humour, so he should work out,' Doug says.

Megaphones mounted on the tower of a distant mosque intone the long and sombre fourth prayer of the day. The believers throughout the city kneel to Allah.

'Damn those drums,' muses Whillans.

The call to prayer reminds us of where we are. Inside the British embassy grounds we are not in Pakistan. We are in 'the compound', a little western oasis, a vestige of that bygone oligarchy called the Raj. Islamabad, Pakistan's capital city, is a metropolis of unfinished government buildings and the opulent houses of diplomats, generals, and businessmen. On the surface the city seems peaceful, yet a volatile atmosphere, as seasonal as the monsoon, springs up from time to time. The embassy people shield themselves from it with walls, with sunglasses, with beer. Even with air conditioning, the diplomatic corps call Islamabad a hardship post.

A few miles beyond Islamabad's collection of manicured embassy grounds is another world—Rawalpindi. There, the women are veiled from head to toe. Like a mirror image of Delhi, earth-toned, shabby, and exotic, 'Pindi's shop-cluttered streets are jammed with cars, bicycles, and horse- and ox-drawn carts. Walls are plastered with acres of Urdu political slogans, among them the occasional faded 'Death to Jimmy Carter' scrawled in English.

An American agent in the Drug Enforcement Agency, whom I'd met the day before at the 'Hash and Curry Run', walks into the club. The Hash Run is a weekly tradition among embassy staff that is a sort of fox hunt without fox or hounds, played in the steamy green Margala Hills that rise above Islamabad. In the run, legions of sahibs run hither and yon like bloodhounds, hunting for a foxily intermittent trail of shredded diplomatic documents. When the trail is picked up, the call of a bugle rallies the hunters, and the search for the next clue begins. At the trail's end a tub of ice-cold beer inevitably awaits.

The DEA agent wears a T-shirt emblazoned with the words 'Survivor of the

Vault'. Not far from the British Club the sponsor of his T-shirt, the ruined American Embassy, bakes in the heat. Marine guards sweat out their duty at the temporary embassy while the new one, a concrete fortress, is under construction. In 1980, during the US/Iran hostage crisis, a Shiite mob attacked the embassy and the flimsy walls of the Great Satan's headquarters toppled under the weight of the crowd. The 120 American staff hid in the underground communications vault, a chamber meant to accommodate only forty. Above, the mob sacked the embassy and razed it to the ground. Inside the vault it grew hot enough to fry an egg on the floor, yet all inside survived.

'How goes the war against drugs?' I ask the DEA agent. His job concerns stopping the flow of heroin out of Pakistan, which since Russia's invasion of Afghanistan had become the world's number-one narcotics exporter. The American smiles curiously, wondering to what extent yesterday's tub of beer had loosened his tongue, and how much he'd told me about his job.

'As long as the Russians are in Afghanistan and the Mujahedein are in Pakistan financing the resistance, there'll be heroin on the world market,' he says in a press-release tone. He seats himself near us, at a table of embassy personnel. Suddenly everyone cranes their necks skyward as a Pakistani F-15 rips through the air. I point out to a British consular official the towering forest of marijuana peeping insolently over the hedge surrounding the pool and he snorts at the anomaly. 'We're locked in mortal combat with the damned weed—can't seem to eradicate it no matter what we do,' he replies. The DEA agent's grin broadens.

We order a final round of cold beers. Ahead there are no bars, no air-conditioned retreats, no swimming pools. Ahead lies the Karakoram Highway, Skardu, and the mountains of the Baltoro Glacier.

The fertile valley of Hunza, with Dhiran Peak viewed from Karimabad.

The Karakoram Highway

Of the two routes to Skardu, the last civilized town before the Karakoram, 220 miles from Islamabad, one is unreliable, the other infernal.

The former is a two-hour Pakistan International Airlines flight past the 26,660 ft high Nanga Parbat. The flight path to Skardu is one of the most treacherous in the world and waiting for suitable weather for this flight to leave may take a week, even two. The Fokkers that service the route turn around at the first hint of bad weather and return to Islamabad. One cautionary tale exists of a hapless load of passengers who failed to reach Skardu despite leaving the ground sixteen consecutive times. With that in mind we opt for the second alternative: The Karakoram Highway by junga bus.

Now, the Karakoram Highway is not really a highway but a dirt road blasted into the precipitous rock walls of the Indus River Gorge. One hundred miles in length, the Karakoram Highway is longer and rougher than the road along the gorge of the Ganges River. Nor is a junga bus a bus in any western sense of the word. A junga is a vehicle that resembles an ornately painted Bedford dump truck with a high pointed prow above the cabin, giving it the appearance of an ancient Phoenician warship, on wheels. It is to such a vessel, piloted by a lanky, grease-smeared driver with a bony face and a rakish smile, whom Whillans immediately christens 'Greasy Chippy', and a chubby co-driver, that we entrust our lives. We load the truck and nestle into positions in the cabin, on the prow, or sprawl about in the back over 5,000 lb of expedition food and equipment. Andy and Don, who'd two weeks earlier driven in just such a rattletrap 900 miles from Karachi to Islamabad with the expedition's gear, look like men returning to prison after a brief taste of freedom as they climb aboard.

'This is a rum way to see the country,' mutters Whillans.

Leaving Islamabad, we pick up Captain Malik in 'Pindi, then weave across town to collect two unscheduled riders who crowd in with the fourteen of us.

'Captain, who are these men that the driver is picking up, and how far are they going?' asks Doug.

'They are friends of the driver, going to Abbotobad.'

A minute later two more passengers cram into the overloaded junga.

'And who are these men now?' asks Doug.

Our junga bus was a clanking contraption that crawled along the Karakoram Highway.

'The brothers of the driver, getting a lift across town,' the Captain replies.

'I see. Nothing is ever simple here, is it?'

'This is Pakistan,' states the Captain, knowingly.

Our parting sight of 'Pindi and Islamabad is of an army helicopter hovering beside a tall building called 'The Very Lovely Cricket Club', dumping propaganda leaflets onto the bazaar. As the sun sets into a purple horizon the spine-jarring journey begins. Hours pass. The junga gears down and zigzags up endless switch-backs. My ears pop, signalling that we are crawling into the foothills of the Karakoram. Sleep is impossible as the junga bounces and creaks from pothole to pothole.

'What the hell is that coming up behind us?' says Steve, pointing to a bright light bearing down on us from behind.

The multi-coloured light, accompanied by loud, inexplicable music, flashes like a Christmas tree. As it closes the gap we see that the vehicle is not a travelling discotheque, but merely the night bus to Skardu. Inside, red, green, and orange lights pulsate stroboscopically, illuminating the tangled limbs and bloodshot eyes of passengers jammed six abreast. The light show is synchronized to the deafening beat of taped Pakistani pop music. Shrill vocals, twanging strings, and thumping drums overtake us and wail on down the road.

'The Bedlam Express,' Whillans christens it.

At daylight the throaty rumble of the junga lumbering over arid hillside roads rouses me from sleep and I open my eyes to see a group of long-bearded Pathan men sauntering along the road. Their torsos are criss-crossed with bandoliers, and they carry Kalashnikovs. The border between Pakistan and Afghanistan is but a short distance away. Over that border stream a constant flow of refugees fleeing the Russian invaders, and of men such as these returning to their home-land to fight.

After twelve hours of driving we enter the Indus River Gorge and the tempera-ture skyrockets. Whillans covers himself with foam pads to insulate himself from the heat: others lean over the edge of the junga to catch the scant breeze, and peer into the rushing waters of the Indus up to a thousand feet below. The proximity of our ragged, bald tyres to the road's crumbling edge mesmerizes us. Riding on the prow, the wind ruffles Jean's long brown hair, tied with a red bandana. He raises his Romanesque nose and sniffs the air, then leans over the side of the truck and peers into the driver's window.

'Ze drivers are smoking 'ashish again,' he calls.

'How long is this truck ride supposed to be?' Roger asks Doug.

'It depends. Anywhere from two to four days, depending on our luck,' Doug replies.

'Couldn't we have rented a real bus?' asks Roger.

'I suppose so, but this was so much cheaper,' says Doug.

'At least this isn't as dusty as sitting in the back of that wretched pickup we rode in across Tibet to Shishapangma. I ate my weight in dust on that trip,' says Roger.

'How was that trip?' I interject.

'Too long,' Roger answers flatly.

'You just get homesick, Roger, that's your problem,' Doug says.

'I enjoy being homesick because I enjoy home,' Roger concludes in his aristo-cratic voice.

Before I met Roger I had only Doug's brief description of him to go on: 'Roger is probably the strongest Himalayan climber I've ever climbed with.' I knew that he'd taken part in a twelve day alpine ascent of Jannu, had almost soloed Makalu, and had alpined Shishapangma. When I finally met him, during the chaos of dealing with the excess baggage tyrants at Heathrow Airport as we departed Britain, he was preoccupied with a long goodbye to Christine, his French fiancée whom he lived with in Chamonix. But seeing his stature I knew what Doug had meant. And, from the first handshake and smile from his shapely, full-fleshed face, capped by faintly red hair, I understood the applicability of Doug's other adjective regard-ing Roger: ' . . . rather cavalier . . .'

The junga stops at a small town.

'Lunch,' calls the Captain. As we enter a restaurant doorway a monkey, hur-tling airborne out of the shadows, propels itself toward Steve and Andy. They leap back just as the monkey is pulled up and catapulted backwards by a chain around its neck, connected to a cement pillar. The proprietors, who sit around a hearth slapping chapatis into shape, laugh heartily. As we dine, the owner 'entertains' us by making the monkey smoke cigarettes. The monkey's eyes bulge as it puffs the cigarettes, then it eats them, burning end and all. Released from the grip of the proprietor, it runs madly around the column, at its wits' end. In some cultures there is a belief that dogs are the reincarnations of the insane, and as such they are treated like dirt; perhaps because the monkey is so near to human it suffers an even greater misery.

The wall of the restaurant is covered with posters of political and religious luminaries: General Zia, the late President of Pakistan Ali Bhutto, Khomeini. On Bhutto's poster a candle, flame extinguished, wafts symbolic smoke into the air. Deposed in a coup in 1977 by General Zia, Bhutto was hanged in 1979. The Captain notices us looking at the poster.

'The evil genius,' he says of Bhutto. 'Yes, a regrettable incident, but Zia had to save Pakistan from destruction at Bhutto's incompetent hands.'

As our gaze shifts to the poster of Khomeini, the Captain shakes his head.

'The evil idiot,' he says under his breath.

The second night falls as we continue along the Indus Gorge. The drone of the engine and the roar of the river fills our sleepy heads until a movement on the edge of the junga catches our attention.

'Now what's going on?' asks Beth.

She points to Greasy Chippy, oblivious to the drop beneath his flapping shirt-tails, circumnavigating the truck by way of the welded railings and ladders that bristle all over the outside of the vehicle. In the moonlight he looks like a ghostly sailor checking the rigging on a haunted ship. I shine my headlamp into his eyes: vein-lined and bloodshot, they look like two spherical roadmaps. He cracks a picaresque grin, then dives beside me to take a nap.

'That lad's a headbanger if I ever met one,' mutters Whillans out of the darkness.

At some dark, time-lost hour that night, the truck stops at a police checkpoint and the policeman wakes us to record our names and passport numbers in a register. The ritual, repeated so far half a dozen times, seems pointless, and I ask the Captain what purpose it serves.

'It is in case we disappear into the gorge—God forbid—or bandits attack us,' he says.

'Bandits?'

'Oh yes. They hide in the hills and prey on trucks.'

I had a vision of a horde of raiders sweeping out of the wasteland, muskets, Kalashnikovs, and scimitars glinting in the moonlight, robbing us down to our underwear, then disappearing into the night.

'Do not worry,' the Captain says, patting his revolver. 'I am prepared.'

'*Chai,*' the co-driver calls, staggering out of the cabin like a zombie and entering a roadside hovel beside the checkpoint.

We follow the drivers into a dirt-floored restaurant, sit at a wooden table, and order the specialty of the house. Greasy Chippy sidles over to Roger and places his hand on Roger's knee.

'Meester Roger, you ride with mee in the front, yes?' Greasy Chippy says seductively in his smattering of English.

Roger wrinkles his nose at Greasy Chippy's oil-stained, orangutang-sized hand and removes it from his knee.

'No thanks. You'd only get grease all over my clothes,' says Roger.

'I will wash these hands,' counters the driver.

'I think he fancies you,' says Andy.

'Surely you've heard the Eastern proverb about a woman being for duty, a boy for pleasure, and a melon for ecstasy,' says Pete. 'Anyway, Greasy Chippy's offer might be the best one you get for the next three months.'

Captain Malik catches the drift of our banter and delivers a translation to the driver.

'Nooo Meester Roger, not this,' he says, most embarrassed, launching into a tirade of Urdu directed to the Captain.

'The driver wishes you to know that his intentions are nothing but honorable,' the Captain says.

The old proprietor of the hovel delivers a plate of chapati and a bowl of stew to each of us. Gristle, bone, and globules of fat float in a tepid swamp of gravy. We stare at the suspicious fare, waiting to see who will take the first bite. The Captain digs in and declares it edible. But Doug sniffs at his bowl and slides it away.

'Captain. This is meat. I'm a vegetarian. Is there no dahl or vegetable to be had here?' Doug says.

'It's deer from the hills—very good.' In roadside stops along the Karakoram Highway there are no menus or substitutions. You eat what you get.

'But Captain. The last place had meat, as did the place before that. Some of us don't eat meat. Some of us haven't eaten all day. How can we be expected to keep up our strength if we don't eat?' Doug says.

'But it's fresh. The deer was shot only yesterday . . .' The Captain had not grasped the meaning of vegetarianism to which Doug was a staunch advocate. Years of vegetarianism had convinced Doug that a meat-free diet relieved the arthritis from his bone-breaks and injuries of the past, and also helped his adaptation to altitude.

Doug became terse. 'Now listen—would you eat pork if I served it up to you?'

To Moslems, pork is unclean and to eat it is a sin. Taken aback, the Captain declared he would not eat pork.

'Then what are we to do about this stew?' Doug continues.

Captain Malik ponders for a moment, then shrugs indifferently.

'This is not my fault,' he says, leaving the vegetarians to stew in their own juices.

After four more hours of driving the junga halts and we take the opportunity to sleep till dawn but the junga starts up again as the sun rises to reveal Nanga Parbat towering far above the haze of the Hunza Valley. The road cork-screws into a dirt-walled river gorge, enters a tunnel, crosses a bridge, then turns right toward Skardu, sixty miles away. Twenty miles in the opposite direction is Gilgit, the fertile centre of Hunza: 110 miles beyond Gilgit the road crosses the Khunjerub Pass and enters China.

At the height of the sun's ferocity the junga halts in front of a road crew repairing a landslide. Across the gorge lie isolated hillside settlements of terraced greenery and apricot groves covered in a lacework of cascading streams and waterfalls. Roasting in the steel-walled junga, we get out of the truck and seek the shade of some nearby boulders on a plain of wind-ribbed sand. The dark, massive boulders, once at the bottom of the Indus, are worn into surreal shapes and rubbed bronze-smooth. They sit beside the road like the fossilized jaw bones of a mastodon, and are adorned with the rock-peckings of some ancient artist, who sought the shade long before us.

Watching the workers chip at the landslide I note that the condition of a road labourer in Pakistan is appreciably better than that of a labourer in India. Along the Ganges River Gorge two men are required to operate a shovel, whereas here it takes only one. In India a piece of rope is tied to the end of the shovel so that a second man can hoist away and assist the shoveler swing his load of dirt.

'It'd take five men to do that in Britain,' Whillans says, putting my observation in perspective: 'Four blokes watching while one bloke shovels.'

On 8 May, after sixty hours in the junga, the narrow Indus Gorge opens out and the lights of Skardu appear. In the dead of night we reach Skardu and become lost in a maze of streets, searching for the K2 Hotel.

'*Mon Dieu,*' screams Michelle from the prow of the junga as the truck hits low-slung power lines and stretches them to snapping point. At this, Al chuckles sardonically, and remarks 'Looks like the whole expedition is about to be electro-cuted on the spot, without ever seeing the bloody Karakoram.' But this, evidently, is standard fare for jungas. The co-driver stands on the prow with a long forked stick and deftly raises the lines. At 2.00 am we stumble across the K2 Hotel, find some vacant beds, and flop into them. But sleep is still a problem.

'Hey Greg, come and see these industrious little bloodsuckers,' says Alan as he lies in bed, shining his headlamp onto the wall.

He points to the acrobatics of bedbugs climbing the wall, linking their many bodies together to span the gap to his bed. As they grapple onto the bedframe Alan squishes them with a candle.

'I'll see if there's some bug-spray in the kitchen,' I say.

I fumble through the darkened corridor toward the kitchen. The hotel echoes with the snoring of our group. A lantern, held by the 'chokidar', or night-man, comes to my assistance.

'Bug-spray?' I ask.

'No, sir, sorry, no bug-spray,' he replies.

Velvet-skinned geckos scamper across the ceiling and walls of the kitchen, dart-ing from behind shelves to snap up insects. I point them out to the chokidar.

'What we need is a few of these in our room. To eat the bedbugs,' I say.

'Acha. Small ones,' says the chokidar, who suddenly throttles one with a fly-swat. I look on horrified, though the chokidar no doubt thinks he has pleased me. With a tatty broom he sweeps the stunned lizard out the door.

The vigil of bedbug watching lasts till dawn. I rise early and stand in the hotel's corridor, watching through a window the rising sun illuminate the white sandy delta of the Shigar and Indus Rivers. At six am I hear the manager tapping furiously at the phone.

'Blasted lines are down. Another bloody fool in a truck has ripped them out again,' he tells me.

I nod, looking out the window as Doug pays Greasy Chippy and his partner and bids them goodbye.

Skardu looks like any dusty town on Pakistan's Northwest Frontier, with its poplar-lined, womanless avenues of crumbling storefronts manned by bearded men swatting flies, squatting amid withered fruits and vegetables and other wares. Surrounding the town, high hillsides of sun-baked rock rise to snow-capped peaks, while dust storms swirl about the delta. Perched high above the junction of the rivers and overlooking the town from the Rock of Skardu is the old Skardu Fort, its stone and clay parapets decaying under the hot sun. Built in a commanding position overlooking the delta, the valley, and the town of Skardu, the fort was the stronghold of the old chiefs of Baltistan. Baltistan itself is a natural fortress, hidden behind gorges, mountains, and raging rivers.

Contact with foreigners in early Balti history was usually by invasion. Surrounded as the Balti were by the Dards, or the tribes of Hunza and Gilgit, to the north and west; the Ladakhis and Tibetans to the east; and the Dogra invaders of Jammu and Kashmir to the south, the Balti had many enemies to fear. Their just reputation as fierce mountain warriors began in the eighth century, when they drove out the Chinese conquerors of Kashmir from Baltistan. At that time, Baltistan's spiritual centre was Buddhist Ladakh. Indeed, the Balti's most ancient roots seem to extend toward Tibet for Balti, as spoken even today, is an archaic dialect of Buddhist Tibet. But just as Buddhism superceded the Balti's earlier pagan religion of Bon, so too did Islam replace Buddhism. By the sixteenth century much of what is now called Pakistan, Afghanistan, Kashmir, as well as parts of China, had converted to Islam under the sweep of the Moslem evangelist, Sikander the Iconoclast. But to reassert Baltistan's allegiance to Buddhism and to Ladakh, a large army marched from the city of Leh into Baltistan.

Using the mountains as their weapon, the Balti allowed the invaders to cross the Chorbat pass, near Khapallu, and enter their lands. When winter snows sealed off the pass and possible Ladakhi retreat, the Balti attacked and defeated the Ladakhi army. The Balti then sent an army of their own into Ladakh and looted and destroyed many monasteries in their wake. Withdrawing to their own lands the Balti and the Ladakhi left each other in relative peace, divided by religion. All that remains of this period in Pakistan today are a few Buddhas carved in boulders scattered around Baltistan.

The peace broke in 1841 when the Dogras, a nation of Sikhs ruled by the Maharajah Guleb Singh, set out to extend the boundaries of Jammu. Under the generalship of Zorowar, the Dogra armies conquered Ladakh and set against Baltistan. As the Balti watched the Dogra armies approach along the Indus and the Dras Rivers they again used Baltistan's natural defences, destroying bridges behind the invaders, trapping them on the wrong side of the Indus. An attempt by a 5,000-strong force to break out from the trap met with slaughter. Without food and with winter approaching, the Dogras looked defeated. But the enemies of the

Balti, the Dards from Hunza, helped the Dogras with their knowledge of bridge building and spanned the river with logs frozen together by the icy winter waters. The Dogas crossed the river and surprised the Balti who withdrew in chaos to their fort. A long siege ensued but, deprived of water, the Balti finally surrendered. The Dogras took Ahmed Shah, the Chief of Skardu, hostage, and the treasures the Balti had looted from Ladakh, back to Dogra-controlled Leh. But before he left, Zorowar planned a spectacle that the Balti would never forget, to ensure that neither Balti nor Ladakhi would revolt against their new masters.

On a field beneath the fort, where wheat is grown today, the vanquished people of Skardu were forced to gather in a great circle. In the centre of the circle were the captured King Tsepal of Ladakh, whom Zorowar kept as hostage; Rahim Khan and Hussein, two Ladakhi rebel leaders; an executioner wielding a huge sword; and a vat of boiling ghee. First, the helplessly bound Rahim's right hand was chopped off and splashed with ghee to seal the wound. Next, his ear was cut off. Then his nose. Then his tongue. Each mutilation was followed by daubings of ghee. Finally he was hacked to bits in front of the crowd, his blood soaking into the dry earth. The executioner then hacked off Hussein's hand and tongue, but stopped at that so Hussein might live as an example of the fate of those who resist Zorowar. Hussein died of his wounds two days later, and, during the winter of that year, so the conqueror Zorowar too died, of gunshot wounds in a battle against the Tibetan army at Titapur, where the Dogra army was finally decimated. The Moslem Balti lived under the yoke of the Hindu invaders for a century until 1947, when Pakistan became a state and split-away from the realm of Jammu and Kashmir.

Today, the invaders of Baltistan are you and I, the foreign tourists.

As we fill the courtyard of the K2 Hotel with our loads, ready for the next leg of the journey—the section by jeep and tractor to Dassu, and the start of the walking—our three Hunza base camp staff, Gohar, Mohammed and Nebi, arrive, as arranged by Doug.

Gohar Shar, a tall, dignified high altitude porter from Ghulkin, near the Chinese border, and an old friend of Doug's from a previous expedition to K2, embraces Doug warmly. After an introduction I accompany the expedition cooks Mohammed, whom Gohar calls *cha-cha*, or uncle, and Nebi, who looks rather like Sammy Davis Junior, into the bazaar to purchase porter rations. We return with several hundred kilos of flour, dried milk, dahl, sugar, ghee, tea, salt, and cigarettes. Tempted by the crate of 500 packets of K2 cigarettes I sample one and, in a fit of coughing that my Hunza companions find hilarious, feel as though my lungs have been momentarily transplanted to 8,000 metres.

Word of our expedition quickly spreads through town. Being only the second expedition of the spring to reach Skardu we attract some two hundred rugged, ragged, work-hungry Balti men, who that afternoon assemble outside the hotel compound seeking enlistment as porters. With an annual income of under $300 per year, expeditions are a boon to the Balti; the men around us have walked from villages up to thirty miles away. The government wage for a porter of $4.50 per day, plus half pay for the return journey, plus food, and a kit of shoes, socks, and sunglasses, means that a porter can earn a third of his yearly wages in two weeks.

We require only 136 porters, and Captain Malik tells Pete that as the doctor, it is his responsibility to weed out the sickly ones and choose only the strongest. Pete rests his hand on his bearded chin, thinking of the most expeditious way to do this. The porters wave their red-covered expedition-record books at him, hopefully.

'I know!' Pete says. 'We'll have a race from one end of the hotel to the other. The first 120 will obviously be the fittest, and we'll choose them.'

Captain Malik is impressed. He orders the men into position. Against the almost lunar background of treeless hillsides and the dusty delta, the 200 Balti battle it out. We count 120 as they cross the finish line, record their thumb-prints on a contract, and hire them, as well as a sirdar, or porter manager. To make the medical proceedings look official, Pete passes his stethoscope to me and I listen to a few heartbeats. Some of the noises I hear in those chests are horrifying, while other men seem without hearts altogether. I report my findings to Pete.

'That's why I'm the doctor and not you,' he says grinning while removing his stethoscope from around my neck and placing the instrument in his bag.

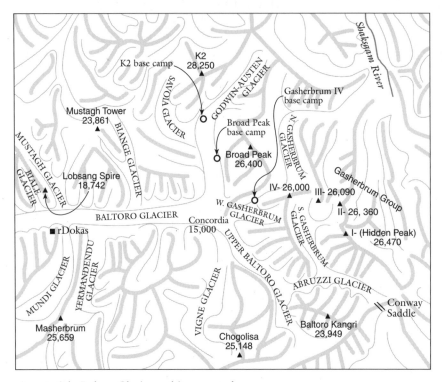

A map of the Baltoro Glacier and its surrounds.

The Baltoro Glacier

From the 1850s to the 1940s, before the existence of the air route to Skardu or the Karakoram Highway, expeditions to the Baltoro Glacier faced a months-long 360-mile trek, from Srinagar in Kashmir. Even in the 1960s and '70s expeditions had to walk forty miles from Skardu to Dassu, and cross the Indus River on *zahks,* or rafts made from inflated goat-skins, before embarking on the twelve day walk to the mountains. Now, a jeep road cuts the journey to Dassu to a day, and a suspension bridge spans the river where the perilous *zahk* crossing forded the raging Indus.

On 10 May our convoy of rented jeeps, Massey Ferguson tractors, and 136 porters leaves for Dassu. The ride over sand-dunes and rutted roads is the dustiest yet, forcing us to shroud our faces with scarfs as we speed past the villages of Bong La and Shigar. But, at the bridge two miles before Dassu, the journey comes to a grinding halt as the local policeman informs us that the bridge is closed for repairs. Although the bridge appears in perfect order, the jeeps and tractors switch off and porters mill about the stony river bank while we enter the police station to negotiate a crossing.

During the course of the afternoon the policeman tells us that the bridge will be open in an hour, in the morning, and not at all. We bide our time taking sweet, milky tea in the austere, whitewashed policeman's hut. Except for a straw bed his quarters are empty, save for a postcard pinned to the wall, of a stunning caucasian woman modelling black lace underwear. The members of our expedition sit around this, completely transfixed. The house-proud policeman carefully dusts it with a handkerchief. Eventually, for no apparent reason, the bridge opens at dusk and we rumble along the final section of road to spend the night at the government rest house in Dassu.

The foot trail towards the Baltoro begins at Dassu and follows the steeply banked Braldu River for fifty miles to the snout of the Baltoro Glacier, the Braldu's source, beneath the flanks of Paiju Peak. From Paiju the undulating, rubble-strewn glacier then leads for forty miles toward the massifs of the Gasherbrums, Broad Peak, and K2. Though the path to the Baltoro Glacier parallels the Braldu River, the valley is sere and desert-dry, baking in the rain-shadow of 21,000 ft high peaks.

Even so, Balti villages sprout up on occasional flat plains at the foot of towering walls of rock and conglomerate.

The Balti irrigate these hard-won parcels of vibrant fertility by channelling mountain streams along hand-dug canals and rickety aqueducts of mud, sticks, and stone that meander across cliffsides to catch otherwise inaccessible streams.

Every stone is sorted from the soil and stacked into walls and the hillsides are terraced and tilled with wooden ploughshares harnessed to great lumbering yaks. Tied to the land in a struggle to eke enough crops each summer to see them through the harsh winter, the Balti are a simple, yet proud people, devoutly Moslem, and mostly of the Shi'ite sect. The origins of the Braldu Balti are clouded by the fact that they have no written language of their own, history being passed on by word of mouth. But according to accounts of village chiefs, the Braldu was settled from 200 to 500 years ago by families from villages in the north, who fled the unjust taxes of the Chiefs of Skardu and the later Dogra overlords. The Braldu settlements were then a hidden kingdom and access to them, by the treacherous gorge or mountain passes, was a closely guarded secret. With Baltistan's turbulent history the Braldu settlers found peace in isolation.

When the first western explorers penetrated the Braldu Valley, beginning with the Munich-born Adolph Schlagintweitt in 1856 and later, in 1887, the Englishman Sir Francis Younghusband, the secret of the Braldu's access was out forever. When Younghusband and his Balti guide Walli, who was born in the Braldu village of Askole, discovered the Mustagh and Shimshal passes, linking Askole to Dardistan, the villagers of Askole were so infuriated that the secret of their isolation had been betrayed, and so fearful of the Hunza raiders who might follow, that the pair left Askole fearing for their lives. It is from these times, when the Balti lived in fear of invasion and distrusted foreigners for betraying their security, that the reputation of the Balti as irascible, hostile tribesmen began.

Balti porter at rDokas.

The scene is chaotic around the rest house at Dassu on the morning of 11 May as porters jostle about to receive their kits of sunglasses, socks, sneakers, tarpaulins, and their allotted rations. Attempts by Captain Malik to create order among the porters turns to anarchy. The lines of men break into disarray and swell, the porters fearing that any hesitation on their part will result in them missing out on their kit. Yet the moment we hand them the kits, most of them rush to the nearest store and sell the items. Driven to despair by the tactless, unruly mob and the impotence of his authority, the captain shouts and yells at the porters.

'These are not my countrymen! My countrymen are reasonable people! What is the point of giving them these shoes, socks and other things when they sell them behind our backs? The regulations state that these items are on loan to the porters!' the Captain says, slapping the Ministry of Tourism's regulations with the back of his hand.

'But what would we do with 136 pairs of used, smelly training shoes even if they did return them?' I ask the Captain.

After the issue of the kits, loads are assigned to the porters. Those porters given loads in anatomically designed packs ignore the shoulder straps, turn the packs upside down, back to front, or sideways, and tie them to their backs with hemp ropes. Nothing we say convinces them to carry the packs as we do, and our demonstrations of the correct way to carry a pack are met with upturned noses and mutterings of 'No good'. Since it costs about $100 to transport a sixty pound load to base camp we have, at Alan's beck, preened away frivolous items. Even simple pleasures such as books fall under Alan's axe of austerity, as every pound in weight costs $2 to transport to base camp, and money is running right. So tight that Alan had been cracking black jokes that we could only afford to buy one-way tickets to Pakistan.

The hike is long and hot, until we arrive at the shaded apricot groves of Chakpo, where we camp the first night of the trek. As we await dinner, Pete leaves for the house of a village man who implores Pete to attend to his sick wife. Meanwhile, I hand Jean and Michelle a tape of French folk songs I have brought. They plug it into their tape deck and listen. Michelle frowns.

'But zis ees not French!' Jean exclaims.

It is French Canadian. The French are very particular about their language. My efforts at detente fall on deaf ears.

At nine o'clock that night Pete returns, accompanied by villagers bringing eggs, a chicken, and apricot kernels, in gratitude for his help. He seems visibly affected by the experience of his house call.

'It was very sobering,' is all he says for a while, until he adds that the woman was desperately ill with an infection following the birth of a child.

He holds his medical bag up and says, 'There is only so much I can do for them out of this. A course of antibiotics here and there, a few vitamins, pain pill. I can't cure them of anything. They need hospitals, schools. They don't even understand the most basic concept of hygiene.' But the hope he gave these people still emerging from the Middle Ages was immeasurable.

The log bridge spanning a narrow gorge between Chongo and Chakpo villages.

After Chakpo, the landscape again becomes barren, though clouds build overhead. Even inches from the silty torrent of the Braldu, vegetation grows unwillingly, and nothing grows worthy of being called a tree. The river and its tributaries are a chocolate brown colour, so turbid that silt particles never settle, but bounce around like never-resting atoms. At rest stops I watch the porters brew tea in this water. I think it impossible to drink such muck, until, handed a cup of tea by Mohammed, the grit crackling between molars tells me that I can, and will, drink it as well.

As the valley narrows the path becomes a precarious trail chipped into steep vertical cliffsides, polished glass-smooth by generations of Balti feet and their herds of sheep and goats. The porters scurry across these sections with the agility of mountain goats, our loads roped to their backs, balancing themselves with staves. In other places the route traverses steep alluvial slopes. Here, the path is nothing more than a set of footprints across an ever-sliding bank. On the slopes that stretch above us puffs of dust appear like sudden grey flowers as stones ricochet down. With each step we slide closer to the river, as if a sand-lion is willing us into the funnel of its trap. One can practically feel the process of erosion happening, as the river sucks at the dirt and rubble.

As droplets of rain pepper the dry earth, we revel in the cool change. But the porters hesitate at the beginning of a long sandy slope scarred with avalanche chutes. They gesticulate and shout about the approaching rain.

'No good, no good,' they tell us in their pidjin-like dialect.

'The porters are worried that the weather will bring rain,' says Captain Malik, himself looking unnerved from the hazardous travel. 'The banks turn to mud and sweep down from hundreds of feet above. Many villagers have been lost here.'

'Yes, I know all about that,' says Pete in a solemn tone. 'It's just ahead that Pat Fearnehough was taken by a slide and lost in the river, right in front of me.'

'That happened here?' says Beth, looking up the Braldu.

The tragedy Pete spoke of had happened in 1978, on an expedition to climb Latok II.

'Ah—the porters have decided to continue,' says Captain Malik as we hear the men chant a prayer. The harmony of their deep voices fills the valley like an accompaniment to the roaring river.

'Shabash, shabash,' cries the sirdar urging the men on. The porters tighten the loads on their backs and take off along the trail at almost a run, keeping an eye on the threatening sky. As we hasten along the trail Pete stops and looks up and down the slope.

'This is where Pat was standing—right here,' he says, his expression flooding with recollections.

'Let's go,' I say, and we hurry away as little stones skip down the slope. As the Braldu swells it cuts one side of the valley off from the other. Because the winter of 1982 had been a severe one the water is still trapped in heavy snows in the mountains and the river is low. This enables us to cross a log bridge to a village on the far bank called Hoto. On the south side of the river we find easier travelling.

Accounts of early journeys along the Braldu describe bridges made from twined and knotted willow stems spanning the river at several points, as well as pine and juniper forests. The willow bridges have long since vanished, as have the forests, felled by the Balti for timber. As we reach Hoto a group of women jabber and giggle at us from a hillside.

'What do they want?' I ask the Captain.

'They want you. They have seen your legs and they like them. The women of this village are very loose,' he answers mischievously.

We westerners, trekking in shorts and T-shirts were exposing hitherto unseen amounts of body to these women. Islamic faith dictates that legs, arms, necks, and women's faces, and all parts in between must be covered. Some of the women shed their veils and smile. Most are toothless with goiters the size of golf balls growing from their necks, a sympton of chronic iodine deficiency. In the Braldu Valley beauty walks a razor's edge, with little sympathy for the Balti.

'You'd have to be a brave man . . .,' Pete says, letting the end of his sentence dangle meaningfully as the women giggle and wave enticingly.

Heat plagues us on the third day of the march to Askole. I walk between Don, waddling along the trail, his walking stick in hand, and Alan, who wears a Skardu-bought straw hat. The brim of his hat unravels as fast as he walks and with a few days of stubble on his chin he now resembles more a scarecrow than the lean and handsome greyhound I'd met in Britain. During a tea break in a desperately hot gulch, we crowd together in the shadow of a boulder, but there isn't enough shade for us all. Steve declines Alan's offer of fifty rupees for his seat out of the sun.

Though it smells of abominations and rodents, the heat is so maddening that I crawl into a nook beneath the boulder. Out in the sun, dressed in layer upon layer of rags and squatting beside fires boiling tea-water sit the porters, seemingly oblivious to the heat.

On 14 May, four days from Dassu, we reach Askole, the most populous village of the Braldu Valley and the last settlement before the mountains. Surrounded by terraced fields and rows of pencil-straight poplars, the village is a bewildering maze of muddy cobbled streets and decaying mud and stone buildings, stacked one atop the other as successive levels fall into disrepair. Oxen, goats, and scrawny chickens root about in the dust. Mangy dogs snarl at us from doorways. Women dash about, veiling themselves from the approach of the camera-clicking infidels. The local men laugh heartily as the women run from us giggling down the streets, herded along like spooked cattle. On seeing Beth and Michelle the women motion to them to cover their faces with veils. These villages—Chongo, Chakpo, Askole—are known to expeditions as the 'Villages of the Rotting Men', a phrase coined by the Italian climber and scholar Fosco Mariani in his 1959 book *Karakoram*. Lacking roads, electricity, sanitation, medical or educational facilities, Mariani saw little charm in these villages, which exist scarcely different today from their appearance in 1958, or indeed, in medieval times. In the faces of the Balti, faces as lined and weathered as old wooden carvings, we see ourselves as we might have lived in another century.

The hodge-podge of racial characteristics that have shaped Baltistan's history lives in the faces of the villagers and in our porters. Some bear Mongolian traits from the Ladakhi influence; others wear the stern, hard-edged features of the people of Northern India; yet others appear European or Grecian. Some have red hair and blue eyes, regarded as a mark of beauty. These anomalous traits fuel the legends that say the soldiers of Alexander the Great intermingled with the Dards and the Balti, though no concrete evidence exists that the Greeks ever visited the region. But legends persist that Skardu is derived from Iskandria, 'Iskander' being none other than Alexander the Great. Poverty, ignorance, sickness, and inbreeding whittle away at the Balti lifespans. Though wretched by modern comparison, the Balti still laugh, live, and love in a parallel world next to our own.

Askole is governed by Haji Medi, the Lambardar, or mayor. A slight man with piercing eyes who looks to have led an easy life, Haji is a despotic, yet popular leader whose family has ruled Askole for generations. Haji has travelled to Mecca, reads and writes English and Urdu, and is as ardent a Moslem as he is a businessman. Expeditions are walking moneybags for Haji. Every porter who passes through Askole pays a tariff of ten rupees; the goats, yaks, chickens, and goods that expeditions purchase in Askole all come from Haji's stables; and all expedition booty scavenged from the mountains lands in Haji's coffers. According to Doug, Haji's men had even climbed up to Camp One on K2's West Face to scavenge a store of goods cached there at the end of the ill-fated 1978 British expedition. But Haji's *magnum opus* of venture capitalism is the cable bridge across the Drumordu River.

This elaborate tyrolean, with winch, pulley, and bosun's chair, was first erected by a French expedition when the Drumordu was in flood. Never one to miss an opportunity, Haji and his men dismantled the rope bridge as soon as the French and their porters had crossed the river, and sold it to the next expedition that

Crossing the "jola" (cable bridge) over the Drumordu River.

passed through. But that had been a lot of work—he had a better idea. He would leave the bridge intact, claim it forever-more as his own, and impose a toll of ten rupees per man and five rupees per load. With up to forty expedition crossings per year, Haji's pockets swelled.

As we meet Haji outside Askole he is all bows and fawning. Doug is no stranger to him, having been carried into Askole with two broken legs after crawling down from the summit of the Ogre and along the Biantha Brakk Glacier, in 1977. Doug had also once given Haji's brother a knuckle sandwich after catching him stealing expedition supplies. Thus, Doug is respected. We give Haji a gift of a coat to placate his avarice and to insure us against thefts and porter strikes.

'Ohhh tenkyoo, tenkyoo,' Haji says bowing obsequiously, holding his hands in a prayer-like clasp and rubbing them together.

We camp in a fallow field on the edge of Askole, but while setting up our tents Alan looks at his watch.

'The flood should hit right about now,' he says whimsically.

Minutes later, water begins to trickle through holes in the stone wall surrounding us. Alan, who'd passed through Askole with Andy in 1982, on their way to attempt the Ogre II, explains that it's standard practice for the villagers to open the sluice onto this field just as an expedition has set up camp. We try to shift our tents to dry spots but there is no stemming the tide. The local sense of humour has a Monty Pythonesque touch to it but in fact it is merely the hour of the day to irrigate this particular section of the fields.

The regulations allow the porters one rest day during the march and they choose to take it the following day in Askole. As we rest that day another expedition arrives.

'It must be Renato Casarotto,' says Roger.

Indeed it is the Italian solo climber and his wife, Goretta, steaming on to solo Broad Peak North, urging their porters on to double marches. Casarotto passes in a haze of dust kicked by his porters' feet, greets us briefly, and marches on.

Meanwhile, Pete and I wander about Askole. Women screech and fling themselves face-first into the dust to avoid our cameras and people peek at us from behind closed shutters. An open window invites us to peer into a Balti home. Through dust motes rising from the dirt floor we see a rope-strap bedframe and smoke-blackened walls on which hangs a picture of Khomeini. Religion is a logical crutch for the Balti to lean on and derive hope out of their barren land, for there is little that comes easily in the Braldu River Valley. Children, dressed in a laminate of hole-filled homespun woollen tunics, sit playing on rooftops. Goats, sheep, and dogs wander in and out of the dwellings. Their acidic urine serves to keep down fleas and lice. Pete corners some Balti women threshing grain.

'*Mitai? Mitai?*' the women say, and they touch their tongues with the tips of their fingers, signalling that they want that foreign delicacy, candy. Pete offers a handful of red vitamins instead. With doe-eyed temerity they take the magic objects from him as gently as if they were diamonds, and let us snap a few photographs.

'If there is such a thing as reincarnation, and you found yourself reborn into a place like this, then you could say with a fair degree of certainty that you'd blown it in your past life,' I say to Pete as we walk down a street.

'It could be worse,' he answers.

I couldn't imagine a margin for optimism. 'How?' I ask.

'Well, you could come back as an Askole chicken,' and he points to a brood of bedraggled and scrawny birds rooting about in the grey muck of a culvert. That fate, we agree, must be reserved for the really bad eggs of society.

'You know, I sometimes think that the best thing I could do with my life would be to set up a clinic in one of these places. God knows, they could use one,' Pete says.

We had wandered through Askole, past a graveyard where the graves were marked with two-foot-by-two-foot ankle-high fences, giving the impression that the dead were buried standing up, to save space for the living to grow crops. As we proceeded into a field of iron-stained boulders a few snot-nosed boys followed us, lobbing stones from their sling-shots at the sleek dragon-lizards that sunned themselves among the bleached ibex skulls mounted atop the boulders.

'If you could stand it, putting a clinic in here would be a worthwhile thing to do,' I say. I felt at ease with Pete. There was no need to put on a front of mild bravado as with the others.

'Yes but it's not as simple as that. Just say someone did build a clinic here. You'd increase the Balti's awareness of sanitation, reduce the incidence of disease and sickness, and decrease the infant mortality rate. The population grows, the village swells. The hillsides are scoured further for firewood, the land overgrazed, overfarmed, the wild game hunted out. This land can't sustain more than a small village. For all the good you'd do you'd create as many ills,' Pete said.

The problem was insoluble. It boiled down to a balance between the natural world and man's world. In Pete's and my world that balance had been lost. Progress had bludgeoned nature into a shape that suited man's needs. The other end of the scale, Askole, retained the balance yet struggled against nature's overwhelming forces. It was as if man was not a native of earth at all, but some clumsy intruder. Perhaps the reasons we were drawn to the mountains was precisely because they were not man's place at all.

On 15 May we leave Askole. Two hours of walking brings us to the tongue of the Biafo Glacier, a towering mound of ice and rubble bulldozing out of the mountains, jutting into the Braldu. We cross the 200 ft-tall glacier and reach the camping spot Korophon, a Balti name that refers to a huge central boulder sitting on a plain. Far up the Biafo rise the stupendous granite fortresses of Conway's Ogre and the Latok Peaks.

On the sixth day we ford the thigh-deep and ice-cold Drumordu River, avoiding Haji's bridge while the river is low, to camp at a desolate riverbank campsite called Bardumal, meaning, in Balti, 'Troublesome Place'. But a few miles before Bardumal we encounter Casarotto's Liaison Officer, with two porters, heading

Porters fording the Drumordu River at low water en route to Bardumal.

back toward Askole. The LO walks slowly, leaning on a ski pole, looking very ill.

'It looks as if Casarotto's LO has had enough and is heading back to Skardu,' Doug says, quickly assessing the situation.

'Well, that'll give the signal to Captain Malik to bail out as well. He's been moaning about the hiking more every day,' says Pete.

The arduous trek to the Baltoro is more than most LOs can take, for officers in the Pakistan Army are accustomed to being chauffeured about in jeeps, rather than grovelling on foot. To accompany his ailing comrade-in-arms back to Askole would be a graceful and strategic withdrawal with minimal loss of face for Captain Malik.

Pete examines the sick LO the moment we reach him.

'It's probably the altitude, but it could be your heart. You'd better descend as low as possible, and very slowly,' Pete tells the man. He is overweight and doesn't look as though he has ever walked anywhere.

Captain Malik and his comrade debate for some minutes in their native tongue, commiserating with each other's ordeals. With the little Urdu I have learned I can work out that Captain Malik is telling his comrade about the anarchy and the erosion of his authority: why, only the day before, Nebi had told the Captain to jump in the Braldu when the Captain had ordered Nebi to take his boots off for him! 'These Hunzas and Balti are a rebellious people,' asserted the Captain. 'They don't know who is running Pakistan.' Casarotto's LO stands, bids us farewell, and marches off into the brown landscape.

'You're not going?' asks Doug of Captain Malik, plainly surprised.

'No. I'll stay until I am killed or injured,' the Captain replies courageously, showing more mettle than we'd given him credit for.

At Paiju campground we find the last trees we will see for three months. Bisected by a clear stream running down a grassy hillside, Paiju is the oasis of the Braldu Valley. Paiju, which, in Balti, means 'salt', derives its name from salty deposits around a nearby hot spring. Above the campsite loom the granite buttresses and ice walls of Paiju Peak. Within sight of Paiju lies the snout of the Baltoro Glacier, the black and chaotic river of rubble and ice that spews the Braldu. Unlike the mouth of the Gangotri Glacier, where thousands of Hindus and Buddhists flock for worship, the Balti fear the Baltoro. It is a place of cold, of crevasses, and a place where spirits live. Yet they go there, for the money and, like us, for the beauty.

The few trees of Paiju are polished smooth around their trunks from porters scaling them to search for firewood. Wild roses bob in the breeze, their pink flowers too heavy for their flimsy stems.The paper-thin petals seem strangely out of place in the arid valley; they belong in a Japanese wood-block print.

After pitching camp we present Don with a bottle of Irish whisky, smuggled into Pakistan for the occasion of his genuine fiftieth birthday. Beth hands him a letter from his wife, Audrey, that had arrived in Skardu. He appears touched by our concern.

'What news from home?' Beth asks, as Don finishes reading the letter.

'The usual business: Water heater is buggered 'n the roof leaks,' he says, keeping his sentimentality in check, yet winking slyly. Don lived his hard-boiled image and loved it.

The porters slaughter the goat we'd bought from Haji Medi and divide the beast into 136 equal portions, giving each man a carefully weighed handful of meat. No man gets more than another, no man less. With bellies full of goat meat they begin a dance, singing and chanting, kicking up a cloud of dust, and insisting that we participate. Don, a non-dancer, trots off uphill, wooden cane in hand. Amid the circle of clapping Balti we take our turns, whirling about in the amber glow of evening, with the orange granite spires of the Lower Baltoro peaks behind us. As the celebration ends the Captain urges the porters into patriotic cries.

'Long live Pakistan! Long live England! America! Australia! France! God is great!'

Before departing next morning Doug decides to clean Paiju up, as the rubbish of many expeditions is despoiling the fragile beauty of the place. Doug organizes the porters into groups and with the Captain interpreting he explains the concept of cleaning up. The porters smile curiously. Cleaning up is as alien to the Balti as the idea of colour to a blind man. In a Balti village there is no rubbish, as everything can be put to use or burned as fuel. The trash on the ground at Paiju represented useful items awaiting a purpose. And as for hygiene, well, the Balti simply never wash.

Led by our example they form a line and begin to pick up a decade-worth of sardine cans and Kodak boxes, depositing them at Doug's feet. Soon sticks and rocks are added to the heap. Handfuls of mud. Live plants. Small lizards and finches flee in terror from the pillage.

'Captain. Order the men to stop. They've gone too far,' says Doug. The Captain shouts but porters continue to scour the hillside.

'I cannot make them stop!' the Captain replies.

Rocks pile up. Laughing Balti trample the streambed, silting the water. The leader has invented a new game and it is fun.

'Aaahaha, the buggers have gone berserk,' chortles Al.

'They'll destroy the place!' says Beth, outraged.

'*Mon dieu!*' mutters Jean, turning away from the imbroglio.

Finally the porters lose interest when they find Doug's game resembles work, and they set off with their loads.

On the seventh night we camp at Lillego, a flat place beside the chaotic glacier, reached by crossing the four-mile-wide Baltoro. Above us stands a huge wall of solidified mud pocked with enormous boulders ready to drop out of the crumbling matrix. The porters lassoo these boulders and secure their tarpaulins to them, tugging on the ropes to cinch knots. We watch in horror, expecting a landslide. Oblivious to the hazards above them, the porters set up camp, light fires, and make chapati, tok, and roti, their wheaten staples. They knead the dough on flat granite stones, porcelain-smooth from years of chapati making.

The clatter of a stone falling down the cliffy alpine meadow far above alerts us to a herd of grazing ibex. These wild mountain sheep with their rich coats command the attention of everyone in camp as they roam in single file across the steep hill. We are in the land of the ibex, the markhoor, the red bear, and the snow leopard.

We drop onto the glacier again next day. Most of the route is on moraine but where we tread on glacial ice Captain Malik looks mortified.

'Will it be like this all the way?' he asks.

'Worse,' I say.

'My heavens—If you have any messages for God, then give them to me now, for today I will surely die.'

We round a bend and Lobsang Spire finally comes into view, at the end of the craggy cluster of Uli Biaho, Trango Tower, Nameless Tower, and the Grand Cathedral. Pointed, slender, vertical, and golden, Lobsang is every bit as well turned as Doug's photograph depicts. We pause to stare at this, our first climbing objective. We have no idea where, if anywhere at all, lies a route up its steep walls.

'There's Broad Peak,' Doug points to a towering mountain in the hazy distance. The peak is massive, high beyond my expectations of what an eight-thousander should look like. I find it hard to imagine that in a few weeks I'll be on its flanks.

That afternoon, 19 May, we arrive at the boulder-strewn hillside meadow called rDokas, at 13,310 ft. The name means, in Balti, 'split rock' and refers to a huge fractured boulder beneath which the porters dwell during approaches to the mountains. rDokas is our first base camp, our home for three weeks while we attempt Lobsang Spire.

The Palmist

The afternoon of our arrival at rDokas the porters gather around us, eager to be paid off so they might hurry back to the warmer valley below. Our plan is to dismiss all but twenty porters who will, under the supervision of Gohar and Nebi, shuttle loads for our next base camp, beneath Broad Peak and K2. The shuttle and the journey back to rDokas will be accomplished in three relays, each taking four days. As part of the ever-diminishing pyramid of our expedition caravan, food and fuel have been consumed and sixteen porters already paid off. Even so, 120 loads remain with us.

Pay day begins. One by one the porters are called by name, handed a wad of rupees, and their conduct books signed by Doug. Captain Malik sits guarding the pack containing the expedition bank, the pearl-handled revolver at his waist a deterrent to any light-fingered Balti. As each man collects his money I notice a perceptible sag in his face that betrays his thoughts: 'For a week I have humped your junk around, breaking my back and suffering for you, and all for this pile of coloured paper. Not goats or chickens, or food, not clothing or bedding or tradeable, usable items, but paper. Now I'll have to go all the way to Skardu to convert this stupid money into useful things, and I'll be fleeced by rupee sharks en route, because I can't count. What I don't spend I'll have to hide, sewing it into my coat for fear of some bandit slitting my throat for it. It's a raw deal, you hear? A raw deal. Ah, why do I do it?'

The Captain selects twenty strong men to remain as shuttlers. As Doug begins to hand wads of rupees to them as well, for their work to date, Alan turns to him. 'I don't recommend we pay the porters who are staying on to shuttle for us. They'll probably go on strike the moment the others leave.'

'It'll be alright. They seem like good men,' says Doug, handing out the pay. As afternoon approaches the dismissed porters gather up their blankets and make ready to leave. 'Captain,' Doug says, 'tell our porters they are the best men I've worked with in twenty years of expeditions.'

The Captain conveys Doug's words of praise, and the porters respond with a final round of patriotic cheers. They are glad to leave. The way ahead is hard and the glacier still in the grip of the worst winter in many years. As they leave, Whillans watches them disappear into the rocky glacier. 'That's the best sight in the Karakoram,' he says.

'What is, Don?' I ask.

'The backs of our porters, heading home,' he answers.

Clouds gather out of nowhere and snow begins to fall as we scurry about erecting our tents. Captain Malik walks over to Doug. 'Leader—These bloody bastard porters! They have just told me they will not work unless we pay them double the official government rate.'

'What?' exclaims Doug. Alan rolls his eyes and walks away. The happy Balti faces of minutes before are replaced with scowling countenances. The porters sit atop boulders, their blankets wrapped around them, staring down on us like vultures. We had brought the strike on ourselves by making the tactical error of having faith in human nature. By paying them for their work to date they had gained leverage over us, an advantage many westerners wouldn't trust even their own kind to remain true to. 'They've got us over a barrel, Doug,' Don says, staring up at the rascals.

'Captain: Tell these men that they are the worst porters I've had in twenty years of expeditions,' says Doug.

The Captain does so and the polyglot argument begins. English, French, Urdu, Balti, and Gilgiti phrases fly about in translation and cross-translation as Captain Malik, Gohar, Nebi, Mohammed, and we bargain with the Balti. Doug applies the patient schoolmaster routine, followed by the call to reason and patriotism, followed by retreating into his tent to let the problem simmer. The porters remain steadfast in their demand for more money. We remain adamant we will not pay them.

'Money is the root of all evil,' I overhear Doug say to himself inside his tent. Captain Malik fumes with anger. He struts about and makes a show of loading his revolver. The porters watch nervously while I dodge the waving weapon.

'Isn't that a bit extreme?' I say to the Captain.

'Stick 'em up,' he says, jokingly pointing the pistol at me, sensing my uneasiness with guns, then shouting for ten minutes at the Balti, his pistol in his hand.

'Maybe we should start burning our rupees. That's what the Americans did in 1975 when the porters went on strike. It seemed to work for them,' suggests Steve.

As the stand-off festers, the unpacking, repacking, and weighing of loads continues as the tempo of the storm increases. Cold fingers, the argumentative atmosphere, and the knowledge that the expedition hovers on the brink of bankruptcy makes us grumpy. We begin to snap at each other and voice our discontent with certain aspects of the expedition.

'This *laissez faire* approach of Doug's to the role of leader is maddening. If he's going to be the leader he should act like one,' continues Alan.

They refer to Doug's belief that if one person accepts the role of expedition leader, like captaining a ship, the others go to sleep and let him chart the course. Doug preferred to let others take the initiative.

'Nevertheless, Doug ends up getting his own way in the long run,' says Roger.

I'd noticed that Doug's closest friends were also his biggest critics. Though warm bonds existed between Doug, Alan, and Roger, formed on climbs of high mountains, there was also evidence of competition and friction between them. It was as if the individuals on the mountain were different people from the individuals on the ground. Doug appears and the conversation ceases. He begins nosing about each load, emptying stuff out, undoing work already done.

'Doug, don't bugger up these loads. We've already packed them,' I say, showing him a list I'd made of the contents of the loads we were to send up the glacier—if the porters ever went back to work.

Doug dismisses the list as an extension of bureaucracy. 'Gotta have it all in here, youth,' he says, pointing to his head, as he pillages another load, plucking stuff out like a raiding magpie. 'I don't need lists. I need a clear picture in my head of what is going on. You've been working in a climbing store too long, kid. You'd better watch you don't develop the shopkeeper's syndrome of keeping lists and accounts.' I struggle to keep the lid on my fermenting frustration and Pete winks at me and smiles. Jean lights a Bidi.

'I'll take one of those, Jean.' He hands me one and lights it.

'But you don't smoke?' he says.

'Only in the mountains. It's the nerves.'

'Ah, *oui*. Me too. The nerves, *oui*.' At last I feel as if I have made contact with the Frenchman.

Captain Malik returns from his discussion with the porters, who are now holed up in a cave up on the hillside.

'It is settled,' he says. 'The porters will work for government rates on the hike up the Baltoro and half pay on the return and on rest days.'

The sudden turn of events is astonishing. Our estimation of Captain Malik rises as we realize he is on our side.

'How did you get them to agree to that?' asks Doug.

'I promised to throw them in jail if they did not resume work,' the Captain says. Threats go a long way in third world countries.

As the snow clouds part and mists waft about the Trango Towers another mob of porters appears, rounding the bend between us and Lillego. It is the Basque expedition to the Abruzzi Spur of K2. The Basques pitch a big communal tent and round the day off with callisthenics to taped music. As Jean interprets his conversation with the leader, Mari Abrego, we realize that our porter problems are mild compared to theirs.

'The Basques have a very big problem with their Sirdar,' says Jean. 'He is crazy, a religious fanatic. He makes the porters whip themselves as penance for their sins, flogging their backs with branches and ropes. And at Bardumal he demanded that the Basques give him boots and clothing. When the Basques refused he ordered the porters to rise up and threaten the expedition with staves and rocks. They backed the Basques up against the Braldu. If it wasn't for the LO stepping in there might have been bloodshed.'

The Sirdar in question, Sher Khan, stands watching us. Tall, with yellow buck teeth and a wild glint in his eye he glares at us with a Charles Manson stare. Mari, a chain smoker, passes around his pack of cigarettes.

'*Gracias,*' I say. 'So, where in Spain are you from?'

Mari turns red and declares vehemently that he is Basque, not Spanish. Jean gives me a brief history lesson to explain that within Spain there exists a strong separatist movement amongst the Basques, and that Basque terrorists frequently blow up Spanish politicans. With a Spanish expedition on the West Ridge of K2 and the Basques on the Abruzzi Spur, I wonder what forms of sabotage we will find ourselves camped between.

No sooner do the Basques leave than two Polish women on their way to climb Broad Peak arrive, Anna Czerwinska and Krystyna Palmowska. We invite them to our camp for dinner. Don even uncorks his whisky. But the women carry themselves with an icy aloofness, rationing their smiles and deigning to talk about much of anything, least of all the situation of martial law in Poland. Intent on opening a dialogue Doug asks, 'Well then, how many times have you ladies been to the Himalayas?'

'Why must you insist on calling us ladies?' Krystyna indignantly replies.

'Very well,' I chirp. 'How many times have you gentlemen been to the Himalayas?' Our guests retire early, and leave quietly next morning, unappreciative of our humour.

Butting into the Baltoro Glacier at a right angle, the Biale Glacier is flanked by the Lobsang Peaks on the west, the Cathedral Peaks on the east, and Biale Peak at its end. The peaks of the Lobsang chain are unnamed, unclimbed, steep rock spires. Though Lobsang Spire dominates the chain, its neighbours are also impressive summits. Lobsang Spire had been attempted unsuccessfully in 1975, by the West Face, by the Americans Don Luria, George Lowe, and Dennis Henneck but no one had returned to try the peak since.

On 22 May Alan, Andy, Pete and I establish a camp on the Biale Glacier and the following day climb an easy snow route to the unclimbed summit of Peak 5547, an 18,205 ft peak in the centre of the Lobsang chain. Even on this minor bump amid a sea of giants there is the elation of treading on new ground. It is my first view of the Karakoram, and my first time to an unclimbed summit. A wealth of abstract feelings, dormant since the day I'd stood atop Shivling, dust themselves off and fill my spirit. From the summit we hear the shouts of Doug and the others as they hike along the Mustagh Glacier below, heading toward Mustagh Pass and the 19,460 ft summit of Karphogang.

We descend as the sun-warmed snow begins to stick to our crampons. Back on the glacier Alan, bitten by summit fever, looks up at Lobsang and declares that he and Andy will try it the next day. Seeing the competitor in Alan emerge, I pretend not to be affected by his urge to beat everyone else to Lobsang Spire. Pete and I decide to team up again to try Lobsang's neighbour, the front-most peak of the Lobsang Peaks, which we christen Biale One. From rDokas the south face of Biale One appears as an imposing 2,500 ft rock wall with a broad knife-edged summit crest. But on the north side the peak is split by a couloir rising from the Biale Galcier, separating Biale One from Lobsang Spire, and leading to within 800 ft of Biale One's summit.

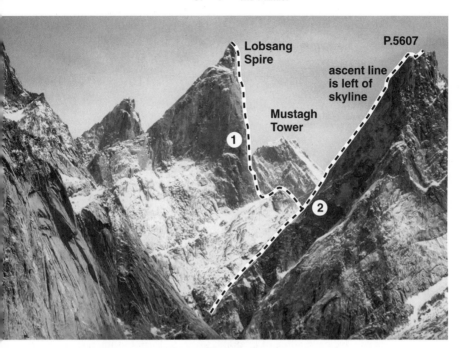

Lobsang Spire, Mustagh Tower and Peak 5607 from Baltoro Glacier.
1. Lobsang Spire S Buttress (British/Australian, 1983).
2. Peak 5607 (to summit crest) (British/Australian, 1983)

At dawn on 24 May Andy and Alan saddle big packs for a three-day attempt on Lobsang by the slabby West Face, while Pete and I plan on a light dayclimb of Biale One. Both teams share the initial couloir for a while, kicking up the firm snow, until Andy and Alan break away onto Lobsang. But, a few hundred feet higher, we look down to see them following our tracks to join us on our route, evidently having had second thoughts about climbing Lobsang after seeing suspicious clouds moving in. They carry no gear, save for a rope.

'Shoot the looters,' says Pete.

We meet at the top of the couloir and without a word rope up together. Pete leads, swinging his ice-axes into a groove of water ice. The thud—kick—thud of his progress resounds about the couloir. After three hundred feet, the rock steepens and the climbing becomes technical, yet the shadowed wall is still thickly coated in winter snow. We bandy about on cramped belays, and move slowly up the snow-covered rock. I take another lead and dig into seventy degree snow to get to a crack. Progress is nearly impossible. My efforts to lead become a case of diminishing returns.

'Let me have a look over here,' says Andy. I come down, give him the lead rope and he veers leftwards. Excavating rock from a thinner layer of snow, he taps pitons behind flakes, levers the flakes outward and slips small wired stoppers behind them. The pins and flakes grip the stoppers like a vise. He clips his etrier-slings to these, and scales the wall, one placement following another. Though difficult going, his progress is catlike. As he digs a deep trench to gain the summit crest, snow bombards us.

'This could slide,' he warns from above.

'Well, that'll be the end of us all,' says Pete.

I follow the pitch, removing the flimsy placements with a light tug.

'Placements like that are rated A5 in Yosemite,' I tell Andy, impressed with his lead.

The ridge-crest is an amorphous, rocky knife edge leading 500 ft horizontally to a summit boulder only 40 ft higher than where we stand. Alan determines that since it is the true summit we had better stand on it, those being the rules of the game. We straddle the knife edge and tear the arses out of our Gore-Tex pants, skirting around gendarmes, and shredding our hands on the coarse-grained rock. The climbing is inelegant. Below we see rDokas and beside us the slender Lobsang Spire. From this vantage Pete and I study the route on Lobsang that Doug had, in years past, seen in profile from the Baltoro: a symmetrical, elegant corner system cleaving the prow of the South Face. That, we decide, is the real prize on the Biale Glacier.

Afternoon clouds scud toward us and sprinkle snow. The wind rises. Nobody mentions the unlikelihood of our making the true summit and getting down before dark. It is late, we have hours of climbing to go, a storm is building.

'Time to bail out, eh?' I say to Pete. He shrugs and holds up the outstretched rope linking us to Alan and Andy. They have forged ahead with our gear, making it impossible for us to descend. So we continue in their wake, like passengers.

'Two hours of light left, Al,' I advise, as Al negotiates a knife edge.

No reply.

'We've got no bivvy gear, you know,' I add.

Still no reply.

'Is it worth it?' I finally ask aloud.

'Yes!' says Al, emphatic and terse.

But we turn about a few minutes later as darkness and snow set in, reverse the traverse, rappel down the wall, and dash down the couloir, to arrive at the tents at 10.00 pm.

Back at camp there is noticeable tension. Nothing is said, but there is a feeling that something up there hadn't clicked. Alan's intensity to succeed and my take-it-or-leave-it attitude has produced a rift.

'I don't get it, Pete. Al is pissed off at me for not wanting to go to the top, yet there was no hope of us getting there before dark,' I say when we are in the seclusion of our tent.

'Al is on a different wavelength,' Pete replies.

As I lie in my sleeping bag that night I think about the day's events and our motives in these mountains. Alan had appeared willing to suffer a miserable, stormy night on a tiny ledge in order to stand a few feet higher, accepting the tenet of climbing that states that a mountain has not been climbed until the summit has been reached. Alan's is an empirical logic, a function of a scientific mind. But Pete and I had shrugged it off, feeling that the ridge crest was good enough for us, that this was an acclimatization climb and as such not worth suffering for. Within each person there are values that make one climb worth it and another not; in the same way it might be worthwhile to carry home a 100 lb sack of gold, yet not a 100 lb sack of manure.

Were we a team? I wondered. A collection of fiery, strong-willed individuals, yes, but not a cohesive group striving for a common goal. We probably couldn't climb 'as one', or 'for the good of the group', if we tried. Alpine-style climbing is a sport of individualists rather than team players.

The seed of competition had also germinated on the Biale Glacier. We all felt the natural urge to compete, whether among friends vying to get a move higher than the other on a hard rockclimb on the local crag, or to beat another team to the foot of an alpine route. I began to wonder how we would make decisions to go up, go down, and when we'd had enough. And who would climb with whom? The silent clash of ideals on Biale One had taught me something: that the challenge to us was not only the mountains we planned to climb but the way we would come to terms with one another's very different views on climbing and living.

Swept out of the Biale Glacier by storm, we reach rDokas next morning. In the main tent Captain Malik entertains us by reading our palms. At first I regard it as a joke, but when I see he is serious I pay close attention as he runs his index finger along the lines on my hand. After a minute he looks me in the eye.

'Ah, my friend, you have very little determination,' he says. I look back at him, glance at my palm, then look out the flapping canvas tent-door to see Biale One swallowed by clouds. I wonder what else he had read about me.

10
The Tip of the Spire

The moment the storm cleared Alan and Andy crossed the Baltoro to attempt Lobsang, leaving rDokas the same afternoon that Doug and the others returned from the Mustagh Glacier.

'There's no need to rush,' said Doug to Alan as he left. Alan's urge to wipe Lobsang from the slate and then move up the Baltoro to the bigger objectives was a source of concern to Doug. The fever to move on to the eight-thousanders had spread through some of the team like a virus, particularly those among us who had no ambitions around Lobsang. The original plan for the trip called for us to use the Lobsang Peaks as an acclimatization stepping stone for Broad Peak, which in turn would be a stepping stone for K2. Doug also hoped to shed the traditional hierarchical structure of an expedition and for us to move about the mountains in pairs or groups, climbing with whoever we felt comfortable with, as one would in Yosemite or Chamonix. The plan was idealistic, perhaps demanding more flexibility from us than we were capable of giving and not everyone agreed that this was the best plan. To some, spending three weeks at rDokas was simply wasting time that could be spent in the higher mountains. Was not the icing on the cake Broad Peak and K2? And, for some, was not the sweetest prize of all to be the first Briton atop K2? As we sat around the tent that night we discussed the issues on everyone's minds.

'Well, Doug,' said Roger, 'I'm afraid that your plan for us all to climb with each other simply isn't going to work. Teams have been formed and I doubt that they'll change. I personally have no intention of taking risks on big peaks with people whose experience in the Himalayas is limited, or who are too old. I mean, let's be realistic—alpining eight-thousanders is bloody serious business.'

Roger spoke openly and honestly, so much so that Don got up and left the tent. But Roger was right. It was imperative that we have absolute faith in our partners for these ambitious climbs. We were a diverse group in terms of age and experience, and the hectic pace of the expedition had left little time for us to become familiar with each other. He was also right about the teams. Alan and Andy were already operating as one team, Jean and Roger another, Pete and I a third.

'This had the potential to be such a productive trip, without the usual divisions of the A team and the B team,' said Doug, who perceived the pairing off of the group as an insurmountable wall that would divide the expedition.

'It still has potential,' replied Roger. 'And what about Gohar—is he the tenth member?' he added pointedly.

The issue of Gohar was a conundrum to us all. Though he'd been invaluable in organizing the shuttle of loads up the Baltoro his presence as one of the climbing team wasn't welcomed by everyone.

'Well,' said Doug, 'Gohar has a lot of experience at 8,000 metres, yet on all his expeditions management has cut him off before the summit. I thought it'd be a good gesture to give him a chance for the summit of Broad Peak. Not to mention the fact that he could team up with old Don.' Doug whispered the last sentence.

'Well I won't be roping up with Gohar or Don. Gohar is a high altitude porter— all he's ever done is jumar ropes and carry loads. And Don is too old and slow. He won't even make a cup of tea,' said Roger.

I admired Roger's frankness and his ability to speak his mind, even though he included me among those not up to snuff enough to climb with him. Roger's openness came from a mental discipline he called 'the inner game', a concept of visualization and self-awareness that he applied to life. By stepping back from reality he could view himself and others objectively and address problems clearly. Doug respected this clarity in Roger, though the criticisms were often levelled at him. Both prized the ability to listen to their innermost thoughts. The 1980s observer would call them 'old hippies'. In fact Alan, whose pragmatism sprang from an analytical mind with a Cambridge education in mathematics, scornfully called Roger's 'inner game' the 'inner joke', and found it nothing less than amusing that Roger had a nagging back problem caused by another ethereal pursuit, yoga. Mysticism, to Alan, was largely humbug.

We were so very different. I wondered if we'd ever tear down the barriers between us. What was it Alan had said about Andy, whom he'd known for years and had attempted the Ogre II with? That 'I'd spent three months with him on an expedition but still didn't know the first thing about him?' Andy's ability to shift with the tides was an anathema to Alan, who sought to shape the course of the expedition, rather than follow it. I was glad that in Pete I'd found a partner well matched in speed and mood.

Finally an agreement on one subject was reached. Since Alan, Andy, Pete, Doug, and I were the only ones interested in Lobsang, we would give that objective another week, then head on to Broad Peak and K2. With that in mind, Doug, Pete, and I decided to leave the next day to attempt the route on Lobsang's South Face. But a sudden two-day storm engulfed the mountains, keeping us at rDokas and causing us concern for Alan and Andy, still on Lobsang.

On 31 May the weather clears again and the three of us cross the Baltoro with packs laden with gear for our proposed climb. We plan to tackle the South Face using the 'big wall' tactics I'd used on vertical rock walls such as El Capitan. Though the route on the South Face would involve several days of aid climbing, load hauling, and the need to sleep on collapsible portable ledges we felt a greater certainty of success on this route than on Alan's and Andy's smooth and indistinct-looking West Face. We would haul hardware, food, and bivvy gear sufficient to weather out several days of storm, while Al and Andy would rely on a single burst of climbing in favourable weather. Since we'd seen no more than three good days in a row since reaching rDokas we preferred the certainty of our method. The difference in styles was the difference between the hare and the tortoise.

As we arrive at Biale camp, after a three-hour hike from rDokas, the weather again breaks for the worse and snow pelts the tents.

'It looks bad for Al and Andy,' says Pete, but shortly after we enter the tents they appear in camp, after a harrowing retreat from high on Lobsang.

'Did you do it?' Doug asks.

'No. But we came bloody close. We got to within a few pitches of the summit. The rock is smooth and plastered with snow,' says Andy.

'We had an awful bivvy last night. The wind is terrible up there,' adds Alan.

Andy, with his British fascination for tatty relics of defeat, sports a rusty old Chouinard chromolly piton and a faded sling from the 1976 American attempt. We admire his trophy, then they pack up and leave for rDokas. 'Will you be back?' asks Doug. Alan pauses.

'I doubt it,' he says.

The storm blows for three days. We lie about our tents as powder slides *wumph* down the gullies of the Cathedral Peaks and clouds boil around the spires. Pete and I share one tent while Doug, bigger and with more junk in his pack, occupies another. We dine together in Doug's tent. As we chat about our very different backgrounds I feel a closeness build between us.

Pete Thexton on Lobsang Spire.

Pete, a Londoner, was raised in an educated atmosphere, his mother a doctor, his father a Methodist minister. Like many intelligent Britons I'd met, he was proper, courteous, yet guarded about his innermost feelings. But he freely admitted he was deeply moved by the experience of climbing to the point where in choosing between his medical career and a life of climbing, he found it hard to distinguish his vocation from his avocation.

'And what about you?' he asked me.

'Bred and schooled in a rough working-class suburb of Sydney. Never went to university. No career as yet. Though sometimes I wonder about the future,' I replied. Then I turned to the other occupant of the tent: 'What are you going to do when you grow up, Doug?'

'Don't know, kid. I'm only 41.'

On 4 June there is a lull in the storm. As we stretch our limbs outside the tents two figures appear out of a halo of rising mists. Unplanned visits usually mean trouble, so we sit on our haunches watching the figures pick their way through the rock-strewn glacier. When we identify Gohar and Nebi we begin to speculate on what kind of disaster has befallen those at rDokas.

'I have one small letter for you, Doug Sahib,' says Gohar in his beautifully lyrical and deep voice as he arrives. The letter explains that a decision has been reached among those in rDokas to continue on to the next base camp while we persevere with our ascent of Lobsang, since our stay on the Biale Glacier had exceeded the agreed time. Beth, Roger, whose back had worsened, Nebi, and the Captain would remain. The porters would return to rDokas after finishing with the shuttle up the Baltoro and await us there.

It seemed a reasonable plan but it perturbed Doug, who felt that splitting the party would desynchronize our levels of acclimatization and make it even less possible for one group to climb with another. He also worried that the lure of K2 might be too great for some to resist.

We return to rDokas for more food and to see the others off, but as we cross the Baltoro we see drastic changes in the glacier. Folds of ice have risen and fallen, like waves moving in slow motion. Lakes we'd seen in one place have drained to another site. Where we'd crossed rubbly, icy hills a few days before, an enormous crater as big as a city block gapes at us where a subterranean ice cavern had collapsed. Nor are we alone on the glaciers. Snowdrifts collect the imprints of animals as small as rats and as big as cats that silently track our scents and visit our camps whenever we are absent.

At rDokas, loads are packed and the porters set off for the third shuttle. The tensions between us dissipate as we each set off to do what our instincts dictate. 'Without the porters watching our every move and half of the team gone, rDokas takes on a new life. Suddenly I see what the perfect expedition is—half a dozen people on a quiet grassy hillside, contemplating the mountains, getting to know each other more intimately.

Roger lies in his tent, bedridden to the point of needing a bed-pan, yet optimistic of recovery. As the days pass awaiting the return of good weather we form a warm friendship with Nebi and the Captain. Though Nebi cannot speak English nor we Urdu or Gilgiti, he has a knack for communicating with his eyes and hands. We sit together on the rocks discussing with the Captain Islam, Pakistan's feud with India, the presence of Russia in Afghanistan, and his life as a soldier. He concedes that military life and war is a 'filthy and regrettable business', yet he feels compelled to serve his country. By nightfall a strong mood of oneness overtakes us as we sit beneath the tarp draped over a boulder that serves as our kitchen. A few straggling porters from another expedition enter to share the warmth of our fire. The Balti chatter happily, their eyes and teeth reflecting the flames. The smell of their bodies, an odour like smoke, fills the kitchen.

'Would you care to hear a joke?' the Captain asks.

'Certainly,' I say.

'There was once a mad hashish smoker who lived beside a well, chanting a different number each day. One day a neighbour asked the hashish smoker why he walked around and around the well, saying 26, 26, 26 or some such number all the time. The hashish smoker merely looked into the well, and continued his intoxicated chant: 26, 26, 26. "You crazy hashish smoker," said the neighbour peering into the well. "There's nothing down there. You've lost your mind." Suddenly the hashish smoker grabbed his neighbour and threw him down the well and continued chanting: 27, 27, 27 . . .'

Laughter pours out of the tent and flows down the hillside, roiling away towards the snapping and popping glacier.

On 7 June we return to the base of Lobsang just in time for another storm. In the tent, we discuss abandoning the attempt and joining the others.

'If we throw in the towel on Lobsang, what guarantee will we have of succeeding on Broad Peak? Will we abandon that too for K2 if the weather doesn't cooperate? It seems that abandoning Lobsang is a certain way to miss all the opportunities,' I say. 'Just because K2 and Broad Peak have more metres, cost more money to book, and have thinner air doesn't mean they are better.'

So we stay, waiting for clear skies until in a fit of pique at four in the afternoon on 8 June we set off up the couloir, in the middle of a howling blizzard, motivated by a momentary glimpse of the summit that inspires us to climb into the storm and out the other side. We respond to an instinctual notion that the weather will clear. There is no other sign, only the feeling that we have to get lucky sometime—*Inshallah*.

A week before, with light packs, Pete and I had climbed the couloir in a couple of hours. Now, with 70 lb each on our backs, in a gale, and with powder snow sloughing about our ankles, we climb only two thirds of the way to the col before dark. In the shelter of a boulder we bivouac for the night. Hopes of a clear day fall flat as we wake to another stormy day next morning.

'Up or down?' Doug asks.

'Up!'

Wind funnels down the couloir like a cyclotron. We reach the col, pitch the tent on a flat knoll, and cram inside. As we remove our sleeping bags from stuff sacks and the down fluffs up, we again notice that mine is so thick it threatens to force us out of the tent. I'd brought the warmest bag I could find, a Marmot Penguin, with a loft almost equivalent to our tent space.

'My God, do something about that zeppelin, will you? It's smothering me!' says Pete.

Doug commences to search for tobacco, preening his pockets until a mixture of two parts fluff and one part tobacco is rolled into a cigarette. As he smokes, Pete discourses dryly about chemical pneumonia induced by the inhalation of noxious smoke.

'I'll be all right, kid,' Doug coughs and splutters.

Next morning, 10 June, is pristine clear. We awake to a barrage of sunlight falling on the tent and emerge to an incredible view of Mustagh Tower, a pyramid of black rock and snowfields rising from a heavily crevassed glacier, framed by the sun-daubed walls of Lobsang and Biale One. Behind Mustagh and a silhouetted ridge of rock fingers peeks the distant yet unmistakable shape of K2. Clouds slowly rise around Lobsang, like a curtain lifting on a work of art. When the symmetrical spire is revealed, it shines like gold. Rime ice and powder snow peel off with the warmth and streaks of melt-water ripple down the wall. In a matter of minutes the wintery hostility of the peak changes to warmth and friendliness. If an expedition could be condensed to its most uplifting moments, it would consist of natural performances such as these.

We pack our gear—foam pads, sleeping bags, windproofs, extra clothing, food, gas, stoves, pots, three ropes, porta-ledges, a rack of forty pitons, twenty stoppers, ten Friends, and seventy carabiners into two haul bags and, leaving the tent on the col, set off with heavy loads to the foot of the spire. By ten that morning we stand before the sharp-edged architecture of the South Face. Doug whoops with excitement at the thought that at last things are falling into place.

The climb begins at a steady upward pace. I lead through a band of shattered rock to the start of the main wall and then haul the loads through a small pulley as Pete jumars up. It is aid climbing here, with nut, Friend, and piton placements being swallowed by the cracks. Pete had done little of this type of climbing before but takes to it like a duck to water, applying himself as methodically as a surgeon in an operating theatre. Reaching a small ledge, he anchors the ropes and hauls the loads while Doug jumars and cleans the gear from Pete's pitch, and I come up on the third rope, establishing the routine we will use throughout the route. Doug then climbs a shallow corner to a 3 ft wide ledge, 500 ft above our tent. While he chops the ledge flat for a bivvy I run out half a rope toward a tenuous thin crack, adjacent to a dark, gaping chimney that seems to plunge into the bowels of the mountain itself. I secure the rope and descend as dusk sets in.

We could have slept out in the open on the ledge, but since we have the porta-ledges Pete and I snap them together and sling them from pitons, while Doug, suspicious of new-fangled contraptions, plants himself on the snow.

'In my day people did all right without portable ledges,' he says. Doug lights the stove and produces cups of soup and tea to rehydrate us. As a parting gesture, the last clouds of the storm ram into Lobsang, rip apart, and empty their snowy

The fin

snowhole
bivvy

porta-ledge
bivvy

porta-ledge
bivvy

Lobsang Spire seen from the neighbouring summit of Biale I. The route follows an enormous cleft of perfect granite.

innards onto us. The wind and snow makes it tricky for Doug to write in his on-the-spot journal, so he zips himself into the smoking-hood enclosure of his sleeping bag to record the day's events, while Pete and I enshroud ourselves in the closures of our porta-ledges.

'I've never encountered as-it-happens reporting on a climb before,' I remark to Pete from within my porta-ledge.

'Nor I. We'd better choose our words carefully in case we're quoted and end up in a book somewhere,' he says from within his.

The sun rises on a perfect day. It is 11 June. Frozen condensation on my porta-ledge storm-fly rubs against my face, rousing me from sleep. I step onto the ledge and pick up the stove. As I replace a gas cylinder to begin making tea I fumble the operation and let half the contents hiss away before the seal is made. It is a minor disaster as we have only three cylinders of gas.

'You're not going to start blowing tents up again, are you?' scolds Doug, reminding me of Shivling.

We get underway as I jumar to the high point and commence work on the thin crack, hammering at knife-blade pitons until I reach an airy site for a hanging belay. I pound in four pitons, clip carabiners to them, and tie off the rope. Twenty minutes later all of us, plus our heavy loads, hang from the four steel spikes and nylon threads. Doug then tensions across on the rope into the gaping flare, and shimmies up till the flare narrows to a bottleneck. He hauls himself around a bulge and into a huge open-book-shaped corner that he aid climbs till the 150 ft long rope ends. In the midst of the corner he slams pitons into the crack to construct another hanging belay. Pete leads th rough, progressing another 150 ft up the 600 ft corner. The angle is suddenly greater than vertical. As Pete whacks and dangles his way up, overcoming bulge after bulge, his trail rope dangles free of the wall by ten feet.

The going is slow, the climbing difficult. Waiting is frustrating. Cold seeps into my hands and feet and Doug's are little better after the sun rounds the edge of the buttress and shadows drape the wall. As I shiver on the belay I notice that the piton that Doug has my rope clipped to, and on which I hang, isn't clipped to the other five pitons that made up the belay. I throw a fit and take Doug to task.

'Bloody hell! Why aren't I clipped into the whole belay? What if this piton came out?'

'I guarantee you it's a good one,' he says.

'That's easy for you to say since you're tied to five. And look at this tangled belay,' I grumble.

'You've got quite a temper, you know,' he chides. We both envy Pete, out in the lead, where necessities channel thinking to the moment at hand. After I lash myself to every available anchor we settle down.

'I enjoy everything about this kind of climbing except the waiting,' says Doug.

'Off belay,' Pete shouts from above, interrupting our introspections as he begins to pull up on the haul line. We unclip the bags, cast them free into the air, and watch them inch up the overhanging wall.

'Here, youth. I'll clean this pitch for you. Take this pack and jumar the free line. You'll be fresh to lead when you reach Pete,' Doug says magnanimously. I shoulder the pack, swing out on the free-hanging rope, and proceed to jumar. The pack pulls at my shoulders and I soon find myself gasping at the thin air of 17,500 ft, exhausted within minutes. I miss my lead.

Porta-ledges dangle off the wall halfway up Lobsang Spire. (Photo by Doug Scott)

By nightfall we stand at 17,650 ft on a foot-ledge in the centre of the corner system, grappling with porta-ledges. We snap them together in the dark and suspend them one above the other. Doug puts his porta-ledge through a rigorous test, bouncing and standing on it to pee, dumping his heavy pack onto it as a pillow. I keep expecting it to crumple, but it survives. After we scrape all the snow off the ledge and render it to water, we delicately remove our boots and tie them safely to the rigging of our porta-ledges, squirm into our sleeping bags, and sleep.

The third day dawns even clearer. Our position is one of dramatic exposure. Sitting on the edges of our man-made ledges we look down over the whole of our route to the speck of our tent on the col, 1,500 ft below. Above, the corner closes off into a crackless seam with overhanging reddish walls on either side. It looks disconcertingly blank, but on the left a hairline crack snaking up a 95 degree wall offers a possible solution. I gulp down a cup of tea and then begin a four-hour lead, using all of our smallest stoppers and pitons to reach a tiny ledge just as the rope pulls tight. The others jumar up. As I look below I see Doug hammering out my piton placements and Pete jumaring up the free-hanging rope, looking like a spider on a silken web, 15 ft out from the wall.

The angle relents to the vertical. Doug leads us up a system of hand-jam cracks that give free climbing, but the rock is verglassed from the thaw-freeze of the last few days, and he moves tenuously over icy holds. We push on into the night, toward the snow ramp at 18,400 ft that we know will provide a good bivvy site. Masherbrum flames in the twilight, the sun sets, then all is dark. Pete puts his headlamp on and grapples with an iced-up body-slot. The beam of light sweeps the rocks, spotlighting holds and flakes.

Greg Child leading the crux A4 pitch on Lobsang Spire. (Photo by Doug Scott)

'Look out!' he calls.

Doug and I huddle against the wall. A rock clatters out of the slot, hits the wall, and bursts into dust and sparks above our heads.

Pete reaches the snow and calls for us to jumar up. He stands on a 10 ft wide, 100 ft long, 45 degree ramp. Moonlight shines on the narrow summit tower. We are but 200 ft from the top.

It's midnight. We are thirsty and tired. Doug and I dig a pit into the snow for a bivouac, while Pete digs a pit below us. But as fast as Pete digs his, Doug and I fill it in. There is a comic element to the operation but Pete only sighs in resignation. After a meal of tea and biscuits we settle down and sleep deeply.

13 June, our sixth day since leaving the Biale Glacier, again dawns clear. We melt a pint of water with the last of our gas, and find our only food is a can of sardines. As we gobble down the morsels Doug pours the oil onto his split and cracked fingertips to soothe them. Then, having eaten, we climb the ramp quickly to Lobsang's shoulder and reach a vibrating shield of rock, fractured to reveal the opposite glacier. We poke our heads through the gap and look down the dark snow-patched walls of Lobsang's Northeast Face. But what we find on the final 100 ft tall monolithic summit block is disheartening. On one side rises an over-hanging, blank yellow wall; on the other it is eighty degrees steep, black, and crackless. A razor-sharp fin divides the two faces.

'It's featureless up there. Impossible,' says Doug.

Greg Child and Doug Scott on the third bivvy, Lobsang Spire.

'We have the capability to murder the impossible,' I say, jingling a little sack containing ten rivets, a quarter-inch hand-twist drill, two skyhooks, and two bolts. Drilling holes in blank walls is a common tactic on granite walls such as El Capitan, where rivet ladders are used to connect discontinuous crack systems. But while it is commonplace to me it is a novel twist to my companions whose more traditional ethics regard such tactics as foul play. While some may say that the 'line' of the route ended there, the spire did not, and if it wasn't the summit that was the object of all our effort, then why bother in the first place? For me, this summit is the bag of gold. I suddenly understand the intensity Alan had felt on Biale One. Pete was keen to go on, I was willing to drill, yet Doug remained ambivalent.

'I can take it or leave it, youth. The summit isn't as important to me as that,' says Doug.

'Remember when Georges told us he'd written to Rheinhold Messner for a place on one of his expeditions? Remember Messner's reply? That because Georges had stopped a few feet short of the actual top of several Himalayan summits Messner asked why Georges thought he could climb the one in question. Well, I think summits count for something and this one is important to me,' I say.

Out comes the drill. I hold it in my left hand, twisting it with my wrist and tap-tap-tapping at it with my hammer in the right. When the hole is a quarter-inch deep I tap in a steel rivet, tie it off with a short loop of cord, clip my etrier into it, and step up. Above it I drill another hole, but this time tap in a tiny spiked hook, or 'bathook', that I retrieve as I move on. An hour passes, I creep closer to the summit.

'Well,' Doug concedes from his perch astride the fin of rock, 'my old mate Dougal Haston used to say that ethics are like erections: No matter how well intentioned they might be they are prone to sudden deflation.'

For two hours I hammer away at the fifteenth pitch, interspersing rivets with sequences of skyhooks balanced on tiny edges, in order that our ten rivets might last the 100 ft to the summit. When I step onto the final skyhook placed on the lip of the knife-edged summit I grab a handful of snow and sprinkle it onto Pete and Doug below.

'A present from the summit,' I shout.

Lobsang's summit is covered with two feet of snow. Beneath the snow is a blank slab, so I drill a hole and place a bolt: the drill snaps with the last twist but I secure the rope. For the last time, I call 'Off belay.' Looking down the 100 ft high face I see the ten steel stubs surrounded in granite dust, sunk deep enough to hold my weight but no more.

By noon we sit in a row on the summit, our legs dangling over the Northeast Face. The day is windless, the view sublime. K2 and Gasherbrum IV loom in the distance, white with snow. Behind us, the uncompromisingly sheer east faces of the Trango Towers rise up in smooth sweeps of 4-, maybe 5,000 ft high. Masherbrum, Mustagh Tower, and the peaks of the Sarpo Laggo Glacier fill the gaps between and I feel a deep satisfaction tingling within me.

Doug draws our attention to the treacherous-looking Mustagh Pass, which the explorer Younghusband and his native companions had crossed using a makeshift

Greg Child leading the fin, a rivet and a skyhook pitch to the summit of Lobsang Spire.

Greg Child on the summit with the hammer and drill that made the final pitch possible.

rope of knotted turbans and horse-reins, 96 years before. Doug points his finger toward the meadow called Lobsang Bransa, on the Mustagh Glacier, where a few days ago he'd found the ruins of buildings and yak corrals from the days when the Dards frequented the pass for trade.

As we prepare to rappel, a huge bird, a lammergeier, circles above us, riding a thermal of warm air. It cocks its head toward us, eyeing the three intruders sharing its airy territory, then it floats away. Doug clips his descender to the rope and sets off down as a second bird, some kind of kestrel, zooms by.

'Have you ever heard that piece of old seafaring lore about the third bird being a precursor to misfortune?' I say.

'I didn't think you were the superstitious type,' Pete says, laughing, then turns and starts down the rope. Behind him a black crow—the third bird—rises on an updraft. I open my mouth to tell him but then think better of it.

At the base of the summit block Doug pauses, turns and wraps his arms around Pete and me in a hug that engulfs us both.

'We must have forgotton ourselves up there, not christening the summit with a handshake.' Perhaps it was the view, or the tension of the past few weeks.

Pete Thexton belays while Greg Child hammers on the hand drill on the last pitch of Lobsang Spire. (Photo by Doug Scott)

Our descent is rapid. Doug rappels first and sets the pace while I lower the haulbag on a separate rope. We pass in minutes sections that had taken days to climb until, a rope-length from the foot of the south face, a shout rises from the couloir. Roger, his back mended, and Gohar are below us, standing on the snowy col.

'Just came to check on you. Did you do it?' Roger calls.

'Of course!' Pete answers.

'See you back at rDokas. And there's mail!'

'Give Beth my love,' calls Pete exuberantly as the pair depart down the couloir and we begin setting anchors for the rappels down.

Fifteen ropelengths later, we stumble down the couloir in darkness. The onslaught of spring has altered the bed of the gushing stream which carves away at the snow. Avalanche debris lies about us. Back on the Biale at ten o'clock that night we find our camp amidst a moonscape of rocks and ice. We quench our thirsts with tea, before coma-deep sleep falls upon us. In the early morning a massive avalanche rushing down our couloir wakes us. The rumble builds for several seconds, getting closer and closer. We sit up, waiting, listening before it dies down, far from us after all. We lie down again and our bodies switch off.

'Now you only have two mountains left to climb!' the Captain exclaims happily as we return to rDokas.

The porters pat us on our backs, glad that they can finally quit this camp, get us up the Baltoro, and be rid of us. 'Good sahibs. Success!' they say.

'Have the porters been OK in our absence?' Doug asks the Captain. 'They demanded more money every morning, and I threatened them with prison every night. I waited and waited for you but still you did not come. Then they threatened to desert us, so I pulled out my pistol and shot a crow. It put the fear of Allah into them. But now you are here and they are pleased,' he says.

Spring greens rDokas with wildflowers, finches, and bumble bees. Near rDokas I lie beside a glacial lake, resting before the move up the Baltoro the next day. Lobsang, now an intimately familiar piece of landscape, stands stark against the blue sky. As I rest I watch dozens of small ground spiders, designed flat to scuttle under rocks, scouring the lakeshore for food. The spiders dart about intently, running onto the surface of the water, then back to land, just before the surface tension breaks and they sink. I gradually see the purpose to their erratic, near suicidal flirtation with drowning: in the lake live thousands of tiny wriggling larvae swimming near the sun-warmed surface of the water. When the larvae rise to the surface the spiders race out to try and seize one and drag it back to land for lunch. The spiders' hunt reminds me of our efforts in the Karakoram: poising ourselves on the glacier, ready to dash into the mountains to snatch the weather's brief opportunities.

On Broad Peak

Glacial penitentes with Broad Peak in the background.

Pubs in Strange Places

Two days after leaving rDokas we pass the desolate glacier campsites of Biange and Gore and arrive at the place called Concordia (15,491 ft), the intersection of the Godwin-Austen and Abruzzi Glaciers. Above us stands Gasherbrum IV, 26,000 ft high, shrouded in storm. The swirling mists lend a dreamlike uncertainty to its steep angled symmetry. Only once, in 1958, have climbers stood upon its summit. Immediately north of Gasherbrum IV, the 26,400 ft high Broad Peak rises from the Godwin-Austen Glacier. And, commanding over all from its place at the head of the Godwin-Austen, looms K2, 28,250 ft high. There in a row, from left to right, stand the second, the twelfth, and the seventeenth highest mountains on earth. We stand, awestruck by the view, muttering monosyllabic, inadequate and irrelevant exclamations.

A final day of hiking on the black scree covering the Godwin-Austen Glacier leads us to our final base camp, a clutch of tents pitched on a mound of rubble at the foot of a brown, rocky peak beside K2. We arrive late in the afternoon of 19 June, three days out from rDokas, with twenty porters each carrying 80 lb loads. Our companions, minus Michelle who had returned to France, turn out to greet us as we arrive. Mohammed embraces Doug, his gravel voice happily croaking, 'My leader, my leader'. He hugs each of us in turn, then steals away with Nebi and Gohar, hungry for conversation in his native tongue. Don stands in the doorway of the main tent, minus his beard, and some 20 lb in weight, shed while travelling about the mountains. Tea is quickly produced and the porters paid off. They wave goodbye for the last time and depart.

Inside the main tent the thirty-odd hams, smoked meats, and salamis that Roger had brought from France dangle around the tent's perimeter, tied to the metal frame by strings. The place looks like a butcher's shop. Captain Malik looks skyward and mutters 'Allah forgive me,' as he enters the pork-festooned tent. We commence to run a gauntlet between legs of ham on one side and oozing pork sausages on the other. As the temperature rises during the day the salamis become huge suppurating things, dripping stalactites of fat onto anyone who dares near them. Doug, being a vegetarian, eyes the meats distastefully, but Pete and Roger waste no time attacking a *jambon* with the nearest knife and gobbling down slabs

Alan Rouse and Don Whillans at K2 base camp in 1983.

of ham. Their faces display an almost orgasmic pleasure, for our stores at rDokas and on the trek had grown lean.

Together in the main tent we relate the stories of the past few days. As Alan hears the story of how we murdered the impossible on Lobsang he eyes me dubiously. 'You're not going to put bolts in Broad Peak are you?' he asks with a grin. When it came to climbing mountains Alan had very concrete ethical beliefs. Foremost among those was the rule that to claim a true alpine style ascent one team should not benefit from the work of another team. That not only meant ignoring the fixed ropes of the other team, even if they were beside you, but deigning to sleep in the other party's fixed tents, if unoccupied, and even avoiding their footsteps!

During our time at rDokas the others had explored the possibilities for new routes on Broad Peak and K2, visiting the east sides of Broad Peak and K2, the Savoia Glacier to K2's West Face, and climbing to 20,000 ft on the South Face of K2, all as acclimatization reconnaissances. During their night on K2, as they bivouaced in a snowcave, an earthquake had rudely rattled them awake, sending ice avalanches crashing down around them. It was on the South Face of K2 that Jean had spent a season in 1981, trying to force a route, only to fail in the face of bad weather and hazardous conditions.

Our companions' reconnaissances found that the only route to the summit of Broad Peak not suicidally threatened by avalanche was the original 1957 route on the West Face but on K2 Don had spied a logical, yet safe solution to the South

Face—an unclimbed spur to the left of the original Abruzzi Ridge, yet safely right of the deadly seracs of Jean's South Face. Doug was well aware of this route from a previous visit and it was on this spur that Al, Andy and Steve had experienced the earthquake. The spur led to the prominent shoulder on K2 at 24,500 ft, and then followed the Abruzzi to the summit. The consensus was that after an ascent of Broad Peak, efforts would turn to this route on K2. Jean felt confident that the mountains would be climbed in short order: 'We 'ave looked at everything. Broad Peak is easy and K2 from ze South Face is straightforward. We will 'ave them done and be 'ome in three weeks, no?' he said optimistically. Roger, for his part, had always referred to Broad Peak as a 'punters peak', meaning it was the easiest of the 8,000 metre mountains.

K2 base camp is a harsh and barren place. A thousand feet above the camp huge seracs periodically break away and crash down gullies to either side of us. Nearby, on the crevassed flats of the Godwin-Austen Glacier, lie the tents of the Basques and the Casarottos. Our camp nestles beneath the memorial to Art Gilkey, a cairn of rocks bristling with crosses and plaques to those who had died on K2. Among the plaques is one to Nick Estcourt, killed on the West Face of K2 in 1978. He and Doug had been fixing rope when the slope avalanched beneath them. The 5 mm rope Doug was towing up the slope had snapped, miraculously freeing Doug from the avalanche, but burying Nick under tons of ice. 1983 is Doug's third year to K2. His investment is high.

The clear running water of rDokas is replaced with glacial pools polluted by the waste of past expeditions. During the heat of the day a rank stench rises from behind camp as antique turds thaw out and go about the business of stinking.

'Leave no turd unstoned,' Don sagely reminds me as I walk toward the designated latrine area behind camp to relieve myself. It is on unstable piles of scree overlying ice that we pitch our tents. Those of us who've just arrived sort among the scree, like prison labourers, searching for flat stones with which to terrace our tent sites. In front of our tent doorways crevasses slowly open and close like giant clams. As days pass, those tents too far from the stable region around the Gilkey memorial drift away a few inches a day, carried by the patient flow of the glacier. Alan stands beside me, looking up the glacier as K2 momentarily clears.

'The mountains are impressive all right, but as far as a place to live it's really an arsehole in the sky,' he says.

I look up from my work of piling stones. The triple-summited Broad Peak rises in a long, lofty chain. Surrounded by a sea of moving glaciers, the cloud-covered island of K2 stands defended by steep rock and ice. Far down the Godwin-Austen rises the truncated snow-pyramid of Chogolisa. The fluted ice faces of a dozen minor summits stand between.

As evening arrives Doug enters the kitchen and directs Mohammed to cook up another bean stew. The others had lived largely on meat since reaching K2, and frown at the notion of a return to a vegetarian regime. As we dine that night in the chill of the main tent the bloating bean stew quickly and vociferously takes effect.

'I've *bean* poisoned,' quips Whillans, reaching for a leg of ham as if it is an

K2 from Broad Peak.
1. SSW Pillar (Polish, 1986).
2. S Face (Polish, 1986).
3. S Face (various parties, including French and British, 1980s)
4. Abruzzi Ridge (Italian, 1954).
5. W Face (Japanese, 1981).

antidote. I chomp onto a chapati. Grit crackles between my teeth. Everyone chews delicately on the tooth-grinding loaves.

'Mohammed, what's wrong with these chapati? They're full of sand!' complains Doug.

'Askole ata, this chapati. Haji Medi no good,' he croaks.

Doug nods. Askole flour is infamous and to be avoided by expeditions and porters alike. Either Haji Medi's millstones are crumbling, or as rumour has it, he throws in sand to increase the flour's weight.

As Roger and Pete tear into a ham the Captain looks on, fascinated. He had stuck to a traditional Pakistani fare of rice, dahl, and chapati ever since we had persuaded him to try a sardine, which had almost made him vomit. Fish are quite alien to the average Northern Pakistani, in particular the Balti from the Braldu Valley. During the approach up the Braldu I had noticed one of the porters watching me gobbling sardines. To sate his curiosity I offered him one. He held it by the tail, suspiciously, and made a gesture for me to explain what sort of creature it was. I described it by pointing to the Braldu, indicating that it lived in water. The porter took one look at the murky river, screwed up his nose, and tossed the sardine aside. Anything that lived in that river, he knew, must be evil.

On the morning of 20 June we split into groups and headed to different parts of the mountains to further acclimatize. Jean and Roger donned their skis and headed for the East Face of K2 and to Windy Gap, while Alan and Andy decided to remain in base camp and rest before going on to Broad Peak. Doug, Steve, Don, Gohar, and I headed up the heavily crevassed Savoia Glacier, to see K2 from the West.

The route along the Savoia Glacier skirts the flanks of Angel Peak, a 22,334 ft outlier of K2, then passes through an icefall known as Death Alley, named by expeditions who have visited K2 from the West. The path is aptly named, flanked as it is by shattered monoliths of ice, melted and twisted by the heat, and festooned with daggerish frozen tears that snap with the wind and tinkle into crevasses. Doug saunters along the glacier, humming to the music on his Sony Walkman, blissfully stepping across gaping fissures. We move quickly through Death Alley, to the open glacier where a well-worn path through the snow leads toward the Spanish West Ridge Expedition's base camp. Roping up to cross the crevasse field we enter a realm of cloying heat, and cover our faces and heads with cotton towels, like a band of Bedouins. The Savoia Valley is subject to extremes of temperature—intense cold when shadowed, debilitating heat when not.

Out of the shimmering noon we come across a scene that looks like a plane crash, with the survivors living amongst the wreckage: the Spanish camp. Tents float in puddles of slush that freeze solid at night. Heaps of rotting garbage and excrement lie everywhere. The Spaniards had even become too lazy to toss their trash into the crevasses surrounding them like a minefield. The constant battle with the harsh environment had been lost, but there was a vestige of civilization amid the squalor.

'Look!' Pete exclaims, pointing to the only toilet in the entire Karakoram. 'The throne room of the mountain gods!'

Perched over a crevasse, with a rising mound of shit beneath it, stood a thunderbox, built from packing crates and surrounded by a ragged wall of wind-tattered canvas to give an illusion of privacy. Within arm's reach a news magazine fluttered in the breeze. We each took our turn to drop our pants and test-drive the marvellous contraption.

Sweat-soaked and sun-struck as we are, the Spaniards thrust cold beers into our hands. The alcohol travels straight to our heads, making us instantly drunk. The Spaniards motion for us to enter their communal tent. Inside, light bulbs dangle from wires leading to a broken-down generator. Whillans's eyes light up as he sees crates of cognac and beer lining the tent walls. The Spaniards ply us with liquor and canned *payella* as cameras flash and a cine camera whirs. We have walked into an interview for Spanish television.

'Signor Scott, do you think Messner will succeed in climbing all the 8,000 metre peaks?' a man holding a microphone asks Doug.

'Yes,' Doug answers, popping open another beer.

After an hour the interview ends. The Spaniards grab their packs to return to the West Face. We all walk together for a while, until they take a sharp right turn toward the West Ridge and we continue to the Savoia Pass. An hour of inebriated trudging puts us at a suitable bivvy spot. The moment that the sun leaves the temperature plummets: our perspiration freezes in our clothing, fingers become blocks of wood, and our noses clog with frost. We pitch three tents and retreat into the wombs of our sleeping bags to sleep.

At dawn, we gasp at the cold again until the sun bounces off the white walls of Summa Ri and bakes us alive. As sweat pours from our faces we frantically strip down to our underwear and dream of the cold as a saviour. Steve clips snowshoes to his boots and breaks trail. Over a snowy rise we see the Savoia Pass, leading into China. A windplume streaks from K2's summit. The Northwest Ridge, attempted by Americans in 1975 and Poles in 1982, rises into a clear sky.

Trudging through soft snow at 19,000 ft, we move lethargically. Sweat drowns my face. My head begins to feel like lead and throbs rhythmically. I begin to fizzle out and soon can go no further. At a bergschrund beneath the ice slope leading to the pass Don and I pitch a tent, at 19,500 ft. The others uncoil their ropes and press on while I languish with heatstroke. My entire body feels as if it is aflame and my thoughts are feverish. With dream-like detachment I watch Steve lead a 50 degree ice slope, belay off his axes, and bring Doug and Pete up to him. Doug leads on, then Pete, until all three are spread out on the slope, the highest of them being only a hundred feet below the border of China and Pakistan. Finally it is Gohar's turn to move from his stance, a few feet from Don and I. He shifts awkwardly, reluctance written on his face.

'Doug Sahib, I have forgotton to bring my crampons,' he confesses. I see Pete, up high, shake his head.

'Aye, well that's bloody typical of this crew. Couldn't organize a fuck in a brothel,' sneers Don.

Doug urges Gohar on with a tight rope. After an hour of Gohar slipping on the ice, they disappear over the col in a howling wind, to camp at 21,000 ft.

Don sits beside me on his sleeping bag. I lie with an ice-pack of snow wrapped in my scarf, cooling my forehead. Slowly, I return to normal. Outside the open tent door we can see the small dark smear on the ice that is the Spanish camp, flanked by K2 on the left and the 23,000 ft Summa Ri on the right.

'Back in the '50s, when I was a lad, it was a real event if you met another expedition in the mountains. Now all you do is fall over every other bugger and his dog. I remember meeting Buhl and his mates in Skardu—now there were a bunch of blokes worth meeting,' said Don. The 1950s had been the golden age of mountaineering, the era when the great peaks of the Himalayas were receiving their first ascents.

'And all this alpine-style nonsense. In my day an expedition was an expedition. Everyone worked for the same thing. On this trip, I'm buggered if I know what we're working towards. All these jaunts here and there—we're all over the bloomin' place, up and down like a bride's nightie.'

'It's a different philosophy, Don, a different time.'

'Aye. Then I'm glad it passed me by and I did my climbs when they counted for something.'

'You ought to write about it, Don,' I urged.

'Ah, no, lad,' he frowned. 'Never write anything. You'll only regret it.'

Don's comment brought to mind a conversation I'd had with Doug regarding writing about climbing, in which he'd made the observation that several of his old partners, Dougal Haston, Peter Boardman, and Joe Tasker had all been killed shortly after having books published. The thought loomed like a sinister totem. Superstition, yes, but mountains are places in which to be superstitious. Up until that point Don had been a caricature of the tales I had heard of him, speaking in a dialect of witticisms and wisecracks. Now that the numbers were pared down he began to talk more seriously. Conversation continued long into the night.

In the morning, as Don and I stomped back to base camp, we watched our companions rappel and lower the cramponless Gohar down from Savoia Pass. We were all back in camp by 22 June, missing by a matter of an hour Alan and Andy, who'd set off for Broad Peak.

Next day Jean and Roger, returned from their journey beneath the East Face of K2 to Windy Gap, a pass on the Sino-Pakistani border, prepare once more to depart, also for Broad Peak. Doug approached Roger:

'Don't you think it's a bit early for Broad Peak? You've been on your back for two weeks, you know,' said Doug, cautious in matters of acclimatization, and concerned that few of us would as yet be adjusted enough to move up to 8,000 metres.

'I'd say the weather is as good as we'll get it. Al and Andy seemed to feel ready,' replied Roger.

Pressured by the knowledge that the spell of good weather was upon us we all felt the urge to give Broad Peak our shot. But it was true that none of us had spent any time above 22,000 ft—a prerequisite for going high. Doug was concerned, but Captain Malik diverted his attention with a pile of mail delivered by a Balti mail runner. By this stage of the expedition, home had begun to seem imaginary, but the letters returned us to reality. The Captain's letters were mostly from his wife, written in neat, closely spaced Urdu script. But one letter, written on military stationery, caused his expression to become grave.

'What is it Captain?' asked Doug.

'I have been promoted to Major and given authority over all the expeditions in the Baltoro,' he said.

Congratulations were expressed. Major Malik looked across the wasteland of his new command—mountains, rubble, ice and snow—and twirled his moustache thoughtfully. Being the King of the Baltoro was the Pakistani equivalent to being Admiral of the Swiss Navy.

'But that is not the least of it,' Major Malik went on. 'I have orders to arrest Casarotto.'

'What?'

'Yes—I have it here,' he said waving the document. 'He is charged with mistreating his porters and his Liaison Officer. The poor fellow we met on the approach suffered a heart attack in Askole, and had to be helicoptered to Skardu. He is very ill.'

Casarotto had already told us of disputes with his porters over his urging them to do double marches. He'd even come to blows with them. Yet the charge was absurd, and with Casarotto soloing at that very moment high on the North Ridge of Broad Peak North, the situation was laughable.

'What am I to do?' said the Major, realizing the futility of his orders, and no doubt fearing the wrath of Mrs Casarotto. That afternoon, Roger and Jean left for Broad Peak. Pete and I began to prepare our gear for an attempt beginning the following evening. I had recovered from my bout of heatstroke and Pete, though complaining of a slight sore throat, felt strong. We trimmed away at our gear, neurotically snipping off grams from the gear we'd carry, even going to such lengths as to cut inches from the straps on our packs, breaking matches in half, and removing labels from our clothing. Anything unnecessary is left out. Even the tiniest details are attended to: instead of carrying a full tube of sunscreen we carry only what we will need—a film cannister full. Immersing ourselves in these preparations removed us from the tensions building among the group. Doug had coupled with Steve to climb Broad Peak, leaving Don with no alternative but to climb with Gohar. This Don regarded as a slap in the face, and he brooded about it for some hours. Once, Don was the world's most experienced high-altitude alpinist, invited on expeditions all over the world. Now, the only partner he could find was Gohar, a paid high altitude porter. But soon we all became pent up with the excitement of launching onto an 8,000 metre peak and the tensions eased.

'I'm quite looking forward to reaching 8,000 metres for me fiftieth birthday,' he finally said to Steve, whose excitement was building no less than anyone's.

Major Malik sat reading *Reign of Blood*, a gory saga of Idi Amin's dictatorship, a popular book in the barracks. As I packed he informed me of Amin's selected atrocities, Major Malik's favourite one being that Amin kept his ex-wives' heads in his kitchen freezer, to keep his current wife in line. Meanwhile, Nebi busily paved base camp with flat stones. Since some of us had tripped on the rubble and almost broken our legs on the way to bed, this was a good idea.

'What are you making, Nebi?' I asked.

'Road,' he said after searching his meagre vocabulary.

'Road, eh? Bus coming, Nebi?'

'Ji! Bus!'

'You, me, we catch bus, go Skardu after Broad Peak, eh?'

'Skardu, ji! Acha, acha!'

Broad Peak West Face (North Summit at left, then Central and Main Summits).
1. Traverse of North, Central and Main Summits (Polish, 1984).
2. W Face to Main Summit (Austrian, 1957). The standard route.
O = Standard locations of Camps 1, 2 and 3 on the West Face route.

The Other Side of Luck

Throughout the calm, clear morning of 25 June we watched the figures of Alan, Andy, Roger, and Jean leave their high bivouacs and head toward the summit of Broad Peak. A thousand feet below them, the two Polish women followed their tracks. Even through an 800 millimetre lens they appeared as mere specks beneath the rocky black pyramid of the main summit. The slant of the sun highlighted their tracks as they zigzagged across the great snowy terrace. They negotiated a small serac, then a steep chute, then gained the col at 25,591 ft between the main and central summits.

'They'll be on the summit in two hours,' Doug forecasts.

As the figures move south on the long summit ridge they disappear behind a rocky promontory. Below them we see the Polish women turn around and descend from 24,500 ft, evidently deciding that the time is not ripe for them to push on. As the women descend they sway and stumble with fatigue. From a distant part of the mountain a savage crack rents the air as a huge avalanche cuts loose and blows up a thick cloud of debris.

Soon it will be time for us to leave for Broad Peak too. Pete and I decide to leave in the later afternoon to climb Broad Peak's initial couloirs by moonlight and reach Camp One while the snow is firmly frozen. Doug and Steve, with Don and Gohar, decide to leave at dawn on the 26th, after a full night's sleep. An hour before sunset, as the afternoon begins to gather and the light on the peaks around base camp softens to a gentle glow, Pete kisses Beth goodbye and we bid the camp farewell, heading across the glacier. Out in the centre of the icy wastes I pause to photograph K2, majestic and clear in the twilight.

'There'll be plenty of time for that,' Pete says, hurrying me along toward the base of the three-crowned giant ahead of us.

Between base camp and the foot of Broad Peak lies two miles of glacier, crevassed and forested with a maze of ice towers, or *penitentes*. As Pete and I pick our path across suspect snow patches, moving from one rubbly island to another, we probe the snow with our ice axes to check for crevasses. We talk of the route ahead and check off items to ensure that nothing has been forgotten. As we make our way we talk about Lobsang. Yes—it had been perfection, and there would be more. We spoke of more climbs—he'd come to Yosemite and we'd climb El

Capitan; I'd visit the Alps in winter; and maybe, just maybe, if Broad Peak went well, we'd find ourselves together on K2. A great warmth radiated from Pete onto me, like the alpenglow clinging to the mountains. His small kindnesses and carefully chosen words told me that I was at last breaking through the carefully guarded barrier with which he surrounded himself.

At a snow patch I probe forward, poking my ice axe shaft into the snow ahead. The snow feels firm. Nothing thuds or tinkles to imply a hollow surface. I deem it safe, but the very moment I assure Pete it is so and move forward, the surface gives way with a crash and I drop into a slot.

'Crevasse,' I understate in the sudden quiet that follows smashed mirrors and glassware. I had the foolish surprise one would feel standing on a glass-topped table that had suddenly shattered. More surprising was that the crevasse had a false floor and I had stopped just a body-length down. Beneath me I could see cracks in the floor that dropped into a black emptiness.

'Thought I'd lost you already,' Pete said, seating himself on his pack as I extricated myself. Scalpel-sharp fins of ice had sliced hairline cuts into my arms and face. I looked as if I'd had a tussle with a wildcat.

Pete points over his shoulder. 'You'll be pleased to know you've got an audience. Some trekkers watched the whole display from their camp a few hundred feet away.'

'How embarrassing.'

'Don't worry,' Pete added impishly, 'no one from our camp saw it.'

As we enter the forest of *penitentes* the sun drops, leaving the air breathless and the summit rocks of K2 burning orange. The gurgle and rush of streams falls suddenly silent, choked by night's freeze. As we emerge from the ice-maze, Broad Peak stands suddenly before us, its silhouette well defined as the Baltoro grows quickly black with night. On a bed of scree beneath the mountain we pause for a drink and a bite to eat. On the scree lies a cluster of old wooden wedges and hemp slings. We fiddle with these artifacts left by some predecessor, perhaps the Austrians Hermann Buhl, Kurt Diemberger, Fritz Winterstellar, and Marcus Schmuck, who pioneered the first ascent of Broad Peak in 1957 or, perhaps, they belonged to the tragic Polish expedition who'd made the first ascent of the 26,247 ft high Central Peak.

In late July 1975, six Poles set off up the face above us, climbing a more direct variation of the Austrian Route to the 25,591 ft col between the Main and Central Summits. That variation has become the *voie normal,* but from the col they planned to climb the South Ridge of the Central Summit. Snow conditions were poor, the going slow. Beneath the col, as night and storm approached, one man, Roman Bebak, descended leaving five to complete the climb. As the storm grew stronger and the five rushed to complete the route, three men—Bohdan Nowaczyk, Marek Kesicki, and Andrei Sikorski—took shelter from the wind on the final rock step below the summit, while Kazimierz Glazek and Janusz Kulis persevered to the top. At 7.30 pm Glazek and Kulis reached the summit, then descended to the others. The storm was now upon them. As the last man, Nowaczyk, made the final rappel to the col, the anchor pulled and he fell to his death, taking the vital ropes with him. Trapped in a raging storm and with no way to descend the steep, avalanche-prone chute beneath the col, the climbers bivouaced out, wearing only the clothes on their backs.

At first light they resumed their search for Nowaczyk and the ropes. Nothing was found; in desperation, they tied all their slings and harnesses together to construct a makeshift rope. In the afternoon Glazek descended the gully to the snowfields and 300 ft down found a site for a bivouac. But behind him the weakened Sikorski slipped knocking Kesicki and Kulis from the face. Sikorski fell 600 ft; Kesicki slid down the snowfields and plummetted thousands of feet over the huge seracs; Kulis, the only one of the three to survive the fall, stopped 150 ft below Glazek. Glazek and Kulis endured a second terrible night in a snowhole, then continued down next morning, their fingers and feet frostbitten. Kulis would subsequently lose most of his fingers and toes. On the descent they found Sikorski, partially buried in snow. Attempts to revive him proved fruitless: he was dead. The only traces of Kesicki were a few tufts of hair and some bloodstains on the snow.

As we enter the first couloirs of Broad Peak the full moon rounds the mountain and douses the West Face in a silvery light that bounces bright as daylight off the snow. We crampon our way quickly over the firm, crystalline surface until a rocky

The view from Broad Peak: the Baltoro Glacier winds around Crystal Peak.

promontory appears, at 18,543 ft. Here sits a small tent—Camp One, established by the Polish women. Anna and Krystyna were climbing the mountain in siege style, placing fixed camps along the route, each stocked with bivvy gear, food, and fuel. We rest here an hour, make tea, then continue into the moonlight.

Step after step, breath after breath, every hour the atmosphere just a little thinner. Behind us, the first hint of dawn turns the Karakoram every shade of blue and gold imaginable, while the moon sits fixed in the sky, great and white, refusing to evaporate. The mountains glow, changing colour by the minute, like a horizon of chameleons. With this view over our shoulders, we zigzag through the gullies and towers of yellow limestone. As we reach the crest of a rocky spur at about 20,000 ft, blinding daylight and heat flood the mountain. Day reveals further relics of past expeditions; shredded tents, bits of fixed rope, and an old oxygen cylinder poking out of the snow. I pick up the steel cylinder to feel what it would be like to hump its weight up a mountain. Weighing at least 20 lb, it feels like an unexploded bomb, but my lungs wish they could have a taste of the cylinder's juicy contents.

The half-melted tracks of our four members above pit the slope. As I slot my feet into their footsteps I play a brief game of pretend that I am following Buhl's tracks, back in 1957, the year of my birth, and the year too that he died, on Chogolisa. Heat dries our throats so we keep chewing handfuls of snow. Tiny black gnats, blown in from the plains, dot the surface of the snow. At first they look dead, but as the sun warms them they spring to life and crawl around.

At about 20,500 ft on the morning of 26 June we meet Alan, Andy, Roger, and Jean, returning from their successful ascent of the previous day. They look tired, almost aged.

'Well done,' Pete says to Andy and Alan, who reach us first and describe their windless summit day.

'It's no punter's peak up there,' Alan says. 'The summit ridge is at 26,000 ft and is bloody long. Technical too. Andy felt sick all the way along the ridge. And Roger nearly bought it on the descent—he tried to glissade down from the col, got out of control, lost his ice-axe, and went sliding down. By a miracle he stopped in some soft snow.'

Andy considers us wearily. 'Now I know what they mean when people say "8,000 metres."' And down they go, sucking at the atmosphere that grew thicker with each step.

From our position on the spur, we can see the jet-black Central and Main Summits far above. To the north is K2. To our left, the 300 ft tall ice cliffs at the foot of the West Face's great snow terrace, above which our route will skirt, appear to threaten our path. This is, however, an optical illusion, for the cliffs are far to the side. Even so, whenever there is a crack and rumble of falling ice we look up in alarm.

At about 21,600 ft Pete stops and points ahead. 'Hey—I see numbers!'

'What? You're hallucinating!'

'No. Look—on the side of the Central Peak—three numbers—666.'

I scan the wall and just as I feel certain that Pete is succumbing to hypoxia I too see a chance play of sunlight on white snow and black rock that bears a perfect resemblance to three sixes.

'Looks as though Crowley left his mark here too,' says Pete, referring to Aleister Crowley, the Irish mountaineer and satanist who'd been on the flanks of K2 in 1902. Crowley believed that the number 666 had magical powers. On K2's Northeast Ridge his party had reached 20,000 ft with a contingent of Balti porters but steep ice had halted them. Disappointed at the decision to retreat Crowley, who referred to himself as 'The Great Beast', got into a violent quarrel with his partner, Guy Knowles, and threatened him with a revolver that he pulled from his pack. A fight ensued that almost dragged the two men over the precipice until Knowles wrestled the weapon from Crowley. Seventy-six years later, a strong American Expedition climbed the Northeast Ridge, shortly after a Polish team had pioneered the route to over 8,000 metres.

We reach Camp Two at 21,998 ft, late that morning, just as the heat becomes stifling and the snow turns to mush. Here stands another tent left in place by the Polish women. We slip into it and begin to melt snow to fend off dehydration. Doug and Steve reach us in the early afternoon and pitch a tent nearby while we begin to sleep off our long night-shift.

The next morning, 27 June, is again clear. We climb a long, low angled spur of snow and ice until noon, when at 22,802 ft we find a third ragged and fluttering Polish tent. Here, we all rest and brew up for an hour. Wind cuts fiercely across the slope and rams into the tent's nylon walls. As we set off again Don and Gohar arrive. Don moves in spritely fashion for all his fifty years. These two decide to bivvy here, while Doug, Steve, Pete, and I set off to camp higher. We agree that while we go to the summit the next day, Don and Gohar will move up and occupy our high camp for their own summit bid the following day.

'Better keep climbing if we're going to make it up this hill,' Doug says, and we set off.

As we gain elevation K2 disappears behind Broad Peak's squarish Central Summit. Occasional clouds now wander across our path, engulfing us and creating eerie contrasts of diffuse light over the stark neutrals of white snow and black rock. We spread out over the slope, carving a diagonal route upwards, Doug striding powerfully in front, then Steve, me, and finally Pete. At 3.00 pm, at the site of Alan's and Andy's bivouac, we pause for another brew. Their snow cave resembles less a cave than a rabbit hole. Steve checks the altimeter.

'24,300 ft,' he announces. It is the highest Steve and I had ever been, short of flying.

We set off again, trudging and gasping at the altitude until twilight begins to darken the mountain. At 24,500 ft, near a jumble of 100 ft tall seracs, I clear a platform to place our tent, light the stove to melt a pan of snow, and await Pete. Doug and Steve climb through the serac and bivvy 300 ft above. Twenty minutes pass. Pete approaches slowly, coughing raucously.

'Hurry up Pete—you've got the tent!' I call, feeling the cold night bite into my fingers and toes. He staggers up to me, panting at the unsubstantial air, then dumps his pack, and sits on it. I hand him a hot brew. He guzzles it and quickly revives.

'How are you feeling?' I ask.

'Just tired. I'll be better with a rest.'

It is late into the night before we finish melting snow for drink. Even then we feel we could have consumed a gallon more. Our stomachs feel queasy with altitude. Out of the sweets, chocolate, Grain Bars and tinned fish we carry, it is a salty can of sardines that sates us most; with the huge fluid loss through breathing and exertion at altitude our body salts are dropping low. Pete's cough disappears as he rehydrates, then sleep descends on us. I begin to realize the deficit in sleep we have amassed by climbing around the clock for so many hours and by pushing ourselves up the mountain so late into the day.

During that night the altitude creeps into our heads. By morning it is bashing away from inside our skulls. Waking is a long and difficult process, cloudy and drug-like. The crack of wind on the tent walls and the crinkle of our frost-covered Gore-Tex sleeping bags are soon accompanied by the hiss of the stove. While I melt snow I hear Pete mumbling in his sleep, in between the sporadic gasping of Cheynes-Stokes breathing.

'What about this rope then?' he asks.

'Rope? Our rope is in the pack.'

'Noooo, not that rope,' he chides.

'Then what rope?'

'The rope we're all tied into.'

'We're not tied in, Pete. We're in the tent, Camp Four, Broad Peak.'

'Noooo, you don't understand,' and I began to feel like a thickheaded schoolboy giving all the wrong answers. I plied him for more clues to his sleepy riddle and got this:

'It's the rope that all of us are tied to.'

'Fixed rope?'

'Noooo,' he whined.

'Umbilical cord?' Any wild guess now.

'Noooo!'

'Then you must be speaking of a metaphysical rope, eh, one that everyone is tied to but no one is tied to?' But before I can get an answer the smell of sweet tea wakes him. 'How is your head?' I ask, as I try to force some hot oatmeal down my throat.

'Terrible.' Both of us squint from the pounding pain in our temples.

'Mine too. Maybe we should go down.'

'No. Mornings are always the worst. We're nearly there. Give me some aspirin. We'll be OK.'

We quaff down three aspirin each and set off, carrying nothing in our packs but a stove. The steep ice of the serac gets our blood flowing and clears our heads. As I pull onto the slope above the serac I see Doug and Steve stomping out the last few feet of the final chute to the col. Following their tracks I enter the steep chute two hours later, wade through soft snow, and arrive at the 25,591 ft col. Here, on Broad Peak's first ascent in 1957, Buhl had almost given up, slumping in the snow until his doggedness and Diemberger's enthusiasm had urged him onto his feet and on to the summit. A strong wind gusted from the north, splashing spindrift over the summit ridge. Ahead, the prow-like summit juts toward Sinkiang China. Beneath me, in Sinkiang, lie the North Gasherbrum Glacier, and deep within a fold of valley, the Shaksgam River. China's rust-coloured landscape contrasted sharply with the blinding white of the Godwin-Austen Glacier and the peaks of the Karakoram.

Pete labours up to me via the chute the Austrians in '57 had found to be verglassed, the Poles in '75 a bed of ice, and we in '83 a ribbon of steep snow. While awaiting Pete I'd fallen asleep long enough for the lump of ice I'd dumped in the pan to melt and boil. As I make a brew, Doug and Steve wave from their position on the ridge a few hundred feet away. We signal back. All is well, the summit a few hours away, and within sight. The sky is intensely clear all across Baltistan. Nanga Parbat, 150 miles away, stands on the southwest horizon. Straddling the border of Pakistan and China, as Broad Peak itself does, lies the pyramidal Gasherbrum IV, immediately to our south, and visible to the left of Broad Peak's Main Summit. Gasherbrum IV is an impressive sight, with its unclimbed Northwest Ridge directly before us and the Northeast Ridge of the first ascent on the left. I recall that an American team is working on the Northwest Ridge and wonder if they are gasping away somewhere on the final rocky headwall capping the mountain.

'That's a beautiful mountain down there,' Pete remarks of Gasherbrum IV. 'We ought to give that Northwest Ridge a shot next season, if it isn't climbed this year.'

I agree and we set off along Broad Peak's mile-long summit ridge at ten o'clock.

Along the summit ridge lies the most technical climbing yet; short steps of compact snow interspersed with rock outcrops. We rope up and move together, pausing to belay over tricky sections. The first difficulties of the ridge lie in skirting a large limestone block, across which an old piece of bleached rope is strung, knotted to a rusting piton. As I lead across, in crampons, mitts, and down suit, I squint at the rock and check my eyes to be sure I'm not hallucinating, for the rock over which I climb is pitted with the fossils of sea-shells. Eons ago, this piece of the earth lay on the ocean floor; now it stands at 8,000 metres.

As we near the summit the strain of altitude grows. Each step becomes increasingly harsh. When we pass through the door of 8,000 metres and enter the region climbers call the 'death zone,' disorientation and fatigue take an exponential leap. At perhaps one o'clock Doug and Steve pass us on their return from the summit.

'We summited at 11.30 am. It's even windier and colder up there,' Doug says, shouting above the wind. Plumes of spindrift curl over the ridge ahead.

'How far away?' I ask.

'An hour.'

'Doug, let's go. I can't feel my feet,' shouts Steve.

Doug yells into my ear: 'We'll get as far down the mountain tonight as we can. Good luck, kid.' They move off, their steps jerky and tired. Pete and I are now as alone as we would ever be.

Moving at 8,000 metres is like wading through treacle. I gradually become aware of a peculiar sense of disassociation with myself, as if a part of me is external to my body, yet is looking on. I feel this most when setting up boot-axe belays or making difficult moves, a strong feeling as if someone is peering over my shoulder keeping an eye on me, or even as if I have a second invisible head on my shoulders.

We traverse for another half-hour to the False Summit, an icy, corniced dome at 26,382 ft. There we sit, looking toward the tantalizingly close Main Summit. By now those sensations of disassociation are punctuated by feelings of total absence: momentary blackouts, when neither I nor the guy over my shoulder seem to be around. I would emerge from these absences a few paces from where they'd struck me, leading to a concern over stepping off the narrow ridge. 'Like a dream,' I mutter to Pete, but the wind snatches my words away before he hears them.

I look ahead: The corniced ridge dips down and curves left in a final long, easy slope to the summit, only 18 ft higher than our position. We are nearly there, thirty minutes away. But my fears about what is happening to me double. A vicious headache rings in my ears and pounds at my temples, and a tingling in my arms grows so intense that my fingers curl into a tight fist, making it hard to grip my ice axe. My last shred of rational consciousness raises a cry of concern over the possibility of a stroke, or cerebral edema. But to articulate this to Pete is difficult, as speech and thought seem to have no link in my mind. Exhaustion I can understand, and given that alone I might have crawled to the summit, but something alien was going on within me and I wasn't prepared to push my luck with it. I get it out that I want down. Pete kneels beside me and gazes at the summit, so near yet so far.

'Go down? But we're so close! Just half an hour!'

The idea of turning away from success when it is so close was maddening to me too, and Pete's ever present determination nearly got me going. I tried to ascertain whether the sensations I felt were imaginary, or were really the beginning of some short circuiting of my body chemistry. There is a state of mind that sometimes infests climbers in which the end result achieves a significance beyond anything that the future may hold. For a few minutes or hours one casts aside all that had been previously held as worth living for, and focuses on one risky move or stretch of ground that becomes the only thing that has ever mattered. This state of mind is what is both fantastic and reckless about the game. Since everything is at stake in these moments, one had better be sure to recognize them and have no illusions about what lies on the other side of luck. It was one of those times. I had to weigh up what was important and what was *most* important.

'It'd be nice to reach the top, you and I,' Pete said. And so it would have, to stand up there with this man who had become such a strong friend in such a short time.

'Didn't you say that summits are important?' he added. Those are my words he is throwing back at me, shouting above the wind and his own breathlessness, harking back to my determination of a few weeks before that we should succeed on Lobsang Spire. I struggled to compose an intelligible sentence.

'Only important when you're in control . . . Lost control . . . Too high, too fast. You go on. I'll wait below.'

'No—we stay together,' he replies.

Strain is written on Pete's face as much as mine. In sixty hours we'd climbed from 15,500 ft to over 26,000 ft. We had found our limits. The decision to descend comes without a word. We just get up and begin the long path down, seeing that those red hills in China are now covered in cotton wool clouds, encircling K2 and lapping at Broad Peak's East Face.

A few hundred feet from our high point I feel a sensation like a light blank out in my brain. I have just enough time to kneel down before I slump backwards onto a patch of snow, then black out into a half-world of semi-consciousness and inaction. . .

'So this is it,' I think with a strangely detached curiosity as the day turns pitch; 'this is where the plunge into senselessness and apathy begins, where the shades of death descend.' Yet at the same time I am conscious of my swaying head and my incoherent mumbling. I think of Salley, whom I have no right to inflict such folly upon. 'Get up you idiot, get up,' I keep telling myself, until vision gradually returns. How long had I been out? I cannot tell.

Next to me sits Pete, observing my state as a good doctor should. He wears a white lab coat with a stethoscope draped around his neck; I double-check; nonsense. He is wearing his red high-altitude suit. I am beginning to imagine things. A minute later I regain control of myself, as suddenly as I'd lost it. Pete puts a brew of hot grape drink in my hands. As soon as I drink the liquid I throw it up.

'See . . . told you I was sick.' The purple stain in the snow forms intricate arabesque designs that grow onto the snow crystals glinting in the afternoon light. I could have watched these hallucinations all day, but Pete urges us onto our feet.

K2 looms in front of Pete Thexton as he descends the summit ridge of Broad Peak.

Pete Thexton at the col on Broad Peak at 25,591 ft; minutes later he announced that he had developed pulmonary edema.

Rapidly I begin to improve. My strength and mental faculties return. I'd made it back through the 8,000 metre door before it slammed shut and locked me in. But I'd cut it close.

In the warm glow of evening I take Pete's photo as we reach the col: the summit stands behind him. Had we made the right decision? Should we go on? Would we have the strength to return later? I feel remorse at having let Pete down, but then the tables suddenly turn: Pete appears over a crest on the col, lagging on the end of the rope. He takes short steps and looks stressed.

'I can't breathe properly,' he says in a whisper. 'It feels as if my diaphragm has collapsed.'

A bolt of fear runs up my spine.

'Are my lips blue?' he asks.

'Yes,' I say, noting the indication of oxygen starvation.

We stare at each other.

'We'll get down,' I blurt out, and we turn and crunch tracks to the edge of the wind-blown col. Things were wrong, very wrong. We had to shed altitude, and fast, but a snail's pace was the best Pete could manage in this thin soup of air. We reach the steep chute that we'd climbed to reach the col. The hour is late, about 7.00 pm, but we seem outside of time: we are simply there. I wrap a sling around a spike, double our short rope, and I rappel 60 ft to the start of the snowfield. Pete follows.

On the snowfield wind and driving snow had covered all sign of our tracks. 'I'll go ahead and break trail. Follow as fast as you can,' I say and Pete nods in response. Dragging the rope behind me I begin loping down the slope. After 300 ft I turn to see that Pete has barely moved.

'Pete!'

No answer.

By the time I light my way back through the soft snow the last gleam of twilight peters out in the sky and night is upon us. Where had the hours gone? Pete has his headlamp on. It shines out to the windy night. He doesn't speak. When I turn toward the glacier I see a pinpoint of light shining up from base camp, 11,000 ft below. It's Beth, his girlfriend far below, giving the eight o'clock signal as arranged, and Pete is returning it.

Conversation is superfluous. We know we're going to be on the move all night, very high, and in rising wind and storm. Already, clouds are blocking out the stars. I tie the rope to Pete's harness and begin belaying him down, length after length, till his strength begins to ebb. Then I talk him down, ordering and cajoling every step out of him. At about 10.00 pm he collapses in the snow and whispers he can no longer see. So I guide him by direction, telling him to traverse 45 degrees right or straight down. Even on the easiest ground he has to face in. Without tracks it's all instinct anyway. And all the time wind and spindrift swirl across the slope, and the bastard moon shines everywhere but on the upper slopes of Broad Peak. There is no time to think of what might happen to us, but only that we must move down, move down, move down.

The hours melt into a pastiche of endless, dreamlike movement. Pete becomes too weak to walk, so somehow I support him, dragging him, lowering him, whatever it takes to move. The sensation of being outside of myself is more prevalent than ever. My watcher checks my every move and decision. I keep turning around, expecting to see someone. As I mechanically work toward getting us down, part of my mind begins to wander. I find myself thinking of that first ascent of the Central Summit, by the Poles. The account I'd read called their stormy descent a 'struggle for survival'. Accompanying the story was a photo of Broad Peak, littered with crosses where the climbers had perished. Those crosses were now underfoot, and the ghosts of history were hiding in the shadows. I find that agnostics also pray.

The slope steepens, indicating that somewhere nearby is the band of ice cliffs we'd climbed that morning. We need to find the low spot in them by which we'd ascended, but where that was was anyone's guess. We link arms and shuffle towards what I hope was our earlier position. The wind howls and Pete inches around uncertainly.

'If only I could see . . .'

'I'm your eyes, Pete—move right ten steps!'

And he does.

It soon becomes too steep to blunder about as we are, so I begin making 20 ft leads, shoving my axe into the soft snow and belaying Pete in to me. At the last belay he lets go of everything and swings down to the edge of the ice cliff. The shaft of my axe droops alarmingly. I lose my cool and yell a mouthful of curses at him as I haul him back up.

Storm on Broad Peak.

'Sorry,' he whispers calmly. Throughout the ordeal he had remained composed, conserving his energy for matters of survival, rather than letting fear take hold. I clip him to his axe and wrap his arms around it.

'Just don't lose it now, brother. Please.'

The wind attacks with unprecedented malice. Waves of spindrift hiss down around us, burning our faces. If my back-tracking is correct, then somewhere in the darkness at the bottom of the ice cliff is our tent, and if things have gone as planned, Don and Gohar are in it. I call till my throat is raw, then shove my ice-axe in to the hilt, from which to lower Pete. Confusion reigns in the seconds it takes to lower him, he is so disoriented that he cannot tell whether he is at the bottom of the cliff or not, I am blinded by spindrift, and feel the axe shifting out of the snow. I wrap the rope around my arm to distribute some of the weight while holding the axe in with my knee. Pete gasps in distress as the rope pinches his waist.

'Are you down?'

'Can't . . . tell.'

'For God's sake, you gotta be down!'

He comes to a stop and digs his hands into the snow. I rappel off my second short tool, moving quickly before it slides out. At the bottom of the serac we again link arms to negotiate some broken ground. I glance about, searching with my headlamp for a familiar lump of ice to tell me that we have descended the ice cliffs in the right spot. Then, suddenly, a light appears, illuminating the form of a tent.

'We've got a sick man here, Don,' I call to the light. Pete crawls a few feet along a crest of snow then stops completely. A bobbing headlamp approaches. It is Gohar, himself groggy, woken from a deep sleep. I lie on my back, sit Pete on my shoulders, and slide us down the last sixty feet to the tent, while Gohar belays us.

As Don drags Pete into the tent it comes around to 2.00 am. We have been moving for 22 hours.

In the quiet of the tent we lie, all crammed in together, rubbing each other's limbs and melting snow to get vital fluids back into us. Feeling takes a long time to return to my hands and feet, and Pete's are ice cold, yet remarkably, not frost-bitten. Warm liquid perks him up.

'How are you, Gregor?' Pete asks with a hopeful spark in his voice.

'Done in. Rest a couple of hours till dawn, then we'll head on down.'

'I'll watch him, lad,' Don says.

I stagger out to repitch our tent, the tent that Pete and I had collapsed and weighted with snow blocks that morning so it wouldn't blow away. It is filled with snow and the foam pads are gone. I throw the rope down for insulation and crawl into my sleeping bag. It seems that a million years have passed since we set out. We've gone beyond mental and physical barriers that we didn't even know existed within us. We'd become a single entity, fighting to survive. Nothing could stop us from getting down now. In a couple of days this will be just an experience we would have shared to become closer. All the bullshit of ethics, ego, competition, and the glamour of big summits has been scraped aside to reveal that in the end everything boils down to one thing—life! My eyelids close under the weight of exhaustion and I dream of grassy places.

But those words of Pete's were the last we ever shared. Two hours later, at dawn on 29 June, he awoke to ask Gohar for water. Gohar pressed a cup of warm liquid to Pete's lips, but Pete didn't drink from it. Don and Gohar looked at each other for a few seconds then called me. I awoke with a throbbing headache. 'Dead,' they were saying. But that was impossible! We'd made it through that hellish descent! We were going to make it down! Then sense prevailed like a sledge-hammer. I rushed into the tent and tried to force life into him, through his mouth, with mine, forcing my own thin, tired air into him. His lungs gurgled loudly, saturated with the fluid of pulmonary edema. I tore his jacket open and rythmically pounded my palms against his chest to squeeze a beat from his heart, but he would have none of it. He would only lie there with an expression of sublime rest on his face, as if dreaming the same grassy dream as I had been.

We sat in silence, our heads full of sad thoughts, our eyes registering that the unthinkable had happened. Don lay back on one elbow, looking at Pete.

'It's always the good blokes that go,' Don said.

Suddenly I hated this mountain and its heartless geology. What about the people at home and below who loved Pete, what about them? Tears filled my eyes. Outside, the Karakoram was ablaze with a clear and calm light.

'Notice that the wind has suddenly dropped?' asked Don. 'Not a breath. It's always the same when death is about, always a lot of noise and wind, but as soon as it gets what it's after it quietens down. I've seen it before and it's always the same.'

I'm still thinking about that, still wondering.

The wind returned a few minutes later, stronger than before, and threatened to tear the tent apart with its claws, like an evil predator, now searching for us. I sat staring at Pete. He couldn't be dead. I wouldn't accept it. But he had gone and I knew it. I closed his partially opened eyelids with my hand and wrapped his sleeping bag around him. Gohar clenched my arm. 'Greg Sahib, we must go,' he said with a look of natural fear. I looked around thinking there must be something we should do—a place to bury him—some words—or get him down the mountain for . . . for what?

'We've got to see to ourselves now,' said Don sternly. 'You're in a terrible state, youth.'

One last glance at Pete. Gohar's lips moved as he softly spoke a prayer in Urdu, then we bade our friend farewell. I crawled out of the tent, zipped it shut, turned into the maelstrom of blowing snow, and started down. We left everything as it was. Gear lay strewn about, none of it possessed of value any longer. It was a long descent, with every step full of a great sense of loss and perhaps a strange feeling of guilt at having to leave our friend as we did. But the snow would soon settle over him and set firm as earth. The snowfield would inch inexorably to the icecliffs and peel away in bursts of avalanche to the glacier, which would carry him within it to the fast-flowing Braldu. His journey would outlive us and no ashes could be scattered more thoroughly, nor a monument exist more lasting than Broad Peak.

Weary legs took us down to the Polish tent at 23,000 ft by late morning. Doug and Steve, two specks 3,000 ft below, moved down ahead of us. We tumbled into the tent, laying about.

'I thought he'd make it,' I said for the tenth time.

'No. I could tell the moment I laid eyes on him that he was bad,' said Don. I kept thinking of what death meant, of how none of us would ever know Pete again. Then there were voices outside the tent. A party of Swiss, heading up, appeared and greeted us happily. I formed words to explain the tragedy, but somehow words had no feeling, no reality. One of the Swiss looked at us with pity. 'Yes, I was on Everest last year and lost a member. We also had to leave him on the mountain . . .' By God, that's not a member who has died, that's a man, a friend. I cursed his practicality, but what could he say?

The Swiss had a radio. They called their base camp and carried the message to ours. In a few hours Doug, himself just off the mountain, would break the news to Beth and she would burst into tears. Then the Polish women arrived. I told them too, but the news didn't seem to sink in. They could only complain that Don had accidentally taken one of their stoves from Camp One and when he'd realized his mistake had left it in Camp Two. They harped about this, while I mouthed words to try and make them see exactly what had happened above.

'But don't you think it's important that there be a stove in every camp?' one of them asked rhetorically. I tossed them our stove and set off down the mountain. Words. They had meaning no longer. No one really understands what we've been telling them. No one is thinking correctly. Nothing is the same up here. It's the thin air.

On 30 June we trace our way down the final narrow couloir of the mountain. Slipping clumsily with snow bailing up under our feet, we see four figures on the glacier below. Andy, Alan, Roger, and Nebi look up and count four figures descending—we have been joined by one of the Swiss—and hope beyond hope that a mistake had been made and we are all coming down alive. I lope through soft snow across the final stretch, sinking up to my thigh with each step.

It is Alan who comes forward to meet me halfway. We look at each other, point-blank. Our gazes penetrate more than flesh and blood. 'Then you know . . .,' I say.

'Yeah. Pete is dead.'

I throw my axe on the scree. I can no longer contain myself. Roger supports me and holds me tightly. 'It's not worth it, it's not bloody worth it,' I say.

'No. It's not,' Roger answers . . .

As the afternoon fell on that last day of June we looked into one another's eyes and for the first time knew each other. I had learned the real rule of this beautiful, reckless, terrible game, the only rule: The mountains are beautiful but they are not worth dying for.

A Long Walk with Whillans

That night at K2 base camp we sat in the main tent discussing what had happened on Broad Peak and what must happen now. Conversation came with difficulty. Every word was spoken, and heard, painfully. Each of us had known Pete differently. Some had known him from past expeditions, some through the daily grind of life around Sheffield. Others only knew him through the context of this expedition. But he had made a strong impression on us all.

Whillans sat quietly listening to the talk then got up and went to his tent, returning with his still-nearly-full bottle of whisky. He opened it, ripped it back, took a gulp that made him gasp, then passed it around. After a nip from each of us he finished the contents in two or three mighty swigs.

'This is how I say goodbye to my mates,' he said, thumping the empty bottle on a crate in front of him. From the moment he had seen Pete, when we dragged him into the tent he'd known that nothing we could do would save him. He now sought to anaesthetize that memory. As the booze coursed through his veins he began to stagger and roar about the tent, his wildness driving all away, to their tents or to Mohammed's stone-walled kitchen shelter.

Doug, Alan, Roger, and I huddled in the dark, chill, entrance to the kitchen shelter discussing what to do next—whether to abandon the expedition or whether to try K2. Inside the kitchen chanting prayers, the three Hunzas wailed tearfully in an unabashed display of grief.

'I should leave tomorrow and get the word out about Pete,' said Doug, conscious of the ominous array of formalities that lay ahead.

'I'll do it,' said Alan. 'The sooner someone leaves, the better. The porters have word of this already. The news will be in Skardu in a week. From there it'll be no time before it's in the press in Britain, and by then it will be a right botch-up. One of us has to get out and go straight to Pete's family.'

In this respect we were conscious of the mess, years before, surrounding the death of Pete's companion on the Latok II expedition. When the jungle telegraph of rumour and word of mouth, rushing ahead of the expedition, finally landed in the hands of the British press the distortion was total, crowned with a headline '11 Britons Die on Latok'. The news that we had to break to Pete's family was immensely distressing, but it would be worse if they learned of it through some second-hand, jumbled source.

'What about K2?' I asked.

Silence. The desire to climb K2 was still inside them.

'Give me a day of rest and I'll go out,' I said, 'I was with Pete. I should be the one to tell about it. All of us leaving won't make any difference to what has happened.' In my thoughts I was firmly convinced that Pete would give approval to this plan.

After a few minutes we decided that Nebi and Gohar would accompany me as far as Askole, to help carry food and a few personal belongings. We would travel as fast and as light as possible. From Askole I would hire a porter and buy food in the villages, while Nebi and Gohar returned to K2. Whillans, roaring drunk, appeared stumbling across the rubble, howled some oath, then collapsed. Nebi and Mohammed hurried over, picked him up, and carried him to his tent. As they tried to insert him into it he began to struggle and rage, almost pulling the tent down, so they left him, half-in, half-out, legs protruding from the entrance, ranting torso inside.

Beth joined us in the kitchen and we told her of the decision that I would leave in 36 hours. I asked if she wanted to walk out with me and she thought for a moment, looking in the direction of Broad Peak. Moonlight highlighted the clouds swirling around its summit: a terrible storm was building, that was for sure.

'It's just too soon. I can't go yet. I haven't even comprehended what has happened.'

And so it was settled.

On 2 July Broad Peak wore a thick lenticular corona that caught the sunlight eerily. As each of us woke, the thought of what had happened again pushed aside all other ideas. But also came the realization that Pete's death was already a thing of the past and that after the grief we had to find a way to live with what had happened. Nebi and Gohar woke me early for breakfast. Whillans, who'd decided to join me on the walk out, after a day of recovering from his awesome hangover, stood ready to leave. There was a long goodbye, then we set out. Beth walked with us for a while along a moraine rib.

'Goodbye lass,' said Don before pecking her on the cheek, and heading off with the Hunzas, but I lingered a moment. As we parted she asked an unanswerable question: 'Why?'

I thought of what Major Malik had said of his belief that every move we make, from beginning to end is predestined by some higher form. I wondered if, on the great blueprint of existence, it had been intended that Pete should come here and never leave. Conversely, I thought of the game of chance and calculated risk that mountaineering is and wondered if we had simply put our heads in the noose one time too many. Finally I looked about at the chaos of the glacier, the breaking down and change all about us, extending into the sky and beyond that into the universe. We were small pieces of a vast puzzle where anything was possible.

'It's random. It's chance. That's why,' I answered lamely and turned to leave. Beth, who had known him far longer than I, sat on a rock and waved for a long time, until a fold of the glacier put her far behind.

What had gone wrong up there? Perhaps our decision to climb through the night and miss out on sleep had disrupted our metabolisms and weakened us. Certainly, the rapid gain of altitude had taxed our acclimatization to the limit, but others had moved as fast and with no more acclimatization than us, yet they had reached the summit in good shape. Perhaps Pete's sore throat at base camp and intermittent cough on the mountain had been a warning he'd wrongly ignored, a precursor to edema, but as a doctor he was aware of the signs and had deemed himself fit.

Other pressures pushed us on to Broad Peak too: the need to capitalize on the spell of good weather; the desire to succeed and not be left out of the running for K2. Pete was, as his friends knew, hard on himself. He relished the physical and mental extremes of life. The risk of soloing a hard alpine route, the impossibility of climbing Everest in winter, were all mirrors that Pete used to see and understand himself, and others. Yet he was immensely level-headed. When I fell ill on the summit ridge he was ready to turn around. I turned these things over in my mind as we walked through snowstorms and forded icy streams etched into the greatly changed glacier. Still, the randomness of things stuck with me. Why Pete, who had been to higher altitudes, and on more occasions, and not me? And what of the timing of events? Were it not for my bout of altitude sickness we would have reached the summit and Pete would have been struck by pulmonary edema along the difficult ridge instead of at the col, in which case we'd have stood little hope of reversing the tricky ridge without accident. And wasn't it odd that I had recovered at precisely the time that Pete had been struck down?

We were hit by things that medical science knows little about. Pulmonary edema seldom announces its onset with any dramatic warning symptons, but is insidious and sudden. Altitude had triggered a reaction that caused Pete's lungs to fill with fluid and smother the alveoli that absorb oxygen from the atmosphere. My condition may have been the beginnings of cerebral edema, swelling my cranium with fluid, exerting pressure against the brain, thus inducing the disorientation and hallucinations. Or, perhaps, I'd suffered a brief ataxic stroke, triggered by the altitude and dehydration. The delicate balances within us had toppled: mine had regained its balance, but Pete's had crashed incontrovertibly. Our only choice had been the arduous descent we had made all night. But for Pete, it wasn't enough.

On the second day of walking, as we passed rDokas, we looked up at Masherbrum's summit poking through the building storm.

'Back in '57 I'd been a ropelength from the top of that one, but we had to turn back when my mate got cerebral edema,' said Whillans. 'A few weeks earlier one of the lads, Robert Downes, had died from the same thing that got Pete. He's buried somewhere in Skardu. In those days pulmonary edema and cerebral edema didn't even have names.'

'While you were up there in '57 I was in the process of being born,' I said.

'Aye, a very bad year was '57,' said Whillans in that beautiful Lancashire drawl.

'I failed on Masherbrum, Buhl died on Chogolisa, and you were born.' He grinned the barest sliver of a smile, to which I replied in kind.

'Come on lad. There's a long walk ahead of us.'

Grey skies followed us for days, sweeping us out of the mountains, disguising the fact that there were mountains there at all. No last glimpses of the Karakoram, no more summits through the clouds, nothing to look back on.

Behind us the huge black tongue of the Baltoro Glacier lolls rudely across the breadth of the valley and dribbles the grey Braldu River from its snout. As I step off it my body feels wrought and knotted, like some piece of gristle that the glacier has spat out, indigestible and bitter.

After three days the mountains yield at last to the village of Askole, lush now with crops of wheat and barley. Here begins the world of men. Haji Medi, knowing of our march, invites us into the dusty meeting chamber of his house, a dim-dark dungeon crammed with the men of the village. Already the news of Pete's death has reached Haji's all-hearing ears, reminding me that the tragedy is outrunning we emissaries of terrible news. Haji Medi kindly arranges food and a porter for us and Don and I prepare to depart, leaving Nebi and Gohar to return to K2 base camp. They walk us to the edge of the village. I feel a lump in my throat as Nebi wraps his arms around my waist, lifts me off the ground and says a single word of English—'friend'. Gohar grips my hand tightly, then we part, carrying fond thoughts of one another back to our daily worlds.

The days pass in a flurry of dust and shuffling, blistered feet. Walking as fast as my legs can carry me I get ahead of Don and Ali, our new porter. Suddenly, in the middle of a sliding scree slope above the foaming river, something makes me stop, halted as if by a mental lasso. There, in front of me, is the place where Pete had paused during the approach, the point at which he recalled the friend he had lost in the landslide. It seemed as if two mirrors had been turned to face each other, reflecting different events with the same end, back and forth, forever. I thought of Pete, again, thinking that it is just as terrible to lose a new friend as to lose an old one.

In Chakpo, one day from Skardu, we buy some eggs and a kilo of *choli*, apricot kernels, to break the monotony of gritty chapati that had been our staple since leaving the mountains. As the villagers gather around us, weighing out their produce, a simpleton spinning a bob of black wool leans against a tree and gazes at us with curiosity. Beside him an old blind man, with a long grey beard like a sheaf of cobwebs, crouches on a rock. Hearing the voice of a foreigner and the hum of barter he begs for money. I put a few paise in his hand. The old man jingles the coins and asks for more. The villagers laugh, then the one who'd sold us the nuts finds a cardboard box; trash from an expedition. He carefully folds and tears the cardboard into a rectangular shape, then peels it into thin layers to produce facsimiles of well handled rupees. Producing several of these counterfeit notes, the mischief-maker hands them to the old man. The blind pilgarlic babbles happy-mad and hurries off, probing the way ahead of him with his cane, while his neighbours laugh until tears run down their faces and slap me merrily on the back as if I were one of them.

In roasting Skardu the phone connection to Britain was down, the PIA flight was grounded due to bad weather, and the hellish NATCO buses were jammed to bursting with people coming and going for the religious holiday, Ramadan. The best we could do was get tickets for the dawn bus to Gilgit, 100 miles away. I paced around our hotel room, concerned that we would get stuck in Gilgit and that somehow the news would outrun us to Islamabad. On the hike out we had deliberately made no mention of Pete's death to other expeditions or, now, to the officials in Skardu. But the word was out that something had happened on Broad Peak. People were even letting us in on the secret. The notion of our mission and my obsession that Pete's death be broken to Pete's family in the best way possible tainted me with a darkness that not even Don's wit could penetrate.

As the bus rumbled to Gilgit the heat descended on us and I grew impatient and insupportable. Once in Gilgit, on the eve of Ramadan, and in the PTDC Hotel, the hotel manager informed us that all transport was indeed at a standstill, for several days.

'I must make a phone call to Britain. Does the phone work here?' I asked the hotel manager, explaining to him our problem, hoping that out of some sense of compassion he might have a solution. Back at base camp, we had formulated a plan to call Jan, Doug's wife, and for her to contact close friends of the Thextons, rather than for me to break the news through the hiss of long distance.

'Certainly you may call Britain. Our hotel has a very fine phone connection. I will book a call for you,' said the manager.

'Thank you. How long will it take to get through?'

'Later tonight. Perhaps tomorrow.' He shrugged. I slumped in my chair.

Day wore into night and the night grew late. I became an insistent, ugly foreigner, asking every hour for the phone call to be checked. It was the religious holiday of fasting, I knew, and the phone operators were probably doing as much work as the bus driver, but all I knew was that somewhere out there, through the air waves, the word was getting out.

As Don and I sat next morning breakfasting in the hotel restaurant I realized that almost 24 hours had passed since I booked the call. The manager had grown skilled at ignoring me by now, and as he walked past and I rose and asked him to try the phone once again, he strode by without even looking at me. Breakdown point. I sat down, thumped the table with my fist, then cleared it with a sweep of my hand, sending plates and food onto the floor with a crash. I exhaled with some sort of release, albeit an infantile one.

Don shook his head, picked up a piece of toast, put it on the table and buttered it. A waiter appeared from the kitchen and picked up the debris without a word, either conscious of what was driving me mad, or simply polite. Outside, a prayer lilted peacefully across the town, backed by a chorus of locusts in the poplars. As we looked out of the window we watched the gardener prostrate himself on the lawn of the hotel to pray. He knelt in the direction of Mecca and bent flat to the earth, completely involved in his devotion.

'Do you suppose he's any better off than us, for doing that?' asked Whillans, genuinely curious.

My answer, or lack of one, was cut short by the sudden arrival of the Liaison Officer of the American Gasherbrum IV expedition. We'd met the Americans in Skardu. They'd failed in their attempt to climb the Northwest Ridge, and their malaise of ambitions failed complemented my mood. The hotel manager had told the LO that there was a crazy foreigner desperate to get to Islamabad. Since he'd secured a Toyota pickup at black-market rates to get his team to Islamabad could he please get the mad foreigner out of his hotel before he breaks any more plates? *Inshallah.*

Our luck seemed changed for the better as we left Gilgit next morning, with nine of us crammed into the overloaded vehicle. But half an hour out of town the rear end of the Toyota began to shudder violently. Peering over the edge we watched a wheel wobble loose and come to within a fraction of an inch of falling off. Not five miles out of Gilgit, we screeched to a halt. The sun beat down on the strip of black tar that led to Islamabad, making watery mirages. It was a breakdown that not even Pakistani voodoo mechanics could fix. This was the straw that broke the camel's back.

'It's just occurred to me,' I said to Whillans. 'I understand at last. We died up there with Pete and this is purgatory. We'll be here forever, trying to escape Gilgit but never quite making it.'

This amused the Americans but Don looked askance at my histrionics. 'Ah, now, lad, you've gone too far this time . . .' And he was right. In resisting the ways of this land I was driving myself mad. Nothing I could do would change a thing that had happened or that would happen.

Finally, we reached Islamabad, phoned Jan in Britain, and notified the British Embassy of Pete's death. Before I handed over Pete's passport to the consul I opened it up to take a final look at the man I had hardly known, yet knew so well. Don and I parted company in Islamabad. I was to fly directly to London, while he had to fly via Karachi.

'Tooroo youth. I'll be off now,' he said, casual as ever, bidding me goodbye at the gate of the residence we were staying in.

'Just a minute,' I called, and thrust my hand into his. 'At least a handshake after all this . . .' He clenched my hand firmly, perhaps thankfully, grinned, then disappeared into the hot night.

As I walked through the arrivals gate at London's Heathrow Airport Jan Scott met me. Within half an hour we were in a taxi, on our way to the Thextons'.

'How have they taken it?' I asked.

'Strong, but it's so very hard for them. They'll want you to be totally honest. They want to know every detail.'

The taxi arrived. As we opened the wrought iron gate it squeaked on its hinges. Michael, Pete's younger brother, opened the door and welcomed me. We joined Pete's parents, Robina and Clive, with Vicki, their youngest daughter, in the yard, and seated ourselves on chairs beneath a tree. After a few minutes hesitation the story began. The words came with difficulty, yet they came true. It was a particularly bright day, and the sun fell warmly on us all.

Phone Calls and Postcards

Three weeks later. Seattle, Washington. A phone call wakes me early in the morning. It's Steve, back in England. He and Alan had hiked out after a nineteen-day storm had pinned everyone down at base camp. No, he knew nothing of the others—they'd remained to attempt K2. Just as I relaxed he paused. His voice was slightly unsteady.

'But I do have some bad news . . .'

'Yes?'

'Georges has been killed in the Alps.'

'What!'

'He was hunting for crystals on the Triangle de la Verte with his cousin and two friends. A massive stonefall hit them. Only the cousin survived. I thought you'd want to know . . .'

This was impossible news. Georges Bettembourg was one of those people who lived a charmed life and moved through the mountains with instincts inherited from generations of mountaineering. He came from a family of guides and alpinists, knew Chamonix like the back of his hand, had been to the Himalayas many times, including Broad Peak. If a stone fell towards Georges he knew it would always bounce left or right, he had that sort of luck. But he knew he was mortal too. I remembered his words from Shivling: 'You 'ave to watch out for yourself in the mountains. They are very beautiful but sometimes they sneak up on you from behind and—*chop*—you get it in the back of the neck.' Not long before his death his first book, an account of his expeditions, had been published. Georges called it *The White Death*.

More weeks passed without news, then a dog-eared postcard appeared in the mailbox, postmarked Skardu. It was Andy, writing that they were safe after their attempt on K2. They'd come close, almost to 8,000 metres, alpine style, on the South Face Spur, but Jean had fallen sick with the altitude and they'd retreated. Roger had tried it one more time with Mari Abrego, had reached 8,000 metres, but deep snow had halted them too.

After four months the expedition was over. We had left the Baltoro with a little piece of each other and, like the prayers sewn into the small cloth sacks that the

Balti wear around their necks to remind them of their faith, the memories of that season are always close at hand for us. It had been a long summer. We would never forget it.

Gathering at Broad Peak base camp, 1983. Front row: Greg Child, Al Rouse, Don Whillans, Gohar Shar. Back row: Cook Nebi, Roger Baxter-Jones, Jean Afanasieff, Beth Acres, Doug Scott, Cook Mohammed (below Scott), Stephen Sustad, Liaison Officer Captain Malik, and another LO.

Gasherbrum IV, West Face. The Northwest Ridge is on the left.

Part Three

Gasherbrum IV, Karakoram, 1986

The Obscure Object of Desire

'An unfulfilled idea is like a worm in the heart.'

—*An old Jewish proverb*

Unfinished Business

I see it clearly, a wall of snow, breaking up and rolling toward me, engulfing me in white chaos. Snow fills my mouth, my eyes, my ears, and the cold relentless tide drags me down the mountain . . .

I wake to the patter of rain on the window, the hiss of cars on slick roads, the wail of a distant burglar alarm. I shift to the present: an April night in Seattle. In a few days I'll be on a 747 roaring toward Gasherbrum IV.

'What is it?' Salley asks, hearing me suddenly wake.

'A dream.'

If we ever have children and they become climbers I'll tell them 'Stay away from expeditions. They'll make you poor and neurotic.'

After Broad Peak I'd promised myself I would never return to the Himalayas. It was a personal, emphatic, and categoric promise. It was also a promise I could not keep. Again and again the symmetrical silhouette of a truncated, pyramidal mountain kept appearing in my thoughts: Gasherbrum IV. My recollection of it from the summit ridge of Broad Peak, and Pete's suggestion to some day climb its Northwest Ridge, remained etched in my memory.

In Seattle, where Salley and I had moved after my return to America in 1983, I grew to know two of the Americans I'd met in Gilgit after their attempt to 23,000 ft on G4's Northwest Ridge. Steve Swenson's and Matt Kerns's accounts of their encounter with the ridge enriched my own knowledge of G4's stark outline and an idea began to grow.

Then, in 1984, another expedition attempted the Northwest Ridge. Among its members was an old acquaintance, Geoff Radford, a geologist from Anchorage, Alaska. Geoff's expedition reached 24,000 ft—2,000 ft short of the summit. But they'd had a good look at the ridge's final obstacles: A 1,000 ft icefield capped by a steep 1,000 ft marble and limestone headwall. Geoff's account of G4's Northwest Ridge confirmed that it would be no simple snow-plod in the clouds. It would be a technical and serious climb right to the top.

The idea of tackling a long rock wall beginning at 25,000 ft was a sobering thought: climbing simple snowslopes at that altitude is difficult enough. But from my hours on the summit ridge of Broad Peak, as hallucinatory as they had been, I clearly recalled the mountain as I'd seen it that day. On one side rose the twilit West Face, shining like a luminous gold plinth, on the other the jagged Northeast Ridge of the original 1958 Italian ascent, and, rising in the centre, the Northwest Ridge. I remembered looking down onto G4's South Summit, tracing my eyes back along its flattish summit crest to the slightly lower North summit, then following a path of snow ramps interspersed with cliffs down the headwall to the icefields and easier terrain of the lower Northwest Ridge. Digging out a photograph I'd taken from the col, I saw that my memory was accurate. Such a path did exist through the headwall.

News of the second failure on the Northwest Ridge rekindled Steve's interest and we began to talk about an expedition. Steve had attempted G4 twice, the South Face in 1980, the Northwest Ridge in 1983. Despite two American attempts on the Northwest Ridge, and British, Japanese, American, and Polish attempts on other parts of the mountain—eight separate parties altogether—only two climbers of an Italian expedition had ever reached G4's summit: Walter Bonatti and Carlo Mauri, in 1958. The focal points of those failed attempts, the Northwest Ridge and the West Face, had attained 'last great problem of the Himalayas' status. By the mid '80s Gasherbrum IV was a coveted summit, with a ridge and a face as challenging as anything on the planet. Yet its difficulty, and the fact that it was just a couple of rope lengths short of 8,000 metres, kept attention to a minimum. While dozens of expeditions sought permits for K2, Broad Peak, and Gasherbrums I and II, Gasherbrum IV remained a lonely giant, but a giant that would not remain inviolate much longer.

In autumn 1984 Steve and I applied to the Pakistan Ministry of Tourism for permission to climb the Northwest Ridge in the summer of 1986. Accompanying the application we sent the peak fee of $800. Six months later we received a reply from the Pakistan Consulate, not quite granting permission, but requesting an additional $600. Peak royalties had increased. We felt like dupes in a mail order scam, but sent the money and set about the business of raising the $(US)30,000 budget for the expedition and assembling a strong team.

It took minimal persuasion to convince Geoff Radford to return to G4. I'd first met Geoff in 1978, when he was 22, in the storm-pot of Patagonia in the southern tip of Argentina. We were both members of expeditions trying to climb a granite tooth named Fitzroy. He succeeded, I did not. To climb Fitzroy, Geoff and his partners had spent three months waiting out storms, enduring stints of up to thirteen days in a snow cave half-way up the mountain. Geoff's talent as a fine conversationalist and his philosophic acceptance of the physical hardships of mountain life left me with a strong impression. After the expedition, as we wandered the streets of Buenos Aires, under the surveillance of plainclothed police driving white Ford Falcons—'the dirty war' was at its height in Argentina—Geoff and I agreed that someday we'd climb together.

Geoff had a travel-hungry soul. Maybe it sprang from his first job, as a deckhand on a freighter cruising the South American coast. When I next heard from him, two years after Patagonia, he'd solo-driven a truck through Nicaragua just after the Sandinista Revolution. Here was an adventurer, a character off the pages of a

Hemingway story. Balding early, with a thick blonde moustache, he had a serious look about him, yet one that could turn to mirth in a second. By 1986 Geoff was owner of a geo-surveying business, Dihedral Exploration. It was a career to which his tenacious disposition was ideally suited, for much of the field-work necessitated thrashing through dense scrub, and climbing and descending peaks in the North American wilderness.

Though Steve, Geoff, and I felt greatly attracted to G4, we found that finding a strong team and money enough was an uphill battle. In December 1984, Steve, a pragmatic engineer not disposed to gambling, decided that the possibility of a third failure on G4 was a spectre too troubling to ignore. Following an invitation to join a well-heeled expedition to K2's North Ridge, he dropped out. This left me with the paper-title of leader, and Geoff as my companion in the venture.

We both agreed that whoever came with us, they should not just be experienced climbers, but easy-going personalities. The combination of diffidence coexisting with the inner fire needed to climb a big mountain is a strange combination, but by mid-1985 we had pulled together five other climbers of just such a mould.

From Seattle, Washington, came Tom Hargis and Dr Steve Risse. Tom, a carpenter and mountain guide, had climbed around the Cascade Range and Canada for twenty years, and in 1983 had reached 24,000 ft on the Tibetan side of Everest. Quietly reflective, given to writing poetry, and powerfully strong from habitual weight-lifting, the 38-year-old ex-Marine leaped at the invitation to climb in the Karakoram.

Steve, as chief psychiatrist at the Veteran's Hospital in Tacoma was, at 33, one of the youngest men in his field. With his thick-lensed glasses and professorial beard he had the look one might expect of an academic. As a climber he had considerable experience in the North American ranges, and had almost reached the 22,500 ft summit of Ama Dablam, in Nepal, in winter.

Geoff invited his partner from his ascents of Mount McKinley and Aconcagua, a lanky, boyish looking building contractor from Vermont, named Andy Tuthill. Though I'd never met Andy, Geoff assured me that as well as being a formidable climber he was 'one helluva banjo player'. When Geoff phoned Andy and asked 'do you want to go to G4?' he received an instant 'yes' in reply. Andy, an amateur pilot, had just that day crashed his airplane. Geoff's invitation to squander more money and take more risks was a release from the doldrums of his costly accident.

From California came Randy Leavitt, my companion in spring 1985 on a ten-day ascent of a difficult new A5 route on California's El Capitan, a rock route we'd named 'Lost in America'. Though Randy had never been to high altitude, I knew him to be a keen adventurer. A retired addict of parachuting, he had jumped not only from airplanes, but from the 3,000 ft walls of El Cap, from skyscrapers, bridges, and antennae. Randy had all the best traits of a Californian—energy, enthusiasm, and a razor wit. A gifted technical rockclimber recently turned to alpinism, Randy's laconic sense of humour had made our ascent of El Cap not simply a good climb but a good laugh. In the often dour Karakoram, humour as much as strength is an asset.

Our seventh member, from Sydney, Australia, was recruited, sight unseen, over the phone. Though Tim Macartney-Snape and I had never met, being both Australian and both interested in Himalayan climbing, it seemed only appropriate to invite him. In 1984 Tim, along with Greg Mortimer, had become the first Australian to climb Everest. A third member, Andy Henderson, had come to within a few feet of the summit, but had turned back with frostbite. They had climbed Everest in exceptional style, using very lightweight tactics on a new route on the massive North Face of the mountain. To top it off, they'd reached the summit without the use of supplementary oxygen—a singular feat. At that time, the few who had climbed Everest without oxygen had either disappeared on the descent, or had staggered down with brain damage snapping at their heels. Tim though had had the nous to make a taped recording on the summit. He spoke about humanity, the nuclear arms race, and the future of the earth; unusually profound stuff for such a brain-numbing place. Knowing that the addition of a secret weapon like Tim would enhance our chances, and suspecting he would respond to my unexpected invitation with a positive leap of faith, I picked up the phone one night, called him at his Sydney office where he managed Wilderness Expeditions, a trekking company and put the question to him. After a second's pause, he agreed to go.

And so we were seven.

Time soon began to close in on our departure date of 25 April. Each day became a frantic scurry to amass equipment and food as well as to tend the mounting paperwork generated by the expedition. But the big problem was getting the cash. Few of us were particularly liquid in our assets. Not only did we need to contribute somewhere between $3–4,000 dollars for the expedition, but we each had to leave money at home for rent and bills. Lack of money rapidly grew to crisis proportions. I approached several corporations for sponsorship but my efforts fell resoundingly flat. Then Tim phoned from Australia to say that he was bringing a cameraman, Phil Balsdon, to film the expedition. A television documentary, Tim assured me, would attract financing for the trip on the Australian end. His suggestion was a glimmer of hope, yet the only sure way to make money was to work, which we did—overtime.

Tom, in Seattle, was guiding and working as a carpenter seven days a week; Geoff was working on Alaska's purgatorial North Slope oil rigs, doing any geological work he could find while weathering a slump in the minerals market; Randy was hanging wallpaper in San Diego while attending nightschool to become a real estate broker; Andy was building houses in Vermont; Steve was on constant call as a psychiatrist in Tacoma, as well as doing research into Alzheimer's disease; and I was doing demolition work and freelance editing in Seattle. The pressure of earning a living was great enough without complicating matters with an expedition. But we were committed to the mountain, and to each other.

In September 1985 I heard startling, yet unconfirmed news: The Pole Voytek Kurtyka and the Austrian Robert Schauer had climbed the West Face of Gasherbrum IV, using pure alpine-style tactics. During eight days on the face they had encountered extreme alpine and rock climbing, often without belays or protection. But, because they had been pinned down for two of those days in storm and had run out of food and gas to melt water, they had abandoned the higher South Summit, mere hours away, in order to save their hides. Instead, in an extreme state of exhaustion, they had staggered toward the North Summit and for three days had descended the Northwest Ridge—our intended route. If the rumour was true, then this climb was a quantum leap beyond anything ever done in the Himalayas. Their effort didn't need a summit; the climb stood on its own merits as a work of art, an inspired creation that had required the commitment of every cell in their bodies.

To say that this news didn't briefly take the wind out of our sails would be untrue. It certainly gave me great pause to think. Two men, without fixing ropes or camps, had taken a great gamble and pitted themselves against the most formidable wall in the Karakoram. They had almost succeeded. We, on the other hand, planned to approach G4 in a manner that would stack the slim odds of Himalayan climbing more in our favour. Using seven climbers, three fixed camps, and fixing new rope or utilizing old rope to the American high point of 1984, we would position ourselves to climb the final steep pyramid in a lightweight burst. From a practical point of view we could see no way out of using light expedition style. Yes, we sought some measure of success, but we also had to acclimatize high, to 23,000 ft, as Voytek and Robert had done by using the 1984 ropes on the Northwest Ridge. But for us there were no other suitably easy peaks in the area for this purpose, nor could we afford the added logistics such a plan would entail. However, those were secondary concerns. The real concern was abstract. Simply put, had Voytek's and Robert's descent of the Northwest Ridge changed our outlook on our objective? The moving force behind this venture was to explore that unknown stretch above 24,000 ft to the summit. Now that Voytek and Robert had rappeled from the North Summit somewhere down the headwall and icefield, the Northwest Ridge was no longer *totally* unknown. Even so, those cliffs and icefields had been rappeled, not climbed, and the summit still only reached once. I wrote to Voytek and two months later a letter and photograph of G4 came from Poland describing their climb and descent. I called Geoff in Anchorage.

'Geoff, it's definite—Kurtyka and Schauer climbed the West Face, missed the summit, and descended the Northwest Ridge.'

'Does that make any difference to you?' he asked, after a pause.

'No. Not really.'

'Me neither.'

If anything, the news made the worm of unfinished ideas corkscrew in our minds more voraciously. Geoff and I had incomplete business on G4. Unknown adventures awaited our companions.

Formal permission from Pakistan to climb the mountain came in February 1986. Even at that late date the expedition's bank account was a pathetic sight. By selling expedition T-shirts, and from appeals through the Seattle media, as well as to the members of the American Alpine Club and generous friends, we had raised $4,500 cash. Mountaineering equipment suppliers assisted us with special gear. I juggled budget figures and cut corners. With each member's personal contribution set at $3,200 we had enough money to get to the mountain and climb it, but, on paper, not quite enough to get back to Islamabad. Gradually, that seemed acceptable. We were too committed to call it off, but we needed a few dollars more. I presented a public lecture in Seattle and raised several hundred additional dollars; while I was lecturing someone was burglarizing our house, and Salley and I lost several thousand dollars' worth of personal items.

My personal obsession with the entire, all-engulfing picture of the expedition gradually began to overwhelm me. My brief attempt to forsake the Himalayas had left a hollow place within me. Now all I could think about was the mountain. I hadn't forgotten how high the stakes in Himalayan climbing could be, but to run away from the mountains seemed to not just deny an urge within me, but in a convoluted way that I only partly fathomed, seemed to cheapen the friendship that had existed between Pete and myself. The idea of climbing Himalayan peaks, inexplicable, useless, and dangerous as it was, was in my blood. So, like an addict, I gave myself over to it. As I ran through Seattle's streets to train for the mountain I would find myself chanting an involuntary, silent mantra: 'G4, G4, G4'. At night I'd dream about the expedition. One night I dreamed that during the flight to Islamabad all the expedition luggage was jettisoned off the plane. Steve, with his expertise in dealing with troubled minds, broke the news to me. I went stark raving mad. Somehow, Salley tolerated this phase.

On 25 April we bade goodbye to the people we loved and, with thirty bags, began a battle by air across America toward Islamabad, fighting off excess baggage tyrants, trying to hold on to every last penny of our budget. In New York we met Andy, loaded ourselves onto a Pakistan International Airlines flight, and streaked into the stratosphere. In my pocket I carried all our remaining funds, $10,000 in traveller's checks, and an additional $4,000 borrowed from the American Alpine Club. The expedition's entire budget, beginning to end, would be $26,900.

Spring 1986 was an uncertain time to visit an Islamic country. Rubble was still being cleared from the streets of Tripoli after Ronald Reagan's bombing lesson to show Libyan-backed terrorists that Jihad, or Holy War, was over. Consequently, it was open season on Americans. My acquaintances in the British embassy in Islamabad wrote to inform me that since Britain had been used as an aircraft carrier for US F-111 strikes against Libya, walls were being erected around their embassy compound. Such a tense climate led some of us to take precautions. On the flight Randy showed me his anti-terrorist device—a gold crucifix on a chain around his neck.

'I didn't know you'd found religion, Randy,' I said, somewhere above Istanbul.

'No, no. The idea is that if we do get into any trouble and the hijackers wonder about my name—Leavitt does have a slightly *Jewish* ring to it—I'll show them this.'

Holding a crucifix up to the barrel of an Uzi seemed about as talismanic as hanging garlic on the door to ward off vampires, but I felt only marginally more confidence in my Australian passport, should such trouble come our way.

The lights in the cabin dimmed for the in-flight movie and *Rocky IV* flashed on to the screen. Sylvester Stallone and a huge hulking Russian scowled at each other inside a boxing ring and pounded at one another's brains for ninety minutes. It seemed an ironic counterpoint to the international situation seething beneath us.

The marks of three years of change to Islamabad and Rawalpindi were subtle to detect. Long years of martial law had been lifted, yet hundreds of police patrolled the capital. 'Death to Israel' had replaced 'Death to America' as the vogue graffiti. Few Pakistanis were aware of or concerned about the Libya raid. If anything, the individual on the street seemed more friendly to foreigners than ever. Pakistan had its own concerns: Benazir Bhutto, Ali Bhutto's daughter, was rallying opposition against the rulers of Pakistan. There were riots in Karachi, and there was always Afghanistan and India.

We esconced ourselves in the Hotel Shezerade in Islamabad and took care of formalities as we awaited the arrival of Tim and Phil. With the $4,000 loan from the American Alpine Club, we posted our refundable helicopter rescue bond, then cashed our traveller's checks at the American Express office. With the exchange rate at nearly 17 rupees to the dollar our rupees filled a rucksack. Of those rupees $600 worth of them went toward insuring our porters and liaison officer, Captain Rab Nawaz Khan, whom we met in Islamabad. Another $500 went toward shoes, socks, sunglasses, and rations for our porters. For $300 we rented a bus to Skardu. $200 worth of staples, such as rice, flour, potatoes, powdered milk, and kerosene, for our use at Base Camp, were purchased in the markets. Accounting for the hotel bill and incidentals in Islamabad I tallied up our projected needs: We anticipated just over eighty porter loads to Base Camp—about $7,000; thirty porter loads back from Base Camp—about $2,600; hotel accommodation in Skardu—$300; rental of jeeps from Skardu to Dassu—$300; and, to feed and transport us along the way, another $500. Total: $10,700. The problem was that we had only $7,700 remaining. Even the figure $10,700 gave us little margin for padding. Our hope was that Tim, due to arrive on 30 April, had clinched the sponsorship deals he had been cooking in Australia and could bring extra money into the affair.

On the morning of the 30th we arrived at the Ministry of Tourism for our briefing with the affable Mr Taleh Mohammed. Taleh went through the protocol of what we could and could not do in the mountains, pausing over the articles prohibiting foreigners from photographing bridges and military installations, warning us of a 'small military presence' on the Baltoro this year. I enquired what he meant.

'Do not worry. It will not affect your expedition,' he answered. The matter was left at that.

The briefing continued smoothly until Taleh announced a 25 percent increase in porter rates. Our mouths dropped. He was telling us that we would have to shell out an extra $2,700, on top of the money we already did not have enough of! At this totally unexpected raspberry I protested.

'But sir, your office sent me the official government porter rates and we planned our budget accordingly. And now you tell us this?' I blathered.

'We never guarantee that rates will not change. The regulations state as much,' he answered with an expansive flourish of his hand. His assistant, Istfahir, nodded slowly and smiled officiously.

No doubt, there was a clause in the long list of regulations that expeditions abide by that stated just that, but, for several years, expeditions had grown accustomed to porter wages being frozen at the rate of about fifty rupees per day, plus food and kit. We'd had no warning. Arguing, however, would be pointless and be likely only to rub salt in our wounds. We were bogged in a quagmire of bureaucracy. During a break in the briefing I caught a taxi to the airport to meet Tim and Phil, and, I hoped, to hear that our money worries were over. As Tim and Phil walked through the gates of the airport into the heat of the Pakistani day, we shook hands. A throng of airport porters milled about us, quarreling among themselves over who would carry our baggage. Tim, at 6 ft 3 in tall, towered over the crowd around him. His straw-coloured hair and lean, honest face carried the uncomplicated frankness of his rural upbringing, on farms in Kenya and Australia. Tim and I knew each other from only a few letters and a brief meeting when he'd visited Seattle on business. He knew no one else on the expedition. That he was standing before me bespoke no small amount of trust, and a willingness to take risks, both important qualities for what we were about to undertake.

'How are we doing for money?' Tim asked after introducing our jet-lagged cameraman, Phil. It boded ill that he should bring the subject up.

'Bad. We've just been told that porter wages have gone up 25 percent.'

He groaned. "Well, the sponsors didn't come through. We're still doing the film though, only I'm bankrolling it until such a time as we sell it. But there's worse.'

'What?'

'In Singapore we got clipped $1,500 for excess baggage.'

'Shit. We're bankrupt. How much have you got left?'

'About $2,000.'

We were back at square one, with enough to get to the mountain, but not quite enough to get out. We returned to the Ministry for the final round of formalities. Finally as we walked out of Taleh Mohammed's office we bumped into the British K2 expedition, on their way in. Their objective was the unclimbed Northwest Ridge of K2.

'Back again, eh, Greg?' said a voice. It was Alan Rouse, the expedition's leader. We smiled at each other like two criminals surprising one another in the act of the same crime.

'Yeah, back again,' I affirmed, adding, 'I almost didn't recognize you, you're so clean cut.' My memory of Alan from 1983 was of a scruffy climber with two months' growth about his chin. We chatted for a few minutes about our plans and the ups and downs of our expeditions. Ever since Alan had seen K2 in 1983, he'd been planning to return to it. The idea had become burned into his mind, and had consumed much of his energy for three years. Now he was back, sponsored by Fuller's Brewery and with a film crew in tow with the media-inspired plan to reach the summit on the day of Prince Andrew's Royal Wedding.

'Why the hell do we do it?' Alan asked rhetorically.

I thought of the months of work required to get here. For all our money and effort, we'd only bought uncertainty. 'Damned if I know,' I replied.

'Well, we've got our briefing now. Let's get together at the British Club for a beer before we head off,' Alan said. We shook hands and parted company.

A hundred details to attend to kept us from having that beer. Early on 2 May our rented NATCO bus arrived outside the hotel, ready to be loaded for departure. The driver hopped out, slapped his hand on my back and greeted me.

'Oh, no! Not you again!' I said.

'You know this guy?' asked Steve.

'He's the driver I had last year, on the trip to Hunza.' I was referring to a singularly miserable trip, to some peaks around Rakaposhi, every member of which had contracted dysentery. We'd spent two months on the pot.

'This guy is insane. He was smoking cigarettes laced with heroin while he drove us up the Karakoram Highway. We blew a tyre and nearly swerved into the gorge, but he didn't even notice, he was so bombed.'

Captain Rab Nawaz appeared. Compact of frame, he twisted the ends of his moustache and smiled confidently. He carried his luggage and a small cardboard box containing thirty cans of food. Already my relations with him had begun to ferment. The previous day he'd presented himself at our hotel and had demanded, to my astonishment, a daily allowance of 150 rupees per day for sixty days, the duration of the expedition. Government regulations do provide an LO with an allowance of 60 rupees per day to procure their own food in case the food supplied by the expedition is not to their tastes. So, we'd bought Rab Nawaz's food for him, to his approval. Now he'd decided this food was inappropriate. He wanted the money instead. Like the increase in porter rates, the Captain's insistence that LO rates had more than doubled was a regulation unmentioned in official negotiations. Tim and I argued defensively, but Rab Nawaz had us snookered. An expedition cannot leave Islamabad without its LO; if an expedition's LO is unhappy with food, kit, or money he will not accompany the expedition; such disputes must be settled at the Ministry of Tourism; and, being the weekend, the Ministry of Tourism was closed: Catch 22. Since the gringo always loses in such cases, and since we didn't wish to waste time negotiating in Islamabad, or begin on a bad note with our military watchdog, we compromised and gave Rab Nawaz a lump sum of 3,000 rupees.

In the hotel lobby, Rab Nawaz and I shake hands. I tactfully resist asking what he'd spent our money on, but I do ask how he planned to stretch his small box of canned food over two months.

'Oh, I'm sure I will find a way,' he says grinning.

It is apparent that we'll be feeding him anyway, despite paying him the 3,000 rupees, which, on top of his military pay, amounts to a tidy sum.

'You're a tricky little fellow, Captain,' I say.

'I think it's best to be tricky, don't you?' he replies.

Rab Nawaz had played the game so well that we could only laugh with him.

The last bag loaded, the bus begins its journey. Hours pass before we enter the desolate Indus Gorge. Here, at a curve in the road, a thousand feet above the river, the bus stops. The driver gets out and beckons us to the edge of the road, to peer down the vertical cliffs. At the bottom, on a ledge beside the river, lie a bus seat and a few pieces of rusting wreckage.

'Down there is the bus you drove in to Gilgit, last year,' the Captain tells me, translating the driver's words, 'It plunged off at night. Everyone was lost.'

I suddenly understand the driver's uncharacteristic abstemiousness.

Surrounded by white dunes and brown hills, Skardu appears after 36 hours. We rumble into the grounds of the K2 Hotel. The hot evening air is filled with a mixture of traffic and prayers. The K2 Hotel is renovated, with hot showers and without the rustic charm of bed bugs.

On 4 May we make arrangements to hire porters but discover that in all Skardu there are only twelve porters, a contrast with the 1983 situation when some 200 had presented themselves for work. We are told that the construction of a road from Dassu toward Askole, and the military activity alluded to by the Ministry, have absorbed many porters to carry material along the Braldu Valley and into the mountains. But more than that, a late spring season has kept the villagers at home, busily ploughing their fields. We have no choice but to hire our porters in Dassu, one day away.

Of the handful of porters we hire in Skardu are four men from the village of Satpara, ten miles from Skardu. They ask to join on as sirdars, cooks, kitchen boys, or mail runners. Satpara porters have a reputation for being hard-working and good tempered, so we agree to hire two of them, as cook and sirdar. We hire an aquiline-nosed twenty-year-old named Ghulam Abbas as cook, but as we negotiate among the remaining three for the position of sirdar, a tall buck-toothed fellow joins us. He introduces himself proudly as Sher Khan, a sirdar. The conversation instantly centres around him. He issues orders to the Satparans with authority. The Satparans back away and tell us that our sirdar will be Sher Khan. Sher Khan, evidently at the top of some pecking order, extends his hand toward me to close the deal. His face is familiar yet I cannot place it. Suspicious of anyone so quick to grab power I retract my hand.

'I don't wish to hire this man, Captain. Please let him know that and ask him to leave.'

There is an exchange of words but instead of Sher Khan it is the Satparans who leave. Sher Khan stands before me, defiant, a strange gleam in his eye.

'The other men will not work. They say that Sher Khan is a good Sirdar. He is an ex-policeman, a very strong man,' the Captain says.

'Or at least a strong-arm man,' I reply.

Reluctantly I negotiate a rate of pay with Sher Khan, shake his hand, and dispatch him to Dassu to muster 83 porters. Three tractors with trailers in tow, and two jeeps arrive. We load them with our baggage for the morrow's journey. I go to bed wondering why Sher Khan's face seems so familiar, and so troubling.

The jeep-road to Dassu is no less dusty than in 1983. We cover the 41 miles in seven hours and off-road in the walled enclosure of the guest house, where another expedition already awaits. Renato Casarotto, his wife Goretta, and two Basques, Mari Abrego and Josema Casimiro also are headed to the Baltoro, to K2. Casarotto plans to solo the unclimbed South-southwest Pillar, the Basques plan to climb K2 via the Abruzzi Ridge after an acclimatization ascent of Chogolisa. I find myself eyeing Casarotto, as if by inspection alone I might penetrate the powerfully built Italian and see what makes him capable of the long, hard solo ascents for which he is so famous.

Geoff, fluent in Spanish, strikes up a conversation with Mari, whom I remember from 1983 when we had shared base camps beneath K2. Late that season, after Doug's, Andy's, Jean's, and Roger's attempt on K2's South Face, when all the expeditions were winding down, Mari and Roger had made a final bid for the summit of K2, only to be halted by deep snow at 27,000 ft. We chat about how Roger had led the way on their final bid, and then, with sadness in his voice, Mari says 'Roger, *finis,* no?' Roger had died in an avalanche in 1985, while guiding in the mountains of Chamonix.

As we speak, Sher Khan enters the compound. His and Mari's eyes connect. Their body language communicates an exchange of daggers.

'This man is not your sirdar, I hope?' Mari asks Geoff, triggering an animated discussion between them.

'Is something wrong?' I ask Geoff.

'We've got a problem with Sher Khan. Mari says that under no circumstances should we hire the guy. He was his sirdar in '83. The moment the expedition left Dassu he made demands for more money, more clothing, more everything. They argued every inch of the way to K2. At Bardumal, during an argument over more equipment for Sher Khan, he ordered the porters to go on strike, then to attack the expedition with sticks and stones. The porters had Mari and his friends baled up against the banks of the Braldu. It came close to bloodshed. Sher Khan is a religious fanatic. He uses religion as a lever over the porters; they do whatever he says. Mari guarantees Sher Khan will do everything he can to disrupt us.'

I slap my head. Of course! I recall Sher Khan's face and remember Mari's story, told at rDokas in 1983. Geoff, Tim, and I confer briefly. We decide to fire Sher Khan. Since Sher Khan speaks very little English, the Captain conveys our decision. Sher Khan nods his head slowly, acknowledges that it is our right to fire him, but in the same breath makes it clear that he will see to it that no porter in Dassu works for our expedition. He concludes each sentence with a curt smile that reveals immense, yellow, rabbit-trap teeth. Sher Khan leaves the compound and rallies the porters into a ranting mob.

'What is he telling the porters?' I ask the Captain.

'That we are very bad men and are not welcome in this place. The porters are shouting against us. They are saying "Where is our sirdar; Give us our sirdar".'

For the next few hours we try to find a way to get Sher Khan out of our hair. It boils down to a matter of pride. His dismissal has caused him loss of face in front of his people, and now he is getting even with us. Though we know the stalemate will end the instant we re-hire him, the risk of having him cause trouble on the approach is too great. Yet like a pit-bull, he won't let go of us without a struggle.

In the dusty courtyard we try to nut out the problem. After several futile hours of discussion with Sher Khan, negotiations break down at dusk, leaving us no closer to a solution. Frustrated, I wander out amongst the porters, who squat about in groups, chatting. The goat-hair ropes they use for securing loads to their backs are tied around their waists or slung over their shoulders. They are just as eager for a solution as we are, for every day without work is a day without money. The porters smile at me. 'No problem leader—tomorrow all porters working,' one who speaks a patois of English declares.

'This Sher Khan—him good man or bad man?' I ask.

He laughs at me as if I am a fool. 'What policeman good man?' he replies with irony. We share a laugh that spans a world of cultural differences.

Next morning, after Casarotto's team leaves, the debate resumes. After a few more hours of futile talk in the baking sun I get an idea and put pen to paper. I write a contract, and hand it to the Captain.

'Captain, we will hire Sher Khan immediately if he signs this contract. Please read it to him.' The Captain reads. Sher Khan listens attentively to ten points that prohibit him from demanding more than his agreed wage and kit, as stated by the government regulations and the terms of the contract. Moreover, the contract prohibits him from causing any physical harm to our team, either through himself or through any instigation of the porters. The contract is written in duplicate. Sher Khan is informed that one copy will be lodged with the Ministry of Tourism's representative in Skardu.

'A contract? What good is a contract out here?' moans Geoff in dismay.

But Sher Khan recoils from the document as if it is a gobbet of pork. Within five minutes he is ready to leave for Skardu to find another expedition. He brings us a replacement sirdar, a shy young man named Shataraff Ali. We give Sher Khan a day's wages for the trouble of troubling us, then assemble the porters for selection. News of the dispute has attracted porters from miles around. Some 120 men of all ages now stand before us. We choose the strongest looking, those whom Geoff and I recall from our past expeditions, and those with conduct books. The Captain records each man's name on a sheet of paper in the following manner: Mohammed, son of Hussein, from the village of Hushe, or, Kassim, son of Ali, from the village of Shigar, for so many of the men have the same name.

As the Balti thrust their conduct books toward me in the hope of being hired I notice the same book repeatedly cropping up. Smelling a rat, I look about the crowd to see Sher Khan distributing the book among his friends, who in turn bring it to me, again and again.

'Captain, get this man out of here,' I shout, pointing to Sher Khan. The Captain orders him away. A few minutes later I see Sher Khan's malevolent grin riding off on a tractor bound for Skardu.

'No problem,' he shouts with a grin as he waves and then disappears into the dust.

The Valley of the Scoundrels

On 7 May we begin the trek along the changeless yet ever changing Braldu River, arriving in Chongo at the end of the second day. In the apricot grove where we set up our tents, a group of villagers awaits our arrival. Ours is the first expedition of the year with a doctor.

I'd heard it said that inbreeding is so rife in Chongo that even the yaks have club feet. The ragged, at times physically misshapen villagers awaiting us seem to bear out this unkind adage. Those seeking medical attention are all men or boys. No women are among them. When a Balti man brags of how many offspring he has fathered he only counts the sons. Steve rests a few minutes, cleans the dust from the lenses of his spectacles, then begins the evening consultations. The Captain interprets.

A man of perhaps fifty cradles in his arms a boy of six. Both are caked with grime. The child's stomach is frightfully distended. Father and son are clad in tunics of earth-toned, homespun cloth. Threads unravel from the old man's clothes, even as he speaks.

'Captain, ask this man when the last time was that he bathed his son,' Steve asks.

Questioned, the father thinks this over, then answers. The Captain translates. 'Not since the day he was born.' The irony of this is that a mile beyond Chongo are crystal-clear hot springs.

'What about the father? When did he last wash?'

The Captain asks, then tells Steve. 'The dirty wretch does not ever remember washing.' The Captain's role of translating the ailments of the wretched to a bunch of foreign eccentrics on a mission to a mountain seems to amuse him, prompting him to alternate his role of translator with that of comedian. The strangeness of our comparative wealth being squandered on an absurdity like Gasherbrum IV is not lost on him. He begins to tell jokes and soon is strutting around the apricot grove, cracking one joke after another.

Doing his best to ignore the Captain's jestering, Steve examines the child. He diagnoses intestinal worms and a resultant nutritional deficiency and gives the father the appropriate drugs and vitamins.

'Come Steve, tell me: What is the definition of noise?' The Captain turns to riddles: 'I can't imagine,' Steve replies while listening through his stethoscope to the railing lungs of the next patient. 'Two skeletons making love on a tin roof.' The Captain crumples with hysteria at his own joke.

'Very funny, Captain,' says Steve, dismissing his patient with a pill. An octogenarian male hobbles up to take his neighbour's place. 'Now, what's this man's problem?'

Another exchange and a translation: 'He has pain in his cock,' blurts the Captain with a guffaw that by now has become contagious. He dons Phil's wide-brimmed stockman's hat, picks up Andy's banjo, and begins an atonal serenade of some bawdy song. He is the perfect fool.

Phil switches on his tape recorder. 'If this is what expeditions are about, then this'll be one helluva strange film.'

Steve struggles to maintain his professional demeanour, while the rest of us succumb to infectious laughter. 'Sorry, but there isn't much I can do for an enlarged prostate gland,' Steve tells the old man, who comprehends not a word, yet gladly accepts the analgesics and vitamins Steve hands him. After all, it is pills he has come for, and the more brightly coloured the better. Modern medicine still lies within the realm of magic to the Balti. Often they will hoard the medications given them by expedition doctors, and instead of taking the medicines will use them for barter, or carry them as a kind of amulet. Even when a villager is mortally ill the Balti seldom travel to the clinic at Skardu. Though they revere the power of modern medicine, they distrust all things beyond their villages. Prayers, poultices of clay or bark or fungus, sacred healing stones, and a few herbs are the extent of Balti medicine.

We leave Chongo. Paths chiseled into the side of the cliffs lead to meadows being tilled by yaks on the outskirts of Askole. The deltaform rock spire of Bakhor Das, still thick with snow, rises above the valley rim. The mountains are still in the grip of winter.

In Askole we camp on the same barren plot of ground as in 1983. Familiar are the muddy culverts and cobbled streets, the walls and dwellings of mud and round stones, the thorny thickets topping the walls to stop livestock straying. Even the scrawny chickens seem unchanged from three years before. The only mark of change is a recently constructed school hut principaled by a young man from Hunza. And, ruling it all, is the lambardar, Haji Medi. Haji recognizes me from 1983, and Geoff from 1984. He invites us all to his house for tea and eggs.

Located in the heart of the village, Haji's house is a spacious mud-walled labyrinth, with old carved wooden posts supporting a mud and willow-thatch roof. In the room where we take tea we sit at a wooden bench. Otherwise, the room is bare save for Haji's well thumbed Koran, which sits in an alcove set into the clay wall. Haji's son, a grubby urchin of about ten, stares up at us with fascination. I give him a winter hat. The Captain looks on with disdain.

'He has a thousand hats, why give him another? Look at this child—Haji Medi is rich but he cannot even keep his children clean,' the Captain says.

'Why don't we ask Haji why the villagers of this valley never wash?' asks Tim. Coming from the homogenized West, the Balti love of dirt was an enigma to even the best-travelled among us.

The Captain puts the question to Haji Medi. An answer quickly follows.

'He says that the more a man washes his clothes, the faster they wear out.'

Pure wisdom, given the local method of washing, by pounding wet garments with a flat stone. But it did not explain why some Balti along the Braldu Valley may not wash their bodies for ten years, or an entire lifetime. We'd discussed this subject that afternoon with Askole's school teacher, prior to taking tea at Haji's house. The teacher told us that one day he'd taught his pupils a lesson in hygiene and washing. For his troubles, the fathers of the children had threatened to beat the daylight out of him if he ever gave such a lesson again. The local proclivity for filth ran counter to the Koranic reverence of cleanliness. I wondered if this stemmed from an abhorrence or fear not of water but of the body, for in order to wash, persons must disrobe and hence witness their bodies. Perhaps, along the murky Braldu, disrobing and washing had evolved into a sinful act because it tempted the Balti to look at their bodies and entertain thoughts of the flesh that might offend Allah. Or, more simply, perhaps these children of the mountains, like all children, saw nothing wrong with playing in the dirt. We had entered a puritan world so different from our own. Men worked separately to women; women lived sequestered away in *purdah;* marriages, decided by elders, occurred not out of mutual love, but to keep land between families and strengthen clan bonds. The harsh environment cast everything in a utilitarian mould.

I veer the subject away from filth: 'What does Haji Medi think of the expeditions that pass through Askole?'

The Captain asks and then offers a synthesis of the reply. 'He doesn't care what you do in the mountains, but he likes the money you bring. His people are poor. The money is very good for them.'

We nod at Haji's pragmatism. He smiles as if impressed by his own wisdom against our naiveté. Age was mellowing the lambardar, time treating him well, weathering away the sharp edges of his nature just as it erodes and smooths mountains. The crafty old bane of expeditions had become a softspoken middle-aged man, watching his children grow. Haji puts a question for us to the Captain.

'Haji Medi wants to know if you will write a book about this expedition?'

'Maybe,' I reply.

'Then he asks that you say only good things about him.'

Dusk gathers. The schoolteacher knocks on Haji's door. He asks Steve to examine a sick man in a nearby hamlet.

It is dark by the time Steve, Geoff, and the schoolteacher run the two miles across wadis and fields to the hamlet of the ailing villager. The three enter a room dimly lit by a flickering tallow lamp. They are shown a gaunt figure laying on a *charpoi*. When Steve and Geoff switch on their headlamps and shine them onto the patient they are taken aback by what they see. A man, not old, but pitifully thin and too weak to even sit up without assistance, lies shaking and trembling. His skin is covered in black blotches from a bacterial infection raging in his bloodstream, multiplying out of control, so populous that they deposit in huge colonies just beneath the surface of his skin. The expression in his eyes is one of helpless horror. He is near to death and he knows it.

The population of the hamlet crowd into the hut to watch Steve do his work. There is barely elbow-room. Coughs and wheezes among the gathering smack of tuberculosis. Smoke rises from a dark pit in the floor. A ladder descends into it. Geoff peers down and sees troglodyte forms tending a cooking fire. Down there, in that foul dinge, is where the women and children live and cook. Steve diagnoses septic shock from the bacteria, which probably entered the villager's body from unclean drinking water. Ooh's and aah's of wonderment rise from the crowd as Steve opens his medical bag. All eyes watch as he fills a syringe with a powerful dose of penicillin and jabs it into the patient. Leaving an oral course of antibiotics with a village elder to give to the patient later, Steve instructs that the patient be given sweet, milkless tea at regular intervals. Just as the unhygienic world of this villager allowed him to become infected, the unresistant germs in his body will succumb quickly to the penicillin. The drug will run its course in a dramatic way that none of us in the west, with its antibiotic-toughened microbes, will ever know.

In gratitude the villagers bring chickens and eggs. The villager is lucky to dwell in a valley through which a few western doctors pass each year. Thanks to Steve the man survives.

Looking toward Trango Tower and the Cathedral Peaks from the Baltoro Glacier.

On 12 May we reach Paiju. Storm clouds swirl about the granite towers of the Lower Baltoro. The river runs thinly from the glacier. Still, the spring thaw has not begun. I sit on a river-burnished boulder, watching the pewter sky stew. At my feet lie artefacts of other expeditions: Bleached goat horns from a feast that filled the bellies of some Balti; a rusting sardine tin that sated the appetite of a climber or trekker; a tent peg; the worn out sole of a boot; a film wrapper, all alternately buried and uncovered by shifting sands and constant wind, until those artefacts break down as well to also become part of the sand and wind.

A group of porters drag the goat we'd bought in Askole to the river bank. The goat senses its slaughter and it struggles and snorts, wide eyed. The kicking beast is wrestled onto its back and faced toward Mecca. Its throat is slit: hot blood gushes out and the sand drinks it thirstily. The animal quivers briefly, before being carved up.

Early the next morning we leave Paiju's smouldering fireplaces littered with charred goat bones, and head toward Lillego. Our caravan covers the six miles along the back of the Baltoro Glacier to arrive at Lillego's towering mud walls at two in the afternoon, just as the vaporous gray wall of a snow flurry erupts out of the valley of the Trango Glacier and brushes past us. The porters hurriedly cover stone circles with tarps to shelter from the squall and set about cooking their evening meal. Ibrahim, a smiling Balti, rolls a wad of flour into a sloppy dumpling and plops it into a pot of boiling water. He calls the resulting ball of stodge *plapu*. It tastes as bad as it looks. He washes this down with a hot drink of salt-butter tea, a brew also native to Nepal and Tibet, probably introduced to the Balti long ago by traders from those lands. Ibrahim finishes off his meal with a pinch of *naswar,* a finely ground, green, tobacco snuff that he wedges behind his lower lip. I know better than to accept his offer to sample it. I'd tried it once before. All I'd gotten from it was a sensation like the top of my skull opening up, followed by nausea and a foul-tasting slime oozing out my mouth.

Just as some of the porters kneel for prayer and commence their deep, ululating chant, the storm clears to reveal cathedral-like spires across the glacier. Meanwhile Randy, while searching for some item in his load, comes across his frisbee and tosses it into the air. The frisbee carves a boomerang path and doubles back toward a group of praying porters. They scatter as it bounces in their midst, then pick it up, examine it, and return it to the air. It flies across the campsite and bashes into the rump of a porter also praying, prostrated face down, end up. The Balti cackle with laughter as the startled porter leaps to his feet as if Allah himself had kicked him in the arse. The porter spins the frisbee skyward and, for the next hour, our 84 porters and the eight of us run about the rubble of Lillego, hooting and chasing after a twentieth century plaything, while Allah above taps his foot impatiently, waiting for his children to return to their devotions.

From the green meadow of rDokas on, Gasherbrum IV dominates the skyline until the view opens out at Concordia to reveal Broad Peak and the greatest lure of them all, K2. In the weeks ahead eighty climbers from nine nations will assemble at K2's base and assail its flanks: 27 climbers will reach the summit; thirteen will die.

Beside K2 is Broad Peak. I crane my neck up at it. Seeing it again is like confronting the reality of a potent dream. The closer we get to our mountain the thicker grows the mantle of snow overlying the glacier, and the more bizarre become the new sights along the way. At our feet, snaking along the glacier and tied every few hundred feet to bamboo poles, is a radio wire, connecting Pakistani army bases at Gore, Concordia, and further into the mountains. At these bases solid-walled fibreglass huts and North Face dome tents house bored, but friendly soldiers. In the air, military helicopters—French-built Pumas—labour up the Baltoro, their rotors and engines straining to stay aloft in the thin air. The Pumas stock a command base at Gore, while smaller, more agile helicopters continue up the Baltoro toward Chogolisa and the Abruzzi Glacier to supply camps twelve to twenty miles from Concordia. From these advance camps fixed ropes lead to the crests of strategic passes such as Conway Saddle. There, at 20,669 ft, armed with heavy calibre weapons and mortars, outposts of Pakistani soldiers guard the entrances to the 46-mile Siachen Glacier.

Why? As early as the mid-1970s Indian troops had been creeping into a region of Pakistan's Northern Areas, establishing armed bases on an almost uninhabited expanse of mountainous terrain bounded west by the origin of the Baltoro Glacier, north by the Chinese border, east by the Karakoram Pass, and south by the entire Siachen Glacier. Though remote, this high labyrinth of glaciers, ranges, and valleys on the southern watershed of the Karakoram is of major strategic importance, linking India and Pakistan and giving access to the Nubra Valley, the Valley of Ladakh, to Kashmir, Chinese Ladakh, Aksai Chin, and to road links between Strinagar and Leh. It is also close to Pakistan's Karakoram Highway. This violation of Pakistan territory has resulted in an undeclared war that has become known as the Siachen Conflict.

The Siachen Region lies in a controversial area where no line of control is delineated. The two border agreements between India and Pakistan—the 1949 Karachi Agreement on the ceasefire in Kashmir, and the 1972 Simla Agreement that followed the 1971 war beween the two nations—never actually defined a boundary in the Siachen, due to the region's inaccessibility. Since no boundary exists beyond the foot of the Siachen Glacier, both sides claim the land, though the area has been under the control of Pakistan from 1947 till 1983 and has been shown on world atlases as either Pakistan or disputed territory. This great intersection of Central Asia has been frequently contested. China and India clashed over possession of the area east of the Karakoram Pass, known as Aksai Chin, in 1959, and seem likely to do so again; India and Pakistan fought over Kashmir in 1965.

India claims that the Siachen, like all of Kashmir that lies behind the 1947 ceasefire line, is Indian land and is emphatic in its claim. Perspicacious observers may have seen trouble brewing prior to the outbreak of fighting in the Siachen: in 1984 two Indian Army mountaineering expeditions disregarded Pakistani sovereignty and entered the Siachen Glacier. The first expedition was in 1980, to Asparasas Peak. The second, in 1981, is recorded in India's journal of mountaineering, *The Himalayan Journal*. 'The Indian Army Expedition to the Eastern Karakoram, 1981,' an article by Colonel N. Kumar, describes an expedition that explored the Siachen Glacier Region and climbed Saltoro Kangri (25,409 ft) and Sia Kangri (24,359 ft). The article's most interesting aspect is that it makes no mention that this army expedition was violating territory regarded as Pakistani.

The Siachen crisis heated up in 1982–3 when Indian troops established fortified outposts on Sia La and Bilafond La, and set up a large base at Saltoro. Discovering this, Pakistan rushed troops into the region. Armed tent-cities were set up, and existing Pakistani outposts across the Siachen reinforced. Soon, battles were waged amid grassless high-altitude rubble. On 23 June 1984, Pakistani troops tried to dislodge the Indian invaders from their outposts. But since India held the high ground the Pakistani forces were beaten back. Subsequent skirmishes have realigned the possession of some of the high passes; Gyong La has shifted to Pakistani control. Troops on both sides are by now well-trained in mountain warfare, and are well supplied. On the Pakistani side it is common to see soldiers kitted out in alpine-camouflage, with white nylon down-filled suits and white rucksacks.

In 1985, while in Gilgit, I'd watched flight after flight of helicopters arrive in Skardu and land in the Gilgit army base. The story on the streets was that a force of Pakistani commandos had launched a midnight raid on an Indian Army camp and had massacred the Indians in their beds. Retreating back toward their bases, the commandos had been strafed by Russian-made helicopter gunships. The Pakistani helicopters landing in Gilgit were full of wounded soldiers.

In a move seemingly to legitimize India's invasion, the Indian Mountaineering Federation has opened peaks in the contested area to foreign expeditions. Sia Kangri, the peak straddling the Abruzzi arm of the Baltoro Glacier on the west and the Siachen Glacier on the east, in 1985 suddenly appeared on the list of peaks newly accessible through India. However, the Pakistani army doesn't distinguish foreign climbers from Indian aggressors: during a climb of Sia Kangri from the Indian side, an American-Indian group found that Pakistani artillery mounted on a nearby pass were shelling the terrain between them and their mountain. The shots were a warning. Wisely, the American climbers withdrew, but the Indians ignored the intermittent barrage and climbed the peak. And, from the Indian side, artillery shells whistled over Conway Saddle, to explode on the south Gasherbrum Glacier, where many foreign expeditions were camped.

What could India stand to gain by snatching the Siachen? To gain a footing to take the entire Baltoro? To steal K2, the jewel in the Karakoram's crown? Militarily, the region is of great importance to both sides. India's moves are to its advantage in consolidating it as a Central Asian power, but is the cost of opening this window to Pakistan's northern areas worth the suffering?

The Siachen Conflict is part of the ongoing friction between Hindu and Moslem: 400 miles from the Baltoro, on the Pakistan/Punjab border, dozens of heavily armed Indian and Pakistani divisions face each other, poised for battle. India accuses Pakistan of aiding the Sikh terrorists agitating for a Sikh state within India; Pakistan accuses India of inventing a pretext for a long-planned invasion. Millions of dollars are being spent in the stalemate. Each year on the passes around the Siachen, men are lost to frostbite, the maladies of altitude, to storms, avalanche, and crevasses.

Himalayan borders have a long history of conflict. Before the 1800s, the Himalayas and their lowlands were divided into small principalities and kingdoms. Borders, often vague, were based on tribal territories, and these boundaries were continually reshaped by wars of conquest. During the 1800s, British and Russian political agents competed to consolidate these boundaries for their respective empires. Britain sought to push north the borders of British-ruled India and gain influence and control over the mountainous trading passes linking the nations of the Himalayas, a move calculated to gain an access to trade, and to stymie Russian and Chinese designs on these remote outposts. This was the period of 'The Great Game', when Britain and Russia grappled to outdo each other in gobbling up as much of the Himalayan world as they could.

Maps from this period were in a state of constant change. Disputed territories were inevitably rugged and largely barren, but it was land for the taking, and strategic land at that. Boundaries were usually drawn along the crests of mountain ridges and ranges, frequently ignoring ethnic precedents. Borders in disputed areas were often represented on maps as simply a wash of colour with the notation 'undetermined'. When the British pulled out of India, and when Pakistan became a nation, the maps left from those empire building days, so full of ambiguities, fueled struggles that would persist for many years.

The Pakistani officer and his six enlisted men lay around their well-stocked base at Concordia in a state of soporific inertia. Our sudden appearance surprises them, but doesn't rouse them from their seats in the patch of afternoon sun. They are like bears emerging from a long winter hibernation. Glad of some new faces, the soldiers share with us a plate of *pakora,* and quiz Captain Rab Nawaz about events in the civilized world.

Suddenly the *whup-whup-whup* of an approaching helicopter lights a fire under the soldiers. Two men hoist a red market flag; a third man cranks the handle on the radio and shouts into the mouthpiece; the rest, including Captain Rab Nawaz, jump about and wave their arms like castaways desperate for rescue from a desert island. The helicopter drones by like a bumble-bee ignoring a pollenless flower. It continues toward Conway Saddle. The long-faced soldiers return to their seats. The commander, who never rose from his throne of empty jerry-cans, shrugs and contemptuously waves the helicopter away with the back of his hand.

'The heli's never land here. The radio has been down since the first snows of winter. I sometimes wonder if we have not been forgotten.' His voice is full of lassitude.

'Why don't you walk back to the base at Gore?' I suggest.

'We dare not leave this outpost! Two men who went walking on the glacier are still inside it!'

'My God, this is hell on earth!' exclaims Captain Rab Nawaz.

We ask the officer if he has confronted the Indians. He grins. The question probably breaches the realms of restricted information, but his appetite for conversation outweighs his confidentiality.

'My men have shaken hands with them,' he tells us enigmatically.

'So you've served time on the high passes?' Tim asks.

'Yes. I spent many weeks last winter on Conway Saddle. It is impossible to do anything there. The cold is so severe that gun barrels stick to the skin. Men who stay there too long go mad. Perfectly good soldiers lose respect, even lose the will to live. They just die.'

Though mountaineers frequently visit high altitudes, military personnel are the ones who have spent the longest periods at altitudes from 14,000 to 20,000 ft, during campaigns like the 1962 border war between China and India, and now in the Siachen conflict. In all cases it has been found that man is an unreliable fighting machine when rushed too fast to altitude, or when forced to endure altitude too long. The Indian army had learned this the hard way in 1962 when Chinese troops, well-seasoned to battle at altitude from their long campaign against Tibetan Khampa resistance fighters, routed Indian troops along a disputed border tract extending from the eastern border of Bhutan to the western edge of Burma. The Indian soldiers were disadvantaged by being rushed in from low altitudes to defend passes 14,000 to 16,000 ft high. Many fought on the wintery passes and ridges wearing only cotton uniforms and with one light blanket apiece. Of the 1,383 Indian soldiers killed and 1,696 wounded in the battle of the Northeast Frontier Agency, as the campaign was called, almost as many succumbed to edema and exposure, as to Chinese bullets.

The day is late. Cold night air begins to chill Concordia. Alpenglow tints the mountains as thin clouds drift across the faces of K2, Broad Peak, Gasherbrum IV, and the fluted ice walls of Chogolisa. Though the view is beautiful to us, it represents hell to the soldiers.

The Balti endure the bitterly cold night huddled in stone shelters, smoking cigarettes, talking and singing all night long. Anxious to move, they wake early. Clouds of condensation puff from their mouths and noses. They stamp their cold feet as they stand around waiting for the sun to appear. The clear night sky leaves the snow frozen rock-hard and easy to walk on but after five days on the glacier, the cold has leached through the Baltis' flimsy rubber boots and ragged clothes and into their bones. By the morning of 17 May and the final five-mile stage before Base Camp on the West Gasherbrum Glacier, the Baltis' senses of humour are as frozen as the Baltoro. Rumblings of mutiny fill the air as we break camp.

Our small bribes of extra kerosene for their stoves, handed out along the way, have goaded them only so far. Their mood is foul. Most have broken their sunglasses and have headaches from snow-glare. They regard our solution of patching the glasses with tape to fashion narrow eye-slits as an insult. They toss the repaired sunglasses at our feet and demand new ones, but we have none to give. Steve distributes aspirin to those porters with headaches. He is nearly mobbed, it is the last chance for *dabai,* or medicine. It's also the last chance for the porters to pilfer whatever they can. Small items like cups, cigarette lighters, and bits of string securing loads begin to disappear.

Shataraff Ali, the sirdar, crunches across crisp snow toward the rock that the Captain, Geoff, Tim, and I sit on. He interrupts our argument with the Captain, caused by a small hole Rab Nawaz has found in the woollen balaclava we have issued him. Gone with the rise in altitude are the Captain's jokes. He is falling apart at the seams. The cap, he insists, is inferior. By giving him such a cap we have insulted him, and to insult him is to insult the Pakistani army. We are arguing over a pulled thread in a wool hat. Trivialities have become the daily bread of our concerns.

Geoff and I try to placate the Captain, but, as we shiver under the bitter morning sky we resort to shouts. I am perversely glad to see that Geoff's usually amicable disposition deteriorates into a rage equivalent to mine. Tim, luckily, is less splenetic than Geoff or I. He quells the argument in anticipation of a new one looming on the horizon.

Shataraff Ali burbles out something to the Captain.

'The porters are ready to be paid,' Rab Nawaz echoes.

'No way! We pay them at Base Camp. Who told them we'd pay them here!' I shout angrily.

'The sirdar asked me this yesterday. I agreed to it,' says Rab Nawaz.

'What? Whose bloody side are you on, Captain? You're supposed to be helping us, not causing trouble behind our backs. We make decisions about money. There'll be no payment yet.'

The porters gather into a huddle. From it rise the sounds of a strike.

'I told you to buy me a pistol in Abbatobad!' the Captain reproves.

Tim sighs, 'That's just what we need.'

'Well, maybe we should pay them,' suggests Geoff in a moment of cornered weakness. 'What could be so bad about that?'

'Because they'll dump the bloody loads and piss off back down the glacier and we'll spend the next week shuttling loads to Base Camp; that's why.'

The Captain, deep in sulk, is instructed to tell the porters they will be paid at Base Camp. This puts us in the absurd position of seemingly having reneged on Rab Nawaz's deal. As recompense, Shataraff Ali asks for a bonus for each man.

'Jesus Christ! We're already paying them an extra 25 percent!' Geoff howls.

'They're just trying it on,' says Tim, who is an old hand in porter negotiations, having accumulated years in Nepal. Even so, he is amazed at the brazenly incorrigible Balti. We concede to give them a few plastic tarpaulins, but they hold out for more money.

'No Base Camp, no pay,' I declare. Faced with desertion it is easy to become a slave driver.

Shataraff Ali consults the porters. He returns with Soolaiman and four other Balti. These men are the ones carrying the loads of *roti* for the porters to eat on the return journey. Soolaiman, a good-natured porter whom we all like, holds his face a few inches from ours and asks that he and his friends be paid now so they can leave for rDokas with the food. Soolaiman's pestiferous breath assails us like a weapon. We find ourselves turning and gasping for fresh air as he makes his long request.

'This fellow is giving us too many of his sweet words,' chokes the Captain.

'Pay him, quickly,' I wheeze. The remaining porters decide that we are tougher nuts to crack than they thought, and they saddle their loads.

Gasherbrum IV is sharp-edged against a blue sky as we leave Concordia. We enter a pitching sea of ice and rubble trapped in still life. Tim, Tom, and I head off in front to find a path through a maze of frozen streams and lakes, while the rest of the team stay with the porters. After barely a mile, the porters stop, sit, and go no further. I turn to hear Geoff and the Captain, 200 yards back, screaming at each other, then see Geoff storming off as the porters uncoil a 600 ft spool of rope.

'What the hell is going on back there?' I ask as Geoff reaches me.

'The goddam Captain told the porters that there are hundreds of crevasses between Concordia and Base Camp. They demanded to be roped up before going any further. I blew my top.'

From 200 yards away, we watch Randy knot the rope around the waist of a man at either end, while in between, the remaining seventy-odd porters, and the Captain, grip the 8 mm rope in their hands. The crocodile of porters rises then follows along behind us, pulling, tugging, shouting. But at least they are moving. We follow the footsteps of Tom and Tim, up and over pressure ridges and into the gaping portals of the West Gasherbrum Glacier. At 2.00 pm we reach the stone-strewn site of Geoff's 1984 Base Camp. An hour later the porters arrive, but they dump their loads at a spot 100 yards from Base Camp.

'Hey—this is Base Camp here,' I shout to them.

Climbers and porters approaching base camp on the Baltoro.

'*Ni!*' Base camp here!' an old Balti calls back. They untie the ropes from the loads, indicating that they have no intention of carrying them the final 100 yards.

'It's getting pretty rough when your porters start telling you where your Base Camp is,' Tim sighs wearily.

Ghulam Abbas, our cook, arrives, shaking his head at the absurd scene. 'These porters all Shigar men; Shigar men no good; Satpara men good,' he informs us.

Tim clips his cross-country skis to his boots and skates down a snowdrift between us and the porters. I join him in urging the porters to pick up their loads. They shake their heads. They are going to be obstinate, simply for the sake of it.

'Base camp over there,' shouts Tim, waving his ski pole.

'This Base Camp!' retorts the old Balti.

'Bullshit!' yells Tim.

'Bullshit', echoes the old porter angrily, raising his staff, threatening to club Tim on the head.

'No Base Camp—no pay,' I shout again. I turn, walk back to the chosen site, and sit on the pack of rupees. If the porters wished to they could make short work of us and steal the money. Though relations between the Balti have come a long way in recent years, I still had last year's memory of the Nagars, at the base of Rakaposhi in Hunza, physically assaulting the expedition over a pay dispute. Some fifty of them had charged the team like a horde of Tartars, staves waving in the air, pushing my companions around until we saw things their way.

Eventually the loads are delivered to the real Base Camp. Time has worked on our side. We are home, the Balti are not. They have a long march ahead of them. Like workers punching the bundy clock at the end of the shift, the arguments cease, their pay is handed out, and they sprint off down the glacier. We scurry about erecting tents as the first snowflakes of a storm begin to fall. Randy, with a broad grin, distributes his business cards amongst the porters. In America a good businessman never misses the opportunity to do a bit of networking with potential clients; on the Baltoro, a Balti never misses the opportunity to scrounge something for free.

Hurricane at Camp Three

Even before reaching the Karakoram, pundits had warned us that 1986 was shaping into one of the worst Himalayan seasons in climbing history. A heavy monsoon in Southwest Asia indicated that the often mild monsoon experienced in the Karakoram could be replaced with a season of fierce storms. Even in late May, the harsh winter from which the high villages of the Karakoram foothills were just emerging had not left the mountains. But every year in the Himalaya is the 'worst season on record'. The phrase is like a broken record to Himalayan climbers. Thus, it was scant surprise to us on 20 May that we awoke from our first night in Camp One, at 18,500 ft, to a temperature of -25 degrees Fahrenheit.

The route from Base Camp, at 16,500 ft, to Camp One is really a journey from one glacier onto another, from the West Gasherbrum onto a high tributary of that glacier. Where the two meet, an icefall like a solidified waterfall crashes down, creaking and groaning, at times releasing in a sudden thunderous roar.

The path to the foot of Gasherbrum IV, along the two mile long West Gasherbrum Glacier, is a portrait in symmetry. Fed by icefalls on the north and south flanks of the mountain, the glacier rolls out from the West Face like a long and treacherous avenue leading from a lofty fortress. Flanking either side of this avenue stand 6,000 ft walls of rock, fluted and cliffed with ice. The summits atop the walls of the south side of the glacier, of Gasherbrum V and its satellites, make constant efforts to disrupt this symmetry, by daily dumping thousands of tons of ice onto the glacier below. These avalanches sweep across the half-mile wide glacier, and collide with the opposing walls in a matter of seconds, leaving car-sized blocks of ice in their wake.

It becomes our habit to hurry past this section, but, on 25 May, as we carry a load to Camp One, we pause for a minute to stare up at the Northwest Ridge, visible in its entirety for the first time in a cloud-filled week. Geoff's gloved finger traces out a line with which he is well familiar. He points past the terrain we have already climbed—the spur of limestone cliffs and ice gullies that take us safely right of the tumbling icefall spilling out of the huge, hidden glacial valley where Camp One sits—to the ground we will cover in the weeks ahead. We stare up toward the hidden valley, a cul-de-sac acres in size, concealed from view from every angle except the upper reaches of the West Gasherbrum Glacier. From this furthest reach,

Looking up the West Gasherbrum Glacier to Gasherbrum IV as an avalanche pours off Gasherbrum V to the right.

we see a great couloir at the hidden valley's end, a deep white gash splitting the walls surrounding Camp One. The couloir, 45 to 70 degrees steep, rises 3,500 ft to the crest of the Northwest Ridge, to a notch where a hurricane wind whips a stream of snow horizontally west.

'See that little boulder at the top of the couloir?' says Geoff. We zero in on a piece of rock on the lee side of the wind, 50 ft below the notch. 'That's Camp Two. The wall is overhanging, somewhat sheltered. We placed a Whillans box-tent there in 1984. Took us hours to chop a ledge out of the ice. The Whillans box is still up there, dismantled, wrapped in a tarp. It's probably trashed, but if it isn't we should make use of it. It's the only tent that'll survive the wind that whistles through the notch.' A Whillans box is the armoured car of tents, cubiform in shape, made from aluminium poles with heavy-duty nylon walls. Don Whillans had designed it for use at high altitude.

Geoff then points out a network of thin ice gullies leading out of Camp Two. The gullies traverse diagonally, sometimes horizontally rightwards across the West Face then re-join the Northwest Ridge at 23,000 ft. There, on a shoulder of ice domes, is Camp Three. The traverse is rocky. Both attempts on the ridge had found this to be a troublesome, difficult section, but the alternative, which is to climb the rocky skyline ridgecrest, looks even harder. We are counting on a third possibility, out of sight, unexplored, that might prove quicker and easier—the snowy slopes of the Northwest Face on the other side of the notch, in China. In his letter, Voytek had suggested that given perfect conditions, these slopes might give easy access to Camp Three. Voytek hadn't descended that way because the snow was waist deep and ready to avalanche, but after a period of prolonged sweeping by the wind, as was happening now, it was possible that the slope would be safely cleared of snow. Camp Three would be our last fixed camp.

'In '84 we got a camp up there in a bergschrund. We tunneled into it and dug out enough room for a few tents', said Geoff. 'Above that we fixed another 1,000 ft of rope, to the top of the first rock band. That was our highpoint.'

The rock band Geoff points to begins above a steep snowfield, at a rock pinnacle with a prominent notch between it and the cliffed ridge. This landmark we name 'The Notch'. Above the top of the first rock band, at 24,000 ft, we see the profile of the unclimbed 1,000 ft icefield, then the final 1,000 ft headwall. The wall is a swirl of geological contact zones, of diorite, marble, and limestone. Atop the headwall lies the North Summit. The final stretch to the true summit crosses the broken tooth of the summit ridge, traversing horizontally for 1,500 ft. That part, at least, looks easy, but from 10,000 ft below, our view is foreshortened. Bonatti and Mauri in 1958 had found the string of rock towers up there guarding the summit to be the sting in the mountain's tail.

In 1958, when Walter Bonatti and Carlo Mauri were stepping onto Gasherbrum IV's summit, most of us on this expedition were still in nappies. As youths we were raised on the stuff of that adventure, inspired by the images frozen within printed time capsules like *Karakoram,* Fosco Mariani's book about the first ascent of Gasherbrum IV, and Charles Houston's and Robert Bates's horrifying tale *K2, The Savage Mountain.*

Gasherbrum is really a mutated word, transcribed from the Baiti, whose name for the mountain, *'rgasha brum'* means literally 'beautiful mountain'. The modern 'Gasherbrum' was officially coined in 1860, when the British surveyor Montgomerie registered the name with the Grand Trigonometrical Survey of India. When Sir William Martin Conway explored the Baltoro in 1892, he called the mountain's West Face 'The Shining Wall'.

The Baltoro was a rarely visited glacier in 1958. K2 had been climbed for the first time, four years before, by Italians; Gasherbrum II by Austrians in 1956; Broad Peak, also by Austrians, in 1957. 1958 saw three more expeditions trek into the Baltoro: Japanese for Chogolisa, Americans for Gasherbrum I, and Italians for Gasherbrum IV. Among the Italians involved in the G4 expedition were two from the 1954 K2 expedition, Ricardo Cassin and Walter Bonatti. Cassin, a famous climber of the generation preceding Bonatti's, had led the reconnaissance expedition to K2 in 1953. Five years later he was back, as leader of the Gasherbrum IV expedition. Bonatti, 24 years old at the time of K2, may well have reached K2's summit but for a night spent sitting out in a makeshift snowhole at 26,000 ft, after misplacing the high camp where Lacedelli and Compagnoni sat, awaiting Bonatti's and a Hunza porter's delivery of oxygen and respirators. Bonatti survived the cold night unscathed. His Hunza companion, Mahdi, lost the front half of his feet to frostbite. Ironically, they were but a short distance from the tent, but their companions could not hear their shouts for the wind. Lacedelli and Compagnoni reached the summit as the weakened Bonatti and Mahdi descended the mountain.

West Face of Gasherbrum IV seen from Baltoro Glacier.
1. NW Ridge (Australian/American, 1986).
2. W Face (Korean, 1997).
3. W Face (Polish/Austrian, 1985).
The 1958 first ascent followed a ridge on the NE side. The Polish/Austrian climbers had to forego the final traverse to the main summit.

It was a defeat that left the ambitious Bonatti bitterly disappointed, but he had seen his strengths on K2, and would not be thwarted again.

In 1958, several heights for Gasherbrum IV held currency. Zurbriggen, on Conway's 1892 expedition, had surveyed the mountain at 26,016 ft. G.O. Dyhrenfurth, with the 1934 attempt on Gasherbrum I, surveyed it at 26,180 ft. Later surveys settled on an even 26,000 ft.

Dyhrenfurth's expedition to Gasherbrum I had failed, but it did bring back the first observations of a weakness in Gasherbrum IV, though he parenthesized this description with the caution that there was really 'no recommended route' up the mountain, guarded as it was on every side by steep walls of rock and ice. Dyhrenfurth had seen that the South Gasherbrum Glacier flowed from a col, 23,294 ft high, between Gasherbrum III and IV. This col could easily be reached without technical difficulties. It was a good start to the mountain, but what followed—a 2,700 ft rock ridge—was, even by 1958, harder than anything climbed in the Himalayas.

To this the Italians marched, with 514 porters carrying some 24,000 lb of supplies, two liaison officers, a policeman, a cook, fifteen Hunza high altitude porters, and eight of Italy's best alpinists. The massive caravan fixed rope on the mountain to within a few hundred feet of the summit, finally seeing success on 6 August, after 44 days in and above base camp.

On 27 May, in the great couloir above Camp One, Tim, Steve, and I slowly move up steepening snows. Behind us our tracks and red-flagged marker wands trace our path. Camp One's cluster of tents in the midst of the vast white valley grows increasingly small, until it resembles an eruption of bacteria on the smoothness of a culture dish. Above us the couloir is a great funnel with subsidiary gullies branching out like spidery legs. Diaphanous clouds race through the notch. As we climb up, fixing lengths of 8 mm rope behind us, we uncover old anchors and sections of rope from 1983 and 1984. The torn, bleached ropes from the 1983 attempt are encased beneath several inches of ice. The 1984 ropes, made of black polypropylene, are buried under snow. Finding a length of black rope threading up the couloir for some 100 ft, I pull it out of the snow and test my weight on it.

'It'll probably break. It's been there for two years,' Steve warns from the belay stance a few feet away. Never an early riser, he's had a bad morning, leaving Camp One with his boots on the wrong feet, hobbling for half a mile before realizing why he'd become pigeon-toed overnight. Exposed to sunlight, avalanche, and rockfall it seemed unlikely that the rope wouldn't break, but the sight of it in front of me and the thought of being able to save our own rope for higher on the mountain easily seduces me.

'Let's give it a good test,' says Tim, and he comes across in my tracks to stand beside me. We plunge our ice axes into the snow, hold them with one hand and the rope with the other, then ease our combined weights onto it. After a promising moment of security, the rope pops out of the snow and slithers down the couloir. The end had long ago been severed by rockfall. We would get little advantage from the 1984 ropes. I continue up through knee-deep snow.

At three o'clock a mire of cloud pours up the valley and envelops us. Tim leads up to the steepest section of the couloir, where a slab of diorite causes the ice to weep down in thin tears. He moves quickly over this unprotected ground to a rockledge at 20,000 ft, where he secures the rope. Steve and I jumar up, then Steve takes the lead, front-pointing up to a bulging rock wall where he hammers in a piton-runner, before traversing 100 ft to the right. His figure disappears into the cloud. As the rope inches out Tim and I begin to feel the cold penetrate us. I feel a moment of sympathy with Captain Rab Nawaz, who had decamped back to Islamabad after only 36 frigid hours in Base Camp.

'Bloody hell, it's getting cold,' I chatter.

'I wonder just how cold it is?' Tim asks.

I point to the rucksack Steve has left on the ledge. A pocket thermometer is clipped to its top flap. 'See what it says.'

Tim looks at the thermometer and utters a familiar antipodean exclamation. The temperature is -15 degrees Fahrenheit. Even as we watch it the mercury drops: with the wind blowing down the couloir the temperature is plunging in leaps and bounds. We hear a shout from above that the rope is anchored. Steve appears rappeling toward us. A wise decision. Powder snow sloughs have already begun to shower the walls around us. We hurry down the couloir and stomp back to Camp One, and our sleeping bags.

After a day of work in the couloir by Andy and Geoff, Tom and Randy kick up through deep snow in deteriorating weather to run the last ropes out to Camp Two. Watching from Camp One, we see their tiny figures pass under torrents of powder snow coming off the 2,000 ft cliffs above them. The volume of the snow torrents is massive, and would severely pummel the unwitting victims in the couloir, but the avalanches are blown off at right angles by the wind. Tom and Randy secure the ropes and begin their descent from Camp Two. It is only twelve days since we arrived at Base Camp and we are pleased with our progress.

Two more days of storm keep us at Camp One or Base Camp, but on the third day the clouds part in brief respite. Wisps of high cirrus traverse from southwest to northeast, a sure sign of storm within the day, but with the ropes to Camp Two now in place, Geoff, Steve, Andy, Tim, and I each set off with a load, hoping to beat the storm and fully stock Camp Two.

The tracks kicked into the slope by Tom and Randy are drifted over with fresh snow. The work of re-breaking trail, in the midst of a howling blizzard, is exhausting: visibility is 75 ft. In 1984 Geoff had found bare ice and firm snow in the couloir, but today, as on every day that we climb to Camp Two, the couloir is filled with deep snow. One by one we reach the end of the ropes after five hours of climbing, dump our loads on the small wind-carved flat beneath the overhanging cliff, and sit puffing at the thin atmosphere of 22,000 ft. Geoff arrives with a huge load, heavier than anyone else's, carried up in his old Kelty frame pack. Cold, or the weight on his back, didn't seem to bother Geoff in the slightest, nor did the level of sophistication of his equipment. While we bolstered our confidence with state of the art packs and high altitude apparel, Geoff carted an antiquated pack half as old as him, and wore the same battle-weary parka he'd used on past expeditions.

Andy had aptly described Geoff as a 'sourdough', a uniquely Alaskan breed of hardened mountain prospector, and recounted some of the surprising things Geoff had produced from his pack in years past. Like a cassette-tape player to the 20,000 ft summit of Mount McKinley, just so he could listen to his favourite Pink Floyd song, 'The Dark Side of the Moon'. As luck would have it, the tape deck refused to work up there.

Though the cliff in front of Camp Two shelters us from the brunt of the wind, it is still difficult to stand, virtually impossible to speak. There is no point setting up a tent. The wind would rip it apart. Hammered into a crack in the wall in front of us are a few pitons, left by our predecessors. We clip our loads to these. Half-buried in ice we find the dismantled Whillans box tent. Sun-decayed and frozen, it is beyond repair, but inside it are some gas cylinders and several days of dried food. As we dig for more usable relics we look down the Baltoro, toward towering Masherbrum, 25 miles away. A fleet of dark lenticular clouds home in on Masherbrum's summit, as if pulled toward it by magnetic attraction. They cluster quickly and blot out the peak, then the craggy horizon. Like a weather beacon, Masherbrum gives us early warning to descend to Camp One. Within an hour the Baltoro is in the grip of another storm.

Phil greets us as we arrive back at Camp One. He'd climbed up to the camp that day to do some filming—up to that point he'd never climbed, cramponed, or jumared! The exertion of getting past the icefall had almost killed him, but his enthusiasm to shoot film is unperturbable.

'Well, we've got company at Base Camp,' he says.

'What sort of company?' I ask, half expecting that the Indian Army had invaded the Baltoro and that we were soon to be interned. The thought had the makings of a good book.

'Another expedition,' Phil explains.

'To climb what route?'

'They haven't decided.'

During the week spent establishing Camp Two an eight-member British expedition had arrived on the West Gasherbrum Glacier and had set up their Base Camp a stone's throw from ours. Meeting them later that day in the hidden valley, I sense that they are as surprised to see us as we are to see them. We had no idea that they were coming, and though aware of the existence of our expedition, they expected us to arrive at a later date. Since we were at work on the Northwest Ridge, the mountain's most obvious weakness from the West Gasherbrum Glacier, they are left with an unappealing array of choices. They could climb Voytek and Robert's committing West Face route, but with this season's heavy snowpack and unstable weather its couloirs would be a deathtrap, or they could climb the circuitous and objectively hazardous South Buttress, which leads to the South Ridge. But seracs at every juncture also make this a dangerous proposition. Finally there is the steep West Rib, jutting out from the West Face, the line of previous British, Japanese, and American attempts. From what I'd heard about and seen of this third option it was loose, dangerous, and difficult. In 1978 stonefalls had constantly bombarded the British team attempting it, cutting their fixed ropes, causing several close calls. In 1980 three Japanese climbers had been killed on it.

'Did you talk with any of the other climbers who'd tried the West Rib?' I enquire of Andrew Atkinson, one of the Brits.

'Yeah, I spoke to Mo Anthoine.'

'What did he say?'

'Spend the summer in Greece instead.'

The Brits must have seriously pondered this sage advice as they set to work on the West Rib, climbing up onto it from the hidden valley. Each day they'd return to their Camp One, a few minutes' walk from ours, with tales of fearful climbing, of unprotected 400 ft run-outs on thin ice overlaying rotten rock.

The morning of 2 June dawns with wispy clouds racing across a blue sky. Tim and I lie about in our sleeping bags, dozing away the morning and our rest day, while Geoff and Andy, who'd left Camp One at first light, jumar up the couloir. A sudden deafening boom and shockwaves ripple through the glacier, literally bouncing us off the floor of our tents.

'Avalanche!'

But where?

We rush outside and look up, searching for the figures of Geoff and Andy. No tell-tale debris lies at the foot of the couloir. We see Geoff and Andy safely reaching Camp Two. A tingling anxiety subsides.

'It's come from the Brits' route,' says Tim. We cast our eyes right, to a crumbled ice cliff, 100 ft tall and 200 ft in width, that had collapsed onto the glacier from 200 ft above. Enormous blocks of ice sit in the centre of a fan of smaller debris sprawling over an area the size of two football fields. On the West Rib, some 2,500 ft up, two of the British team stand shocked, looking down at a lone figure, motionless on the trail close to the edge of the debris, evidently pondering the preciousness of life. The tracks from their camp come to within a few feet of the avalanche.

'Bloody close,' I later comment to one of the Brits.

'Well-planned tracks,' he replies casually.

Geoff and Andy return on 4 June from their foray beyond Camp Two with encouraging news: the route to Camp Three via China is viable. They had dropped over the notch onto the Northwest face and traversed easily across low-angle rock, scree, and ice to the beginning of an 800 ft ice slope, about 45 degrees steep. Above him, Geoff could see the ice-dome where he'd made Camp Three in 1984. One more day of work and we'd be there. But we are set back again when we wake next day to the sussuration of falling snow. Not wanting to consume the camp's food and fuel, we descend to Base Camp.

Back down on the West Gasherbrum Glacier that afternoon, we immediately set about the business of eating. Himalayan climbing has very few certainties but one fact is that the human body rapidly deteriorates at altitudes above 15,000 ft. In an effort to conserve its reserves, the body slows down. Small wounds heal slowly. Toenails and fingernails grow at half speed. Meanwhile, body fat and weight drop steadily. When body weight drops it is only a matter of time before the climber begins to burn muscle tissue and to weaken. The higher a climber sleeps and climbs, the more rapid this deterioration becomes. A climber has six-to-eight weeks after reaching Base Camp to acclimatize and summit before this weakening process makes activity on the mountain a case of diminishing returns. We combat this deterioration with an intensive program of gluttony, consuming high quantities of dahl, rice, and chapatis, cooked nightly by Gulam.

During the evening meal of 5 June the British team's leader Dave Lampard, and co-leader Andrew Atkinson visit our tent. They wear serious expressions on their faces and after a few pleasantries they get down to business.

'We've got a problem,' begins Dave, 'It's our route. We've decided to abandon it. It's just too dangerous.'

'It looks like a horror show,' Tim agrees. 'What are your plans now?'

'Well, that's the problem. We'd like to come onto the Northwest Ridge.'

There is a moment of awkward silence while everyone waits for someone to say something. The request isn't exactly a surprise to us. Even on a glacier there is gossip and scuttlebutt. The Brits' Balti cook, Ros Ali, had told Gulam the day before about their intentions, and Gulam had duly told us. The situation is difficult. On the one hand the mountains are for everyone. On the other I had no intention of jeopardizing our chances on the Northwest Ridge.

'It's very cramped up there at Camp Two. There's barely enough room for our two small tents, and there isn't much room at the bivouac sites above that. I just don't see how another eight people on the route will work,' I say.

Dave and Andrew offer every possible suggestion in defence of their plan: to fix separate ropes, to allow us first choice of bivouac sites and first shot at the summit. If the mountain had been one of snowy expanses, like Broad Peak, with many choices for bivouacs, we may have relented, but I felt more certain as the conversation went on that to compromise would assure failure for us all. I shake my head. 'Sorry, but I just don't see how it'll work with all of us up there together. But you're certainly welcome to take over the route after we've had our shot.' It wasn't a very satisfactory offer. It was gambling with time. None of us knew when the weather would be good or bad, or what the climbing would be like, or how long we'd be on the mountain.

'Look, if we'd got here first it'd be us on the Northwest Ridge and you in our position. After all, our permit is for any route on the mountain,' Dave says.

'And ours is for the Northwest Ridge and nothing else. We're not about to stop you from going up there, but I think it would compromise us all if you did,' I reply.

You pay your money and you take your chances, as the saying goes. I understood the Brits' frustration, and knew we hadn't won friends by turning them away, yet I felt I spoke the minds of everyone in our team.

'Well, that's it then,' Dave says, rising to leave.

'What will you do now?' I ask.

'It looks like we quit this side of the mountain, get some porters, and try our luck on the south side. But right now we're going to consult a bottle of whisky.'

It seemed like a fair decision—the whisky bottle, that is. Certain climbers might consider their future at such a moment by tossing the I Ching, or by meditating. The wisdom and inspiration found in a bottle of whisky moves some people just as powerfully. Anyway, their expedition was far from over. It was from the South Gasherbrum Glacier that the Italians had launched their ascent of the Northeast Ridge. And the possibility of an entirely new route to the summit, by the South Ridge, was still an appealing alternative. From the end of the South Gasherbrum Glacier the 22,139 ft col between Gasherbrums IV and V, where the South Ridge began, could quickly and easily be reached. It's an alternative that in the coming weeks they will investigate, to 23,400 ft.

After this discussion we turn to our own plans. Though high cirrus has filled the sky all day, Geoff and Andy decide to return to Camp One the following morning. Geoff, with an important job awaiting him back in America, is running to a deadline. He has timetabled his entire trip, and has 23 days left in which to climb the mountain and trek out. Sitting around base camp is making him anxious.

'Gulam—Geoff and Andy leave for Camp One tomorrow. Bed-tea for them at 3 am, breakfast at half-three—okay?' I tell our cook.

At this instruction Gulam laughs. The suggestion to rise in the perishing cold of 2 am, fire up a recalcitrant stove, brew a pot of tea, then bring it to our tents, seems to him a joke. He breaks into a meek laugh and shakes his head.

'No bed-tea,' he says, wagging a finger.

'Yes Gulam, bed-tea,' replies Tim firmly.

Gulam had taken all our requests for bed-tea to that point as a joke. Those of us who'd been on expeditions to Nepal and India knew that bed-tea is a duty synonymous with the role of cook, but Gulam didn't think so. I began to wonder if his claims of cooking for so many expeditions weren't a fiction. After all, he had come to us from the crooked sirdar Sher Khan.

Tim, for the tenth time, explains to Gulam our expectations of him. Gulam looks aghast as he realizes we are serious about bed-tea.

'Hey, I can live without bed-tea,' Geoff interjects.

I glance coldy at this soft-hearted heresy. I'd noticed before on expeditions that Americans have a moral opposition to the perks and benefits that cooks bring to an expedition—probably a guilt reaction left from the days of slavery. But Tim and I, perhaps with a trace of Raj ancestry in our blood, suffer no such qualms. We stand our ground.

Gulam, however, was no fool. To the contrary, he was the sharpest young Balti I had ever met. Perceptive enough to know that to humour us now is to gain later, he relents to the ritual of bed-tea. The shyness that Gulam cloaked himself in belied both a considerable desire for upward mobility and a capacity for shrewdness. Whenever we were up on the mountain and he was in Base Camp with Phil, he would build up his knowledge of English. In the four weeks he'd been in our employ he'd quadrupled his vocabulary. Already he'd learned how to ask for a pay rise. Phil had also taught him to write his name in English. Consequently, 'Gulam' was scrawled in black marker pen on nearly every storage barrel, box, pot, pan, and stove in camp, to let us know that these were the items he wanted at the end of the expedition. Some westerners, jaded with the affluent, gadget-filled rat-races they inhabit, like to entertain the fantasy that given half a chance they'd go back to basics, and trade places with some simple, rural folk. They wouldn't last long in Baltistan. On the other hand, an enterprising young fellow like Gulam would probably become a successful businessman if transplanted onto the streets of some western city. Poverty can be admired by the affluent, but only the poor endure it.

Two snowy days later, on 8 June, Tim, Tom, and I head off at dawn from Base Camp to Camp One, where Geoff and Andy await. The sky is clear, and we hope to push the route out to Camp Three during the next couple of days. We wake Gulam, hand him a cup of tea, and set off.

As Tim, Tom, and I ascend the slopes to Camp One, I hear the sickening whoosh of something sliding down the snowfield, gaining momentum. A blue object flashes past me, highdives off the 200 ft cliff behind me, thuds into the ice fall, and disappears into a crevasse. The thought that enters my mind is an awful one, that Tom, carrying a blue pack and out of sight above me, has fallen off. It seems absurd that a careful climber like Tom could fall off an easy slope but I hurry on up to see what has happened. There, at the base of the next set of gullies, I meet him. He is safe and with his pack. Beside him stands Andrew, descending the mountain after dismantling the British Camp One. He too is safe, but without his pack. He'd hung it by a strap from a bamboo marker-wand stuck into the snow. The wand had snapped, and gravity took over. When I inform him that his pack, containing all his personal gear, has disappeared in the icefall, he sighs. The blows are falling hard and fast for him. We chat for a few minutes.

'We'll be gone by the time you next come down, so best of luck with the route,' says Andrew, shaking my hand. In view of his recent bad luck, I thought his attitude incredibly stiff-upper-lipped. 'Oh yeah, if you dig around our camp up there you'll find some bottles of kerosene,' he adds. This generosity was a boon to us as we wouldn't have to transport any more of the weighty fuel from Base Camp.

As I plod through the corridors of broken ice that lead to the hidden valley I meet the last of the Brits heading down. Amid soft snow and century temperatures we exchange farewells. Again they remind me of the kerosene they'd left us.

Geoff is already in the process of excavating their campsite when I arrive. His dig is a thorough one, and reveals the relics of ten days of British dining, with all the scraps burned and buried to be absorbed by the glacier. His efforts reveal three one-litre bottles of liquid.

'Great. That's a week's fuel on the MSR stove.'

'Weird looking kerosene,' he says, twisting open the lid of one bottle.

'Er, Geoff . . .,' I say, sensing we are about to get the punchline.

Geoff sniffs the bottle's contents then empties it in disgust. A large yellow stain flowers on the snow.

'It's piss,' he says.

'It's British humour,' I explain.

Touché.

On 9 June Tom, Tim, and I, in Camp Two, watch night engulf the mountains. The weather is clear but wind buffets and flattens the two small tents we have lashed to the ledge. As we cook our meal, condensation instantly freezes on the tent walls, and is shaken off onto us. The pot of snow boils, I make three cupfuls of hot chocolate. When I open the tent door to pass Tom and Tim their drinks a gust of wind blows a deluge of spindrift into the tent. It's going to be an uncomfortable night, full of the din of flapping tent walls. Already that day, we had carried a load from Camp One, then had surmounted the crest of the notch, entered China, and followed Geoff and Andy's ropes to 22,200 ft. Amid snowy whirlwinds swirling across the icy face, Tom had led out a 600 ft length of 8 mm rope and secured it to two ice screws. Only 200 ft remained to the crest of the ridge and Camp Three. Though we are tired and the wind relentless, the weather now blows from the northeast, a favourable direction. So, with three flashes of a headlamp, we signal to Geoff and Andy in Camp One that we will push on to occupy Camp Three the next day. We pass the night with only snatches of sleep.

The wind, however, is no kinder at sunrise. We set off up the ropes through searing spindrift, and reach the highpoint at noon. Above the end of the ropes we see the crest of the Northwest Ridge while behind us the flat, wind-polished North Gasherbrum Glacier encircles the East and South Faces of Broad Peak. I see the profile of the rib on the West Face of Broad Peak that Pete and I had climbed in 1983, and the long ridge leading to the summit. White plumes, like windsocks, stream off Broad Peak's summits.

Tim unravels a rope and leads on. Though the slope is only 50 degrees steep, steel-hard blue ice lies below the surface of soft snow. Tim kicks hard to penetrate the ice, front-points toward the ridge, then disappears over the crest. A few minutes later he waves, signalling us to come up and at last we stand on the wind-lashed ridge crest. We look around the icy hump for a place to bivouac, and in so doing see our storm beacon, Masherbrum, piling up with black lenticulars. The wind has reverted to the southwest. Masherbrum is warning us.

'What do you think? Stay or go?' I shout into my companions' ears.

They look at their watches—it's 2 pm—and look at the approaching storm. 'Stay!'

'Well, we'd better find a place to dig a snowcave. A tent wouldn't last five minutes up here,' shouts Tim.

We crampon a few yards across wind-scalloped snow to the place Geoff said had been the 1984 campsite, in the hope of finding a deep bergschrund in which to find shelter and dig out a cave. We find nothing but solid ice. In the two years since Geoff's attempt, the bergschrund had either filled with snow, or had broken away and peeled off the ridge. We poke our ice axes into the armour-plated mountain, but all around is concrete-hard. As we roam about, poking and prodding, the wind grows stronger and the clouds around us thicken, mantling the summit pyramid of G4 with a grey morass.

'Down here! We can dig here!' Tim calls.

At the place a few feet from where he'd anchored the ropes we begin shovelling out a tunnel. Three feet in, Tom, digging, strikes solid ground.

'Goddamit! Ice!'

We each take turns at chiselling, hoping that the layer of ice will give way to softer ground. An hour later it does. Another two hours of digging produces a cave big enough for the three of us to crouch inside and escape the freezing wind. Two more hours of chipping at the walls and ceiling and we have a habitable cave. We push the snow out of the entrance, seal the tunnel with our packs, and settle down to rehydrate ourselves. We are soaking wet. The perspiration trapped in our windsuits freezes. Outside, the storm blows at a frenzy.

When we wake next morning everything in the cave is dusted white from spindrift creeping through cracks in our makeshift doorway.

'How is everyone feeling?' Tim asks groggily.

'Seedy. And cold,' I reply.

All of us suffered from heavy heads and queasy guts from the sudden shift to altitude. The best remedy would be to get liquid into us, but when I lift my head to inspect the chilly scene, a great lassitude overcomes me. I doze off after shaking off the half-inch of powder covering my sleeping bag. My sleep had been filled with Tom's coughing. He'd had a bad night, constantly spitting up mucus from a lung infection that had set in the previous day. His cough had a suspicious wet sound to it, like fluid in the lungs.

'You okay, Tom?' I ask from my sleeping bag.

'Yeah. Just a cold,' he replies.

'Not edema?'

'No, it doesn't seem that way.'

Tom was one of those lucky people with a high pain threshold who never complains about physical discomfort or minor injuries. In fact, I suspected he respected pain as a challenge to endure. But his suppression of the messages his pain receptors sent to his brain was no stoic recklessness. Tom was tuned in to his body as few people are. If he said he was okay, then he was okay. Only if he said he was sick did I worry. Perhaps Tom had learned to endure discomfort during his service in the United States Marine Corps. There, as a patriotic young man, he'd survived boot camp and Vietnam. The wiser for his service to America and democracy, he now went through life with a healthy cynicism to both. His tales of boot camp, where the minds of young men are warped and twisted to fit the shape of the military machine, struck me as particularly horrifying.

Geoff Radford, Andy Tuthill and Tim Macartney-Snape in the snowcave at 23,000 ft the night before the summit push on Gasherbrum IV. Tim is playing harmonica.

'You see the whole idea is to weed out the guys who don't want to get with the program,' he'd explained to me about boot camp training, speaking in the John Wayne drawl that is Tom's signature. 'So the drill sergeants have devised these special "tortures" for those kind of guys. Like the sand box. Now, with the sand box they get a bunch of guys who don't want to get with the program and they tell them "Okay you guys, it's time to play in the sand box." So they march them into this big pit of sand and order them to start throwing sand up in the air. They march around, tossing sand over each other. They make them do this for a long, long time. This torture works best on really hot days. Enough of that, and the guys get with the program pretty fast.'

We shiver the morning away in our sleeping bags, listening to Tom's worsening cough. At 11.00 am he pokes his head out of the tunnel to check on the weather.

'How is it?' Tim asks.

'Whiteout. The wind is worse,' Tom replies, then launches into a fit of coughing.

'You sure you aren't getting pulmonary edema?' I ask again.

'Certain. But just in case, I'm gettin' outta here. This infection won't get any better in this place.'

This was true, yet the idea of descending in such a storm seemed as unhealthy as staying, cough or no cough. But Tom was already packed and out of the door. Over the next few hours he would blindly crawl from rope to rope and be tossed about in a hurricane wind. He would later describe his descent as being the most desperate thing he'd ever done.

For 48 hours more, Tim and I lie about the cave, seldom moving, except to make hot drinks or prepare food, which we do sparingly, to conserve our small amount of food and fuel. For two days our feet have been numb. Even cold-resistant Tim, who two years before had climbed to the summit of Everest in a pair of Asolo cross-country ski boots after his regular Koflach mountaineering boots had been lost in an avalanche, was massaging his bloodless feet and shivering. Cold seeped through our foam pads into our backs, causing our kidneys to ache. Even the Gore-Tex fabric of our sleeping bags began to crinkle like tin-foil as droplets of body-generated water vapour froze solid amongst the feathers, turning the cocoons of our bags to ice-filled sacks. But our imprisonment isn't without purpose. By sleeping three nights at 23,000 ft our body chemistry was altering. Complex changes in our haemoglobin levels were adapting us to the altitude. Our blood, thick and sluggish with an excess of red blood cells when we awoke that first morning in the snow cave, was thinning. We were becoming better acclimatized every hour.

On the third storm-bound day in the snowcave I develop an unpleasant accompaniment to cold feet: swelling bowels. Try as I may to put it off, after some seventy hours I have no choice but to relieve myself. I look up and burrow head-first out of the snow-clogged exit to emerge in a maelstrom of blasting snow and wind, with a wad of toilet paper streaming in one gloved hand. Unzipping zippers, I shed layers of pile and Gore-Tex. The wind, thick with spindrift, makes it impossible to breathe. Snow quickly fills my pants, my goggles ice over. To execute even this simple, urgent business proves out of the question. In no small distress I burrow back into the cave.

'Can't do it! Too windy out there,' I report to Tim.

'Oh dear,' he replies.

'But I still have to go. Look, sorry about this but I'm going to have to settle this in here.'

'Oh no!'

I grab the shovel, fill it with snow, drop my pants, squat astride the shovel, and commence the awful deed. The stench is spectacular. Tim retreats into his sleeping bag and emits strangled gasps of protest. Finished, I zip myself back into my windsuit, crawl back out the cave with the shovel at arm's reach, and pitch the shovel-load over the West Face. The gale atomizes the turd and broadcasts it in equal amounts over China and Pakistan.

Back inside the cave I pant breathlessly. It is the most exercise I'd had for several days. Tim slowly pokes his head out of his sleeping bag, as if emerging from a bomb shelter after a nuclear explosion.

'It's over,' I tell him.

'It's time to get out of here anyway,' he declares.

The cave is becoming a refrigerator. We pack up, and head out into the maelstrom.

Visibility is nil. I grope for the rope a few feet from the cave, find it, clip my figure-eight descender to it and back down the slope. After a few feet I find myself waist deep in powder, wrestling the ropes out from under the snow. I hesitate briefly, wondering if we should retreat from our retreat, but the momentum seems to pull us toward Base Camp. We descend slowly down the heavily laden slope.

After about 800 ft we arrive at the place where the traverse to Camp Two begins. Here the ropes run horizontally across a deeply loaded slope. A deluge of powder washes over the cliffs and down the slope in waves. As I rappel sideways across this slope I feel my feet slip involuntarily. I lock the rope off in my rappel device, but still I move down, as if in quicksand. It takes a second to fathom what is happening, that I have cut the slope loose from its moorings. Under the full weight of the slope, the rope stretches like a rubber band. The snow, now a liquid, moving mass, builds up around my neck. Behind me a faint rumble indicates that the slope is breaking up and sliding 3,000 ft onto the glacier below. The roaring of the storm suddenly stops in my head as every other sensation is banished to make way for fear. Then, the movement suddenly stops, storm again fills my ears. I grapple, sputter, and heave on the rope. I wipe the snow from my face and continue to the end of the rope. When Tim reaches me he has no notion of what has just occurred. I breathe a sigh of thanks to the fixed ropes, and hurry away from the snow-trap of the Northwest Face.

At 1.00 pm we stagger onto the flats of the hidden valley. A sound like pounding surf fills the ravine, as avalanches roar down the West Face. Camp One is almost drifted in. Its occupants—Geoff, Andy, Randy, Steve and Phil—have spent the last two days constantly digging it out. The feeling at Camp One is akin to being a sailor on a sinking ship, bailing, bailing, bailing. It is time to abandon that ship. If the mountain wants to eat Camp One, then we had no choice but to let it.

The Gamble

As we lay about Base Camp, waiting out the storm, I considered our progress: 28 days had passed since our arrival at Base Camp. In those 28 days the weather had been a pattern of almost constant winter storm, with snow falling on all but six of those days. To reach 23,000 ft, the point where the difficulties of the Northwest Ridge began, we had accumulated 45,000 ft of altitude gain and loss. In reaching Camp Three, still 1,000 ft below the 1984 high point, cold had drained us physically, had left us all with frost-nipped fingers, toes and noses. If a score was being kept between us and G4, it would seem that G4 had the advantage.

My intuitive assessment from the way that we spoke about the mountain was that we had ample resolve for a summit bid, yet I doubted whether we could muster the energy for a second attempt should the first fail. The effort of constantly breaking trail through deep snow and cold was beginning to wear us down, physically and mentally. We had reached that point on an expedition where circumstances were forcing us to look deep within ourselves to find the objective truth behind our motivation. Yes, we all wanted the summit, but the physical and mental pain we had endured and would yet endure was so great that we had to force ourselves onto the mountain. Too much more of this masochism and the motivating forces within us would dissipate. Sometime in the next two weeks we would either make the second ascent of Gasherbrum IV, or become the ninth party to fall short of that goal. Doubts about our chances for success began to creep into my thoughts. I felt like a priest losing his faith.

For two days after our retreat from the mountain, storm buffets Base Camp. Wind flaps the tents and rattles the contents of the kitchen, bringing gusts of Andy's banjo playing with it. A desolate ambience pervades camp and the place feels like a ghost town. On 14 June the clouds filling the valley rise to admit the sun, but Gasherbrum IV retains a cover of swirling blizzard. The glacier is coated with snow, wall to wall, till the laser sun pierces through, melting the snow down to scree and ice, uncovering rusted tins and old porter stoves abandoned by other expeditions. Rivulets of melt-water criss-cross between tents and lubricate the glacier, loosening stones and sending them clattering down slopes. Scrap-fattened ravens, or *poroks,* as the Balti call them, roost on the edge of camp, watching our movements, keeping their distance.

Amid tropical palm trees graffitied on the kitchen tent wall, Tim twiddles the radio dial. Chernobyl is the big news again on the BBC, but Radio Moscow keeps silent about it.

'I wonder if we're sucking in fallout up there?' Tom asks.

'You'll probably know in about ten years, when you either have lung cancer, or you don't,' Steve replies.

Geoff returns to camp from a stroll along the glacier. He strains under the weight of yet another enormous lump of high-grade ore. It is dumped with a metallic thunk beside the growing pile of rock specimens beside his and Andy's tent.

'Hey Tuthill, look at this beauty,' Geoff calls. Andy stops picking on his banjo to ogle the rock. Like Geoff, Andy has a degree in geology. They chatter in the tongues of science. Gulam, who is still trying to puzzle out the sahibs' fascination for these rocks, squats beside them to observe the adoration of yet another stone.

'Now look Gulam,' Geoff says, pointing first to the ore and then to his steel ice axe; 'this stone will give you *this* steel, see?'

Geoff Radford nursing frost-nipped toes at Base Camp.

Gulam scratches his head and grins with bemusement. He points from one object to the other, trying to solve the equation Geoff has confronted him with. The scene reminds me of a picture I'd seen in a school textbook, of the transition of civilization from the ages of barbarism to the age of metals. In the picture, a wise man explains the technique of smelting ore and manufacturing tools to an astounded neighbour. The wise man's face has the certainty of ideas, his neighbour's is lit with wonder.

Somehow this scene on a remote glacier emphasizes our isolation. Fifty days have passed since we left our homes. No letters have arrived from the outside world; we are too remote an outpost to attract a mail runner. Yet I no longer feel homesick. Home seems like an imaginary thing. What stands in its place is this strange, almost mad desire to climb Gasherbrum IV. The notion of placelessness disturbs me. I feel uprooted from the vital connections to Salley, to home, stranded with only the mountain and my fellow madmen as company. These thoughts appear like a mirage, a hallucination, a symptom of the schizophrenia of expeditioning. The image that the mountain reflects back into my face shows a different being from the one who lived back in civilization.

Talk from the kitchen jolts me out of these thoughts. Randy is discussing the partnership contract of the real estate business he will enter into when he returns to California; Steve is talking about buying a television and a VCR when he gets back home. He's never had a television before, a point he takes pride in. Perhaps the deprivation of this valley is making him hungry for images. The things they speak of are realities. It's the thin-aired world of the mountain that is dream.

'My God,' I think to myself, snapping out of introspection. 'I own three televisions.'

By nightfall the weather implies improvement but with high cirrus above, Tim passes this off as another ruse. During dinner, conversation shifts to the days ahead.

'I think we should go back up as soon as possible. We have a lot of work to do above Camp Three,' says Geoff, mindful that he has only two weeks left before he must quit the expedition and return to Alaska.

He's right. We do have much work to do. Only Tim and Tom and I are acclimatized to 23,000 ft but all of us need to spend a few nights at Camp Three. So, Geoff, Andy, and Steve decide to move toward Camp Three if the weather is clear in the morning. The plan is logical. It will get us all to the same level of acclimatization. But we don't all share the same view of how to execute the phase of the climb following acclimatization. In Geoff's mind the best way to invest our time is to stock Camp Three with more food and fuel, and fix more rope. The idea has its merits for there is undeniable security in fixed rope, but the plan presupposes that there'll be multiple days of good weather. What if there are not? Perhaps the time spent fixing rope and shuttling loads could be better spent by simply making a dash to the summit. Speed, rather than prolonging the siege, seemed to Tim and me the best option in view of the brief clear spells—none more than 48 hours—we had experienced. And, we were soon to enter a period where many expeditions reach the summit. Statistically, mid June to early July saw good weather in the Baltoro.

'You don't think we should fix rope above Camp Three?' Geoff asks Tim.

'No. Just sleep in Camp Three a couple of nights to acclimatize, then go for it.'

'Well, how fast do you think we can get to the summit?'

'From Camp Three I think we could make it in two days: one day to your highpoint of '84, leave the tents there, then summit the next day. The moon is coming around now. We could descend by moonlight and be back at 24,000 ft that same night, back in Camp One or Base Camp on the third day. If your old ropes are still intact we could move fast. If we go light we could go even faster. Fixing too much rope will just bog us down in logistics, I learned that on Everest. Up there, we stopped fixing rope at 24,300 ft and reached the summit in two days from the end of the ropes; on Annapurna II we moved on the summit day without any gear on our backs. After we reached the summit we descended through the night to our high camp. I'm convinced that the best way to climb big mountains and get back safely is to cover as much ground as fast as possible and spend as little time up high as you can.'

More than any of us, Tim understood his capabilities at altitude. A remarkable physiology allowed him to move over alpine terrain faster than anyone I'd met, tackling slopes in bursts of sprinting rather than the steady metered pace most climbers move to.

'That's a pretty optimistic view of how long it'll take us to climb this thing,' Geoff says and while we all had our theories about speed, Geoff had seen the difficulties above Camp Three. I detected a tone of 'just you wait and see' in his voice.

'Anyway,' Geoff continued, 'the altimeter reading has been dropping all day. I think we should get ourselves in position at Camp Three and be ready for the summit the moment the weather clears.'

'I still don't trust this weather. Acclimatizing is one thing, but it'll just burn us out to vegetate in that snow cave waiting,' said Tim.

Thus, Tim, Tom, Randy, and I decide to remain in Base Camp, observing the altimeter, moving up only if the reading swung in a favourable direction.

Until that moment we'd worked together as a team. Now we were splintering into groups, governed by the different levels of our acclimatization, and by the tactics we thought would get us to the top. But our different ideas converged at one point: when the weather changed we had to grab the opportunity, and grab it quickly. These ideas were instinctual convictions ruled by our knowledge of survival, for, eventually, Himalayan climbs become exercises in precisely that.

The mountain had a hold over us, yet we feared it at the same time. Somewhere between fear and fascination lay a balance. So far, we'd played the game conservatively and more conservative than some: French climbers on Gasherbrum II had reached their summit during one of June's early storms. Two of the French had frozen their feet solid. We'd seen the helicopters droning down the glacier, evacuating them. To have hands, fingers, feet, or toes, amputated seemed a high price to pay for a summit. Cold was the enemy. Frostbite needed only a minute of carelessness to set in. One of Tim's companions on

Everest had lost all of his fingers, and all he'd done was remove his gloves to adjust his crampons.

I found myself thinking of a character I'd met as a teenager, a gnarled old Russian expatriate named Nic, a foreman on a construction site where I'd worked one winter in Melbourne. Nic's hands were calloused from a lifetime of labouring, a career that began as a teenager, on wartime Europe's Russian front, digging trenches, fighting the Nazis. One wet, cold day he found me standing with limp, frozen hands, defeated in my efforts to dig a pipe-trench in mud.

'You think this is cold?' he scoffed. 'I'll show you cold,' and he held up his right hand. The first two joints of his index and middle finger were missing. 'That is cold,' he said. He went on to tell that when he was defending Stalingrad he had to dig trenches in frozen earth, all day, all night, working and fighting on an empty stomach, in sub-zero temperatures. Everything was in short supply. Officers didn't issue gloves till the temperature reached -20 Fahrenheit. Nic had lost his index finger by keeping it too long on the trigger of his rifle. After it was amputated he learned to shoot with his middle finger. Then that froze and was cut off. When he returned to the trenches an officer took pity on him and let him wear gloves until the spring thaw.

But that was war. G4, supposedly, was a vacation. I watched Randy wriggling his fingers, examining them, feeling his numb tips. He was a gymnast, skilful and graceful on rock. Like a pianist, fingers were the tools of his trade; without them he'd make no music. I studied my own fingers, no less precious to me. Unlike a lizard's tail, fingers don't regenerate.

The next morning, 14 June, Geoff, Andy, and Steve leave for Camp One; 24 hours later, during another bout of storm, they move up to Camp Two. There Steve remains overnight to acclimatize, while Geoff and Andy press on into the clouds to Camp Three.

On 16 June the storm lifts enough for us to see the mountain. Randy sets up his telescope and trains it on Camp Three. 7,000 ft above us, two small figures stand outside the snowcave, stamping their feet and slapping their hands to get their circulation flowing. Around them, streamers of snow fly off the ridge. The weather seems about to break, again.

'They'll be down soon,' Tim says.

We turn toward the mess-tent. Randy keeps his eye on the scope.

'Hey, wait on—they're heading up!' he exclaims. As they disappear over the ridge, we are left wondering if they are going for the summit.

The air has a different smell on 17 June. Very suddenly, clouds begin to evaporate. The wind, still gale-force up high, shifts from southwest to north, blowing out of Sinkiang. Light dousing Mitre Peak behind Base Camp and G4 ahead, penetrates a dry, hazeless atmosphere in which a waxing moon shines regardless of day or night. The feel of the snow changes from soft and damp to firm and crisp. We watch the altimeter needle drop steadily all day as it registers the arrival of a high pressure system swelling out of the deserts of China and over the mountainous border into Pakistan. The time to move up has arrived.

Tim, Tom, Randy, Phil, and I head to Camp One. The hidden valley is a cauldron 115 degrees hot. Sweat pours from our brows and salts our eyes. Progress slows to a trudge. Ahead, deep fresh snow all but buries the tents of Camp One. Further on, the couloir is streaked with the claw marks of sloughs cut loose by the sweltering heat. Conditions look bad for those above.

'Christ, there's a lot of new snow. We'll have to wait for the couloir to clean itself out, it's a goddam death-trap right now,' sneers Tom. As we slog into Camp One we are surprised to find Steve awaiting us. Wind had blown him out of Camp Two, almost wrecking his tent. He'd descended the couloir in a whiteout and become lost for an hour between the foot of the couloir and the tents until he stumbled across a wand.

'Geoff and Andy still up?' Tom asks him.

'Last I saw them they were heading to Camp Three.'

'Well, they must be going for the summit by now unless the snow is too deep,' Tim says.

'Or the wind too strong,' adds Steve, turning our eyes to the thick mane of spindrift blasting off the ridge.

The hidden valley is calm and clear at dawn on 19 June. All but Phil, who remains in Camp One with his cine cameras to film us, commence the slog up the couloir. He bids us good luck as we depart. For the fifth time we break trail to Camp Two. The snow is deep: the ridge, I suspect, will be just as laden. Hopes are not high.

At noon we exit the couloir and reach Camp Two's battered tents. The wind is tolerable enough for a pair of *poroks* to sit on the col between us and China. I look behind me. The message from Masherbrum is good: the weather has stabilized. But for how long? A week? A day? In a moment of optimism I rate our chances for success at 40 percent.

Inside the tent we find a brief note from Geoff, pencilled on the back of a cereal packet: '6-18-86. 9.00 am Bring more rope, food, and fuel.'

'It's dated yesterday. They haven't gone for the summit after all. They must have come down here and carried a load back to the snow cave. When we saw them through the telescope they were probably heading up to work on the route above Camp Three,' Tom observes.

'This is no time to be sieging the mountain. We've got to go for it, now,' Tim says with conviction.

We three eat a hurried lunch, pack some supplies, then depart. Steve looks disappointed as he watches us cross the notch into China. He and Randy, who is still jumaring up the couloir, must yet acclimatize to Camps Two and Three. To wait for all of us to be equally acclimatized would be to wait too long. Those who can must seize the opportunity now.

'There'll be tracks and maybe more fixed ropes above, Camp Three will be stocked, tents will be set up high if you catch us in time,' I tell Steve in recompense.

'I know, I know. But if Randy doesn't acclimatize there won't be much chance for me,' he says.

'We've got to look after ourselves now. We've got a chance and some of us are

Steve Risse on Gasherbrum IV at 22,000 ft. Broad Peak's west face route is visible on the skyline at left. (Photo by Randall Leavitt)

Tom Hargis, leading, and Tim Macartney-Snape at 23,000 ft on Gasherbrum IV on 20 June 1986.

going to go.' Monomania was taking over. Steve just looked at me as a psychiatrist would, as one who understood obsessive behaviour. We bid each other good luck and I cross into China.

The slope to Camp Three is not covered in chest-deep snow as we'd feared but is wind-scoured and clean enabling us to make rapid progress. The afternoon sees us surmount the crest of the Northwest Ridge to the snow cave, 56 hours after leaving Base Camp. Gone is the gasping, sickening feeling of our first trip to Camp Three. We are optimally acclimatized. Geoff and Andy sit on the ridge, observing our ascent. When we reach them they hand us a flask of warm juice. Clear skies persist, but the wind is severe. We crawl into the snow cave.

'Welcome to the Gash Palace,' Geoff declares with a sweep of his hand. The cave is now large enough to house a Volkswagen. During the storm Geoff and Andy had chipped away at the walls, even sculpting shelves on which to store the food and fuel they'd carried up from their supply-run down to Camp Two. They had also climbed up to 23,400 ft, uncovering some ropes from Geoff's 1984 attempt.

'What condition are the ropes in?' Tom asks.

'Like new,' Andy replies.

I increase our odds to an even 50-50.

As we dine on a feast of cheese, sardines, and crackers, Tim serenades us with a tune from his harmonica. Meltwater dripping from the ceiling patters a syncopated beat against the Gore-Tex shells of our sleeping bags. Outside, the wind is now a gentle breeze, a good sign, but we know that daylight will again bring blustery winds. We decide to wake at 2.30 am and, if the skies are clear, start toward the summit at dawn.

Anticipation breeds insomnia. I lie awake watching moonlight refract through the snow cave walls, but my mind sees only the uncertain 3,000 ft above. Anxiety gnaws at the pit of my stomach. Part of me hopes for the reprieve of a morning storm.

At 3.00 am a hint of dawn filters through the entrance of the snow cave. As Andy pumps up the MSR stove and sets about brewing tea, shafts of light angle across a hundred valleys and a thousand mountains: the sky is cloudless. We pack a little food, a few gas cartridges, headlamps, bivouac gear and tents, four coils of 7 mm and 8 mm ropes, and a handful of pitons and ice screws. Tim carries the additional weight of a super-8 cine camera, a small Sony professional tape recorder, and batteries, films, and tapes. I add a small soundless movie camera to my pack.

Geoff and Andy enter China and lead the way across wind-polished snow. The 1984 ropes run beside a spine of rock. A two-year-deep snow pack has preserved them well. We pull sections of rope from the snow, and jumar steadily upwards. A few hundred feet above Camp Three, Geoff plants his foot onto a rock to step up.

Snap!

'Damn! Broke a crampon!'

It has snapped at the junction of the strap-post and the front points. He fiddles with it.

'Will it work?' I ask.

'Maybe,' he says. 'This is the same spot that I broke a crampon in '84.'

This is no place for omens, I think to myself.

At noon we reach 'The Notch' at 23,500 ft, where the 100 ft limestone pinnacle stands in front of the first rock band. Sun-bleached, tattered ropes chafed to the core stretch above for 500 ft. We uncoil our own ropes to re-lead the rock band.

Tom climbs first. He moves carefully up the 65 degree diorite cliff, tearing off loose blocks and tossing them aside, dusting snow from hand-holds, grinding front-points into smears of ice. Ninety minutes later he reaches a ledge and secures the rope to a piton hammered into the wall by our predecessors. Icicle-covered coils of rope and clusters of pitons and carabiners dangle from the belay. We consider adding a few to our small rack, but decide against it, since every extra pound on our backs will soon feel like ten. We uncoil another rope. I lead out while those behind arrange the fixed ropes.

My pitch bristles, with frost-shattered fangs that I pluck from the snow like decayed teeth. After 200 ft I sink in a pair of ice screws beneath a 200 ft vertical rock wall. The time is now three o'clock. Somehow, twelve hours have passed since leaving the snow cave. Tim joins me, ready to lead the next pitch. He looks to our right, to more tattered ropes swaying in the wind. They hang down a very difficult looking wall. Geoff had mentioned this section. It had presented great difficulties in 1984.

'That'll take hours to lead,' Tim says sceptically.

'What about the gully on our left?'

We lean out from the belay and peer around the corner to a narrow ice chute flanked by a row of jagged 100 ft tall ice towers.

'I can see why they didn't go that way. Those things'd wipe you out if they collapsed,' he says warily.

'Well, whatever we do it better be fast. Time is getting on. We should bivouac as soon as possible. We haven't had a drop to drink all day.'

The need for speed makes Tim reconsider the ice towers.

'I'll check it out,' he says after all.

He front-points left and disappears into the chute. Sounds of smashing ice tools fill the air, the rope inches out.

'How does it look?' I call.

'Good! I think I can make it to the top of the cliff!' he shouts back.

At 5.00 pm he calls down that the rope is secured. One by one we jumar up the chute and onto a snowy promontory atop the cliff. The altimeter reads 24,140 ft. We pull the rope up behind us, fixing two lengths of 8 mm rope on the first part of the cliff, leaving us with two 300 ft lengths of 7 mm rope. Against an intensely amber sky, we begin to hack tent platforms into a bank of snow. Every few swings with our ice axes brings on a fit of gasping and we try to pace ourselves but there are hours yet before we can rest. Our three tiny tents must be pitched and anchored, crampons and boots removed, damp socks replaced with dry ones, foam pads and sleeping bags laid out and crawled into. Only then could eating and the slow process of melting snow for drink begin.

Tim Macartney-Snape at the site of the Camp 4 bivvy at 24,140 ft. Mustagh Tower rises distinctively on the right, Masherbrum is on the left.

But it is impossible not to be distracted by our surroundings. Alpenglow saturates everything, even us, and the wind has fallen to a whisper. In Sinkiang, countless nameless mountains in the Aghil Range rise high from unexplored valleys. In the opposite direction, the horizon shines from Chogolisa to the jagged spine of Broad Peak, around which peers K2. High on the horizon above Indian Kashmir rise the anvil clouds of the monsoon. And right beside us, so close we feel we could touch it, stands the West Face of Gasherbrum IV, golden, steep, daunting. Seeing it awash with light, I understand why the old explorer, Conway, had called it 'The Shining Wall'. Inside the tents, we settle into the night. Tim pulls out his tape recorder and plugs a tape into it.

'Planning to record some of our banter, for atmosphere in the movie?'

'No,' he says, handing me an extra set of headphones, 'I thought we'd listen to some music.'

I laugh. We were about to rock out at 24,140 ft. I didn't doubt that Tim had chosen something apropos to the moment. He flicks the 'play' button. The name of the band is the Talking Heads. We smile broadly at each other and I give him a thumbs up sign for his stroke of genius, lie back, and listen. Sleep soon overtakes me.

Strong wind flaps the tent walls at first light on 21 June, but the skies are still clear. We leave the tents in place and take only the bare essentials for our attempt on the summit. Between the five of us we take one stove with two gas cylinders, some tea bags, and a few energy bars. We concede the possibility of a forced bivouac on the descent by packing two foam pads and three sleeping bags, just enough insulation to drape under and over us for a night on a small ledge. Our climbing rack consists of two light ropes, twelve carabiners, nine pitons, two wired chocks, an ice screw, and a few slings. We also carry the movie camera.

We head off, unroped, with Andy in front, zigzagging up a steepening snowfield packed firm against the spine of the ridge. We follow in line, our heads down, our steps in concert to our breathing. Not 200 ft above camp a startled shout of 'Help!' comes from Andy. I look up to see him up to his armpits in a slot where the snowfield has separated from the rock and then has dusted over with a thin layer of powder. He grapples with the crumbling edge as the hole tries to suck him down. We hurry to his aid, but in a second more he has his ice axe planted into firm snow and claws his way out.

'Okay?' Geoff calls.

'Okay.'

Andy continues up the slope, following the line of most gentle angle, veering diagonally across the Chinese side of the ridge.

Whumph!

Acres of slope groan around us.

'Jesus!' Our hearts explode, we stop rigid in our tracks. Our combined weight has caused the tension of the snowslab to release and an air pocket to vent itself. The slope quivers for a split second. I await the first ripples of avalanche and select options as to which way to run. But the slope remains intact. We stand rigid, staring into each other's eyes.

'It's okay. It's settled now,' says Tim.

Bloody optimist, I think to myself.

We'd been lucky. A few miles away, on K2 luck was less lenient. At that precise moment, at 5.30 am, two Americans, Alan Pennington and John Smolich, walked toward the great couloir at the foot of K2's unclimbed South-southwest Pillar. Just as they reached the first ropes a boulder toppled from a pinnacle at the top of the couloir, crashed through the frozen surface and sent a shockwave deep into the bed of snow and ice. As the crystalline bonds that held the slope broke, a catastrophic chain-reaction began. A fracture line as deep as 20 ft fanned out along the 1,700 ft long couloir. Thousands of tons of snow and ice crashed toward the climbers. They turned and tried to run for it, but the surging mass of debris over-took them. Everything was over in a matter of seconds. K2 claimed its first victims of the season.

We continue up the ridge, Tim now in the lead. With every foot gained, the tempo of the wind increases. The slope steepens to 65 degrees. We follow Tim's foot-steps, kicked into a frozen surface of perfect consistency. I marvel at the parking-lot size imprints his size 12 feet leave behind, but, as I stretch my shorter legs to match his lanky stride, I begin to hyperventilate from the effort.

The slope crests out on a narrow horizontal ridge at 24,500 ft. We catch the full force of the wind here, and crampon for 100 ft to shelter in a rocky outcrop at the ridge's end. We pause to examine the options. The continuation of the ridge above is steep, rocky, difficult. But to the left a band of ice curls toward another icefield. That is the way.

'Rope up?' I ask.

'No. Too slow. We can handle this,' says Tim after a moment of consideration.

One by one we front-point across the traverse. Nothing holds us to the face but the inch-long steel fangs of our crampons and the tips of our ice tools. A slip and we'd be sliding down the Northwest Face, toward the glacier 5,000 ft below. Exposure and exertion create a tingling feeling that runs up the back of my neck. I try to relax. A nervous, thumping heart is an inefficient mechanism up here. Around the corner of the rocks Tim begins to climb up a 300 ft prow of 65 degree ice. Tom and I linger behind. The unroped climbing is increasingly unnerving. Our calves ache from front-pointing. I see Geoff and Andy 100 ft below. Their faces read a mixture of unease and intense concentration. Geoff, front-pointing on a broken crampon, looks particularly concerned.

'I don't like the looks of where Tim is going,' I say to Tom.

'Me neither. I'll try out left.'

He traverses 80 ft to a more gentle slope but ends up in waist-deep snow. He shakes his head. The wind-polished ridge crest is the only safe path. We return to Tim's prow. At 10.00 am we exit the icefield and huddle into a wind-carved niche bounded by a ridge wall of sun-warmed orange-brown marble. The altitude is 25,000 ft. In front of us, the final 40 degree ice slope to the headwall glints in the

Tim Macartney-Snape climbing unroped and travelling light on steep ice at 24,500 ft on 21 June 1986.

Greg Child, Tom Hargis and Geoff Radford soloing the icy ridge above the Camp 4 bivouac. We're on the Chinese side of the ridge, without visas.
(Photo by Tim Macartney-Snape)

sun. But for the snow ramps I'd seen from Broad Peak, switchbacking up the wall, interspersed by vertical cliffs, few weaknesses break the smooth headwall. Somewhere left of our line is Voytek's line of descent. One look at the wall tells us that we won't be back at the tents tonight. In the niche we brew up and talk turns to tactics.

'It looks like hard going above,' says Tim. 'I reckon we dump everything here and go light. We should be able to make it to the summit and back to here by nightfall.'

Geoff, fiddling with his broken crampon, listens on with reservations. If Tim reasoned by leaps of optimism, Geoff reasoned by clear-headed pessimism. We had ten hours to climb 1,000 vertical feet to the North Summit and traverse 1,500 ft horizontally to the true summit. Just by looking at the headwall it was obvious that there'd be climbing as hard as grade 5.9. We'd be pushing to do all that, and rappel down, in ten hours. Even with our light packs, we'd move slowly, yet without bivouac gear up there, we'd be committed to bivouac in the niche. If we were caught out on the headwall, it wouldn't be pretty.

The water in the pot heats up and we share a drink of hot chocolate. 'Well?' Tim asks.

'Okay, we go light,' I say.

We stash the stove and bivouac gear in the niche and head to the base of the headwall with only climbing gear and headlamps. We each carry a partially full water bottle stuffed inside our down suits. Tim carries the cine camera, shooting film as he goes.

The icefield butts against the headwall. We arrive at a steep crack in a 50 ft cliff. Above this, the snowramps begin. It seems like the best place to start. Tom hammers in a belay piton and I tie in to lead. After a few easy feet I stand beneath a bulge. I hammer in a piton, strip my mittens down to my liner gloves, and begin jamming my fists and feet into the crack, hauling myself around an overhang. The marble is glass smooth. Crampons scrattle and slip as I inch up, gloves become sodden, hands cold and wooden. The amount of oxygen I need is more than I can suck out of the air. A heady lightness, like a glimpse of unconsciousness, washes over me in waves. Gasping desperately, I pause above the bulge, with one foot wedged into the crack, the other stemmed out onto a flake. It's a rest, of sorts. I will myself to breathe more slowly, and suck on my fingers to warm them. I find myself thinking of Voytek's letter. 'Do not fear the headwall, it is nice surprise,' he'd written. Some surprise.

As I creep up I hear a shout from Geoff: 'I'm going down.'

I know what he's thinking. That we're too slow and we'll never make it before dark, that the weather has been good for five days and can't last much longer, that to be caught in a storm without bivvy gear on this wall will be the end of us, that with his snapped crampon it's too risky. I try to shout to him that I'm nearly on the snow ramp, that it looks easier for a long way above, but only a croak exits my dry throat. I see him zigzagging down the slope, toward the niche, where he will bivouac and await us. Watching him descend is like losing a piece of my own body. He'd given his all to get us here but he knew where to draw the line. I hoped we'd be as clear-headed as the day wore on.

I continue up the crack for 20 ft, to a point where ice fills the cracks and the footing again becomes insubstantial. I try for ten minutes to rig protection but nothing works. Finally I take my ice hammer and swing it into the frozen crack. Half of the pick bites. I clip the hammer's wrist-loop to the rope and gasp and grasp onto a patch of snow 10 ft above.

'I'm okay now,' I shout, turning to crampon up the ramp.

'Well done. It looked hard,' calls a voice over my shoulder.

I turn to see Andy, just a few feet away, wobbling onto the snow ramp after soloing up another crack.

'Jesus, Tuthill. Why didn't you tell me it was easier over there? I thought I was gonna die on this crack!'

'I thought I was gonna die on *this*.'

I inspect the verglassed wall he'd just climbed. If anything, it looked more difficult than my crack. He just felt like moving, that's all. 150 ft later I reach a large block and secure the rope around it. Andy, followed by the others, jumars up. Tom is coughing wildly again, his lung infection back in full force.

Andy leads a second long pitch, then Tim takes over for two leads. 'The route alternates between steep ramps covered in snow and short vertical rock steps. Marble, limestone, and occasional lenses of diorite collide. Protection is minimal, the climbing tricky. We grow more and more tired, move slowly and slower. At 3.00 pm I join Tim on a ledge: 100 ft above us the headwall ends and the ridge to the smaller North Summit begins. I tie in to the lead end of the rope and begin to pull up over some blocks. After a few feet I return to the ledge and, gasping and weak, hand the task to Tim.

'You lead it. I'm exhausted. I need time to rest.'

Tim disappears into a chimney. Thirty minutes later he reaches the ridge.

As the four of us jumar up and gather on the narrow crest at 25,850 ft, we consider our position. About 150 easy feet higher and some 700 horizontal feet east is the North Summit. From there, due south by 1,500 horizontal feet, we see the true summit, 40 ft higher than the North Summit. The time is 4.00 pm, the skies are still clear but on the ridgecrest we are exposed to a wind that makes conversation almost impossible. No one needs to be told that we will not make the summit and get back to the foot of the headwall before dark.

Our bodies burn with fatigue. We stand there, watching dusk gather over the Karakoram. The realization that we've blown it begins to sink in. If we descend, we'll never climb Gasherbrum IV, yet to press on seems like insanity. Everything seems about to turn to shit. Then the worm of unfinished ideas begins to twist in our heads. The crazy talk begins.

'I'm certain I can make it through the night without frostbite,' says Tim, the words ripped out of his mouth by wind.

'Bivvy out?' I ask.

'Either that or go down.'

We have nothing but the clothes on our backs. No water, food, or stove. I'd read long ago about Hermann Buhl sitting out a night just below the summit of Nanga Parbat. It seemed to me then something only a superman could endure or a madman conceive. I'd also heard the separate tales of Nazir Sabir and Jim Wickwire, both of whom had sat out nights near the summit of K2. Nazir had suffered memory loss for months. Jim's bivouac had cost him a piece of lung when fluid had frozen in his chest. And there was Bonatti and Mahdi on K2. Even with an oxygen cylinder, Mahdi had lost his feet. A bivouac here would be harsh, but at the same time I felt that our chances were good; the weather was clear, and we still had some strength left. Instinct condoned the idea, the ambition put words in my mouth.

'I'll risk it,' I hear myself say.

Our own private epic begins to take shape.

Tom and Andy look with uncertainty about the clear horizon. That hacking cough is hammering Tom's ribs again. He's running on sheer determination. Andy, who'd frozen toes in years past, looks about the icescape, justly concerned.

'Don't be talked into this by us. It could be a bad night. Maybe frostbite. Think hard,' I say.

They bat it about for a few moments, torn between the rationality of descent and the irrationality of success.

'I'm staying,' says Tom.

'No, it's not worth it to me. I'm going down,' says Andy, seeing the enormity of the gamble.

'Alone?' Descending the rock band unaccompanied seemed dangerous.

'You're worried about me? I'm more worried about you! Anyway, tonight is the summer solstice, the shortest night of the year.'

'Yeah? At least we've got that going for us.'

Andy rips a 12 in by 24 in foam pad out of the back of his rucksack and hands it to us. We divide the hardware: he takes three slings, five pitons, a wired chock, and a rope. We give him the larger share of the gear in order that he should have enough to make five or six rappels. We hope that the next day we'll find his anchors, maybe Voytek's as well . . .

Tim (in front) and Tom chopping out a bivvy ledge at 24,140 ft. Sinkiang, China, in the distance.

Looking across the West Face of Gasherbrum IV, 'the shining wall', to Chogolisa (on the horizon) and Gasherbrum V. Monsoon clouds rise on the right, over Kashmir.

'Good luck.' He turns and leaves to descend to Geoff at the niche. Now we are three.

'Well, this is a grand idea but what do we do now?' I ask, as if reproaching myself.

'Gotta dig a hole. That's the only way to make it through the night,' Tim replies.

We continue along the narrow ridge for another hour, looking for a suitable site to claw out a snowcave. Just below the North Summit, we find a cluster of snow drifts and cornices. We poke our axes about, to see if the drifts allow a snowcave to be dug into them. All are solid ice. Time creeps by. Despite our leg-heaviness our search for a place to endure the night becomes laced with a certain desperation. To sit out the night on the bare ice and rocks could be fatal if the wind didn't drop. I begin to chop into the ice at my feet. Even crouching in a pit would be better than nothing.

Tim crampons down the side of the ridge to a point where a steep spur joins the Northwest ridge. It's the ridge the Italians had climbed. Somewhere on that ridge, at the site of the Italian Camp Six, at 24,770 ft, the climber Giuseppe de Francesch had left a statue of the Madonna of Lourdes, given him by his wife, to invoke a blessing for the mountain. Perhaps even after all these years, the Madonna was still there, propped against the rock. It occurs to me that we could use a little divine intervention right now. Then Tim shoves his ice axe into a triangular mound of snow perched on the narrow crest of the Italian Ridge and the shaft sinks deeply.

'Hey, we can get a cave down here.'

Tom and I descend. Digging begins.

We scratch out little handfuls of snow with the adzes of our ice axes, digging for five minutes each, then kicking and clawing the snowy payload toward the entrance for the others to remove. The effort is almost more than we are capable of. As I take my turn at digging I think of the bridge we have burned, of what might happen, and what might not. Framed in the entrance to the cave is Broad Peak, where Pete had died and where he still lay. It is almost three years to the day since our struggle to get down the mountain. As oxygen starved as my thoughts are, the essence of my reason for returning to the Karakoram falls clearly into place, as never before. It seemed that finishing that idea I had shared with Pete, to climb G4, would close a circle, would somehow set a cruel score a little more even. Why had I taken so long to understand that this was the fundamental reason I'd come here? And what of my two companions? What drew them here? The beauty? To be able to say they had done it? Did they too have hidden compartments inside them full of thoughts pounding for resolve? Or was adventure enough reason? No time for thoughts. I return to digging.

'Greg, come out here. Look at the sky,' Tim calls.

Sky? How can he stand there looking at the sky when night will be on us in a matter of minutes and the snowcave is only half dug?

I back out of the cave. The wind has dropped. Gasherbrums I, II, and III poke up like huge tusks, their snows pearly white, their rocks shining amber. The shadow of Gasherbrum IV is cast across them and the sky is indigo blue, fading into a deeply pink upper atmosphere. Stars penetrate the fading daylight, led by Venus, glinting in the north. Low on the horizon the rising full moon blasts a surreal glow across the Karakoram, from the monsoon thunderheads over Indian Kashmir, to Nanga Parbat in the west.

We stand looking, breathing. For a moment all our doubts vanish. We are quite certain we have chosen the right place to be. As we settle into the cave I feel like a stranded astronaut bedding down for the night on a hostile planet. But no, it's our own wild and beautiful earth.

The Summit

Cold is the immediate sensation that overcomes us as we seal the entrance to the snowcave with Tim's pack. Height, length, and width, the cave measures four feet in each direction. As the day's last light filters through the thin walls we remove our crampons, then take stock of the few possessions we have. The foam pad from Andy's pack goes beneath us. Whoever is in the middle gets a full seat, while those on either end get one buttock on the pad, the other on snow. We decide to rotate positions during the night.

A mouthful of water remains in each of our bottles. We mix the water with snow to stretch it further and sip it down. The water soaks into our tongues, then is gone. We search the pack and the pockets of our down suits for scraps of food. A mangled energy bar comes up from the bottom of the pack, and from Tim's pocket a stale, crumbling lump of fruitcake. He breaks the cake into three portions. Tom and I sample it and gag: it has the consistency of sawdust.

'Can't eat this shit up here,' I grumble.

'That's my mother's fruitcake you're talking about,' counters Tim.

'I'm sure it's very nice at Base Camp, but up here it's shit.'

Nothing is palatable at altitude. We have no appetites, only a great thirst. Tom and I store the cake in our pockets till we can find a use for it. We contemplate the energy bar.

'Save it for 'ron,' I mutter.

'Who?' Tom asks.

Tim chuckles at a familiar Australian wordplay.

'Later-ron,' I explain.

We continue the search for anything useful. Tim checks his cine camera. I notice the sheepskin insulation jacket surrounding the camera and suggest someone could sit on it, or we might take turns wearing it as a hat. Tim rejects the proposition, concerned that the motor in the camera might freeze. He is determined to film us on the summit, but if the temperature keeps dropping as fast as it was, we wouldn't see any summit. Teeth were already chattering. Tom was coughing at full force.

'What about the rope?' asks Tom. 'We could sit on that.'

'I anchored it in the rocks above us. I thought we'd want to be tied in,' I reply, grabbing the strand that runs through the door. The snowcave was burrowed into a precarious mound of snow. Its walls were thin enough to knock down with a misplaced elbow. It didn't seem too remote a possibility that the entire cave might fall to bits during the night, emptying us out of it. With that thought, we keep our headlamps ready. We pull what slack is left in the rope into the cave, clip our harnesses into it, and put the rest behind our backs. Then, zipping our suits up and drawing our hoods and balaclavas tightly around our faces, we sit tight.

'What's the time?' Tom asks. His voice wakes me from a snatch of sleep. I notice that Tim is singing.

'Don't ask that, Tom,' Tim begs.

I check my watch. Little more than an hour has passed since we entered the cave. I announce the discouraging fact. It seems as though we'd been there longer. Tim resumes his singing, louder, some school song by the sound of it. We begin to shiver violently. I rock my body back and forth, slapping my thighs to the beat of Tim's song, wriggling my toes at the same time. The movement produces a trancelike effect, takes the focus off the cold. I notice Tom moving to the same beat, see him rubbing his hands and banging his feet together, mumbling as he

Exhausted after the summit, Tim Macartney-Snape, Tom Hargis and Greg Child in the Camp Three snow cave on Gasherbrum IV. (Photo by Randall Leavitt)

June 22, 1986 dawns clear outside our snowcave at 23,000 ft. We crawl out into the cold and begin the final ascent to the summit.

counts sets of a hundred wriggles, loses count, and starts over. My shivering gradually becomes a low wail that sounds very much like someone in constant pain. I begin to think about this pain, the pain we are feeling now, the pain of cold. What is it like, how to quantify it? Like having a tooth pulled without anaesthetic, all day.

'What's the worst bivvy you've ever had?' Tim asks, prompting me to think back on years of cold, wet bivouacs.

'This is,' I reply without reservation.

Tom coughs again. Something like a pale green, blood-spattered tadpole flies out of his gullet, hits the wall, and freezes solid. He retreats into himself and takes on the countenance of a zombie. The luxury of conversation, even of the occasional caring 'How are you feeling?' drops away. Suddenly I cannot feel my toes.

'My feet—they're going!'

I kick off my boots. Tim unzips his down suit. I put my socked and lifeless feet against his chest. We squirm and shift positions in the tiny hole, like a *ménage à trois* in deep freeze. All we need is a few more hours of windlessness to survive. As we sit shivering, a state, neither sleep nor wake but more like a sedative overdose, full of strange, restless dreams, carries us into our own worlds. All grasp of the flow of time falls away. The night fills with strange mumblings.

As 22 June dawns, sunlight creeps into the snowcave and onto our stiff, hurting bodies. A miniscule veil of frozen moisture momentarily clasps my eyelids together, then releases. We look at each other. Faces are puffed and bloated with mild edema. Capillaries bulge red and angry on our brows. Lips and noses look like peeling sausages. Icicles hang from beards and noses. I recognize none of this ugly crew. Still, the mountain has been kind to us. No one is frostbitten, our lungs breathe free, our heads are untroubled by pain. Outside, the daily wind is building, but the skies remain clear. We enter the daylight, clip crampons to boots, and plod like machines to the nearby North Summit.

Between the North Summit and the summit proper is a long ridge of wind-polished ice that on our right drops over the two mile high West Face, and on our left plunges to a snow plateau 4,000 ft below. The wind from China slams into the East Face and tumbles over the ridge like surf pounding a seawall. At the end of the ridge, somewhere amongst a series of steep-faced limestone towers, is the summit.

We traverse the ice ridge unroped, reaching the cluster of towers in an hour, sheltering from the wind beside the first rocks, where we break out the rope. I tie in and lead off, traversing a snowfield beneath the 80 ft towers, peering through my iced-over goggles, looking for the highest tower. But any one of five separate points above me could be the one. It's a puzzle my altitude-addled brain can barely cope with. I decide we have two choices to the summit: either climb a crack directly in front of me and straddle the jagged summit crest until we reach the highest point, or traverse across the foot of the towers, over verglassed slabs, until we see the summit, and then climb directly up to it.

For some reason I choose the crack. The limestone is solid, 80 degrees steep, the wall sheltered from the brunt of the wind. In the half-hour the tower takes to climb I become so completely involved with the task of pulling up on handjams and flakes that I ignore the bigger picture I'm painting until I reach the summit crest and see a long double-corniced knife-edge ahead of me. I've climbed into a deadend.

'This is the wrong way!' I shout down to Tim and Tom. Spindrift blowing over the ridge sprays them. Watching through openings in their tightly drawn storm-hoods, they've been aware I was heading into a deadend for several minutes, but, like me, have been too lost in their windy oxygen-starved dream-world to be overly concerned.

Cursing my mistake I drape one of our precious slings around a rock spike and rappel down. Tim takes over, heads toward the low traverse, balances unroped across the 50 ft wide verglassed slab beside us, toward a snowfield. His crampons creak shrilly against the rock. One mittened hand pads over the holdless wall, the other holds his ice axe, which he hooks into smears of ice. Neither Tom nor I like the look of the traverse. We rope up. Tom leads across, placing a piton for protection two-thirds of the way across.

On the other side of the traverse, the wind is moderate. There, we stand in a small snowy bowl, directly beneath the true summit. Tim, ahead of us, is already at the end of the snow slope, clambering up the summit rocks. Tom and I follow, towing the rope behind us. Deep pockets in the rock form sure holds for the final steep moves. Meanwhile Tim sits sheltered from the wind by a boulder, the cine camera fast against his face, filming our every move. He holds his breath, shoots a sequence, then gasps wildly. A few steps to his right is a pointed crest of snow encrusted onto the summit rocks. I look around, expecting some final obstacle to surmount, but no, we are on the summit. It is 10.00 am.

Tom, coughing at every step, moves a few steps behind.

'He's a determined bastard,' Tim says in admiration.

Seeing the end of the climb, Tom's ashen face breaks into a smile. The obscure object of desire is reached, the worm within us is satisfied. Too exhausted for clever words we simply clasp one mittened hand in another, shake, gaze about us, and turn to our own thoughts. We'd gone beyond words two days ago, forced by necessity into a state in which we functioned as a single being. Now on the summit, that being, drunk with euphoria, felt suddenly as if it had merged with sky and mountain as well to become a single, elemental entity, like some rare particle, formed in an atom smasher, existent for a millisecond in time.

The catenulate shapes of Broad Peak, K2, the Gasherbrums, and Chogolisa loom around us. The Trango Towers stand like distant castles at the head of the Baltoro. The sky is cloudless right up to Nanga Parbat. A few photographs later, we jam a stone in a crack on the summit rock-fin, sling it, loop the rope through this, and rappel off the summit. As I back down the rope I feel a moment of regret for not having left something up there in memory of Pete, for the summit we never reached. Instead, I leave a fond thought. It's the best thing I had to give.

It's still there.

Greg Child (left) and Tom Hargis on the summit of Gasherbrum IV.

Looking down the Baltoro Glacier from the summit of Gasherbrum IV. Concordia is the great glacial intersection in the center.

Tim leaves the summit last. I wait at the foot of the rope, to help him pull it down. But when I look up I see him wandering off on the summit rocks like a mad lost thing. He turns after 30 ft, and descends.

'I saw it! Bonatti's old rope, clipped to a carabiner and piton!'

'Where?'

'50 ft from the summit. I tried to get to it but it was just out of reach.'

Eager to shed altitude and quell his coughing, Tom solos back across the verglassed traverse. The thin patina of ice is by now scratched away to slick limestone. His feet slip about. He shakes his head at its end.

'Rope up. It's bad,' he calls, then heads for the North Summit.

Tim belays me as I lead back across the traverse, clipping the piton left by Tom, then sinking my ice axe into a snow-patch on the other side. The tip bottoms out on rock beneath. I place my boot on top of the axe, then loop the rope over both, to facilitate a belay.

'It's a lousy belay. The snow is shallow,' I caution.

Tim signals that he understands, then starts across, pausing at the piton to hammer it out. The piton is well seated, but it gives slowly. Using his ice axe as a lever he begins to reef it out. I stand there, holding the rope. My eyes wander. Then, the momentarily incomprehensible sight of Tim's ice axe and the piton flying through the air, then jangling down the rocks, wrenches me to attention. I look across to see a red blur—Tim—cartwheeling backwards over the West Face. He seems to fall in slow motion. I haul in a yard of rope. Still he's falling, 40, 50 ft, dropping down, swinging like a pendulum towards me. The boot-axe belay seems a token gesture, a text book theory incapable of holding a fall. I await a grand tour of the 10,000 ft West Face.

A jolt torpedoes boot and axe into the snow. The axe tip grates against the rock and shifts under the force of the fall. I close my eyes and brace myself for whatever comes next. But everything stops. I open my eyes and look to my right.

The rope has hooked over a tiny knob of rock 15 ft away. Tim dangles out of sight, 50 ft below.

'Tim!'

I scream his name into space for five minutes. No answer, only the ripping wind. I look around for somewhere to anchor the rope. Damn! I'm 20 ft from the nearest piece of rock to hammer a piton in, to clip the rope to take Tim's weight, and the snow around me isn't solid enough to take an ice screw. All that holds us to the mountain is my boot and ice axe.

'Tim! God man, are you okay?'

I glance about. Tom is long gone, down-climbing the first rocks of the headwall, half an hour away if he were to return right then. I tug on the rope. To haul Tim up is out of the question. Rope begins to slip through my hands. I begin to think: if Tim is unconscious or dead I'll be stuck there, holding him forever, as *in-situ* as Bonatti's rusting piton. Ah, no, I realize, that isn't true; gradually my hands will weaken and the rope will inch through until Tim's weight comes tight against the knot at my waist. Then we'll be in base camp in ten seconds flat. I experiment with the dexterity of untying the knot with one hand, and wonder if it's worth bothering with, since without a rope, Tom and I will never get down the mountain. Another foot of rope slips through.

'Tim!' I scream again.

A final option comes to mind as I feel the outline of a pen-knife in my pocket. I'll have to make a choice about this soon, I tell myself. The idea is horrible to contemplate, but as more and more rope slips through my hands, I find myself thinking with the cold practicality of Clint Eastwood. But the rope moves. I cast the knife out of my thoughts and pull the rope in, and in, and in. Tim appears. Feathers fly out of his ripped down suit. He looks as if he's been blasted with buckshot.

He grips my shoulder with his hand. 'Thanks for saving me from the biggest tumble of my life.'

'Thanks for saving me from the longest wait of mine,' I mutter back, relieved. 'God, it's good to see you! Are you hurt?'

An hour later we are at the snowcave. Tom is still ahead of us, wondering where we are. My legs begin to cramp from dehydration. The pain has me growling, stopping every few steps to uncurl buckling legs, locked with knotted muscles, as the glucose in my body flows from liver to muscle, and converts to lactic acid, the compound of fatigue. I stop, try to breathe deeply, to force oxygen into my blood to oxidize and subdue the crippling lactic acid. But the air is too thin, and I carry on with a solid knot in my thigh, like a bullet lodged in my flesh. Soon, my eyes begin to play tricks on me. I start seeing tussocks of grass in the snow.

'Keep an eye on me, Tim. I'm on the verge of hallucinating.' Dehydration now, and oxygen starvation were pushing me into a dream world. I wondered how long I could maintain, how long my friends could maintain. We staggered like drunks. I look across at the West Face, glowing now. What time is it, anyway? Morning? Noon? Night? Hallucinations. Over there, on the West Face, Robert Schauer had, the year before, watched a raven hovering in front of him. The more he looked at that bird the more he became the bird, until he *was* that bird, staring back at a poor, flightless human wreck.

Tim hands me his water bottle. Somehow a teaspoon of snow has melted in it.

'Drink it.'

'We'll share it,' I say, as if we speak of a banquet.

'No. Drink it all.'

I swallow it.

We reach Tom at 11.30 pm, above the headwall. He is coughing wildly.

'Where've you been?' he asks.

'Almost killed ourselves. How are you feeling?'

'My ribs. I think I've cracked some. The coughing,' he says, grimacing.

We're in bad shape. Fatigue and dehydration conspire to detach our minds from our bodies. Another night out without sleeping bags or water will probably finish us off. We begin rappeling down the headwall, swinging about on the rope, searching for Andy's anchors. But we find only one, and begin using our own small supply. As these disappear we strip cord from jumars, ice-tools, anything, jamming knotted slings into slots and cracks. Something compels me to take a photograph of us. I snap the scene, slip the camera into my windsuit. It shoots through an open zip and ricochets into China. Oh yeah, I remember; I used the sling that kept it around my neck for an anchor an hour ago.

Late in the day we reach the base of the headwall. Our throats beg for water. We crampon hurriedly toward the stove we know Geoff and Andy, now at Camp Three, have left at the niche. We find it and light it. Propane spurts from the valve onto our fingers, blanching our skin. The stove explodes into a ball of flame.

'Bastard!'

We kick the stove off the mountain. There will be no water. For a moment despondency has its way with us.

'This place is like a pub with no beer. Let's keep going.'

More rappels down the icefield. Night falls. We scan the face with our headlamp beams, searching for anchors, wandering about the face unroped. I wonder if we *know* we are unroped? I pound the last piton into an amalgam of ice and rubble. No gear is left, yet two more rappels await us. We'll have to start chopping the ends off the rope soon. Tim descends first, leaving Tom and me leaning against each other, propping ourselves up, asleep on our crampons. Tim calls from below for us to descend, but we are out for the count. Awaiting our arrival, he sits on a flat spot, and falls asleep as well.

We all awake simultaneously, suddenly shivering. The moon has traversed far across the sky. Tim calls from below and I look at my watch: we've slept for an hour. The difference between sleep and wake has become barely distinguishable.

Down we go. One rappel left. Out of slings and pitons now. As we make ready to chop into the rope to make a sling, an old frozen piece of Voytek's webbing appears in the beams of our headlamps. We rappel off it to the easy slope leading to the moonglow-lit tents. At 10.00 pm we crawl into them, drink our first water in 36 hours, and sleep a deep, deep sleep.

My eyes open to violently billowing nylon on the morning of 23 June. Wind sucks air in and out of the tent, increasing and decreasing the pressure. I feel like I'm trapped inside a heaving lung. We keep waking, then slumping back into a deep sleep, but finally, concerned that the wind heralds a storm, we make ready to leave. Outside, the sky is still clear for miles around, but the wind is colder, and clouds pave the spaces between mountains in the south. The fine weather is on the way out.

I gather up my possessions distractedly, thinking over the dream, or hallucination, I'd just woken from. It had come to me in the snowcave first, then last night as well, in the small hours of the morning, the same sensation of someone familiar, an old friend, lying close to me, wrapping his arms around me, lending his warmth. I sat staring at the wall of the tent thinking about this. To that point I had an explanation for every sensation up here, as some symptom of oxygen starvation, dehydration, fatigue, or chemical imbalance. My mind was a mess, likely to imagine anything. But then this, so vivid. Tim rallies me as he starts to take down the tent. We break camp, take one last look at this place, then turn our backs to put it as far behind us as possible.

500 ft below we meet Steve and Randy. The sight of their smiling faces confirms that the worst is over.

'Did you make it?' Steve shouts.

'Yeah.'

'Congratulations! Everyone okay? Any frostbite?'

'No. Just exhausted. Are you going up?' I ask.

'No. The weather is crapping out. When Geoff and Andy told us what you guys had done to get to the summit we thought we'd better check on you.'

The air is warmer, thicker, with each step down. We clip the ropes and scoot past Camp Three, past Camp Two, down into the couloir.

As we descend, K2, twelve miles away, is a flurry of activity, with climbers hurrying to reach the summit in the fast-disappearing spell of good weather. On the unclimbed South-southwest Pillar, Renato Casarotto is standing at 27,000 ft, watching the horizon thicken with storm haze, deciding that the weather is not stable. Playing it safe as always, he calls off his summit bid and rappels to the foot of the pillar, passing by the gaping gash in the couloir and crossing the debris that had buried the two Americans. As he hops across the crevasses of the de Filippi Glacier on his way back to base camp he must have thought it a stroke of luck that he was out of the couloir when the avalanche occurred. But luck and good instincts were two things Casarotto had always had in abundance.

Meanwhile, 1,700 ft south of Casarotto's pillar, on the Abruzzi Ridge, six climbers of two different expeditions—the Basques Mari Abrego and Josema Casimera, and a French/Polish group comprised of Maurice and Liliane Barrard, Michel Parmaentier, all French, and Wanda Rutkiewicz, a Pole—move up K2's final ridge, reaching the summit by afternoon. Wanda and Liliane become the first women to climb K2. All reach the top without supplementary oxygen.

On the descent from the summit, the Basques hurry down, but darkness soon overtakes the French/Polish group. At 27,200 ft they reach the bivouac site of their previous night, the 22nd. They had hoped to get to a lower altitude, but the Barrards are so exhausted that all four are forced to spend a second cold night in the same bivouac, crammed into a two-man tent, without sleeping bags.

On 24 June, the Swiss/Polish continue descending through heavy skies, moving at their own speeds. Parmentier forges ahead to Camp Three, at about 24,300 ft, to melt snow, while the Barrards, reeling with exhaustion, fall further and further behind. Rutkiewicz is the last to see them alive, in the vicinity of the 'bottleneck', where seracs on the east side and rock cliffs on the south pinch the Abruzzi route into a steep, narrow chute. Rutkiewicz, already with frostbitten fingers and a cold-blackened nose, continues down to Camp Two with the Basques. She waits two days more for Parmentier while he stays at Camp Three, waiting for the Barrards. His waiting is in vain. Liliane Barrard's shattered body is already at the foot of the Southeast Face; no trace of her husband is ever found. Perhaps a small avalanche swept them off their feet, perhaps exhaustion caused one of them to stumble, dragging the other away as well. The result is the same.

Bad weather set in during Parmentier's vigil at Camp Three. On the morning of the 25th he awoke to complete whiteout and vicious winds. Below him, Rutkiewicz battled her way down, the Basques as well. He radioed Base Camp to say that he was descending, but the fixed ropes and any tracks left by his companions were buried in fresh snow. Soon he became lost on the broad expanse of the south shoulder of K2, staggering about, muttering *Grande vide, grande vide*— 'big emptiness', 'big emptiness.' As he searched frantically for landmarks, climbers in Base Camp tried to guide him by radio. Finally he radioed that he'd located a dome of urine-stained ice. British and French climbers listening at Base Camp remembered this insignificant landmark at the top of the fixed ropes, and could safely guide him to the chain of ropes leading to the glacier below.

With the Barrards, K2 had now claimed four lives.

Days of sunshine have melted out the guts of the couloir leading from the Northwest Ridge of Gasherbrum IV to the hidden valley. Our ropes hang suspended on the walls, at times out of reach. Stones clatter down the couloir. I hope that our luck will hold just a little longer.

Down, down we descend. Small dots of tents, people, and tracks grow larger. Tim, furthest ahead, reaches the last fixed rope, unclips from it, then slides down the last of the couloir on his backside using his ice axe to control his speed. Tom lopes toward Tim's slide-track, stumbles, somersaults down the slope, then arrests himself with his ice axe. Blood trickles down his face from a cut brow. They join the group far below me. I see them shaking hands with Geoff and Andy. Phil films them. Their hands wave about as they search for words to tell the tale. Then they walk back towards the camp.

I feel no hurry. I go slowly, safely to the place where Tim had glissaded and Tom tumbled. As I slide down I hear only the shush of the snow beneath me, the grating of my ice axe rudder to my side. Peaks and wispy clouds are pink with alpenglow. Night will be on us in a few minutes. Venus shines already, to my right, above the serrated ridge bordering the hidden valley.

The events of the past few days mean something different to each of us. Seven different people, seven different stories. The lines of our seven lives had converged briefly to help each other find a path through a strange, hostile place, a jungle of ice and danger, a forest of experience. Now that the journey was over we were free to drift apart again.

Geoff waits for me at the foot of the couloir. I take slow, wobbly steps over a mound of avalanche debris. 20 ft from the end of the couloir my left leg plunges thigh-deep into a hole. I topple forward with a crash. When I lift my head and spit out a mouthful of snow, I see Geoff, smiling, walking toward me.

'It's always the last step that gets ya,' he says, and reaches out to lend his hand.

Heavy Return to Earth

Our world at the foot of Gasherbrum IV had been blissfully isolated. When we rejoined the mainstream of the mountain world at Concordia, weary climbers and straggling porters told us tales of success, and tragedy, on K2. The euphoria of our days on Gasherbrum IV was quickly replaced with a sobering after-shock. The deaths of the two Americans brought home to us just how close we'd come to triggering that avalanche above Camp Four. As for Tim's fall, nothing but chance hitching the rope over a small piece of rock had saved us from a similar disaster to that which befell the Barrards. Freaks of luck had saved us from fates that, by any ratio of odds, should have been. Maybe luck was a slimmer commodity on K2, maybe there were too many climbers vying for the same amount of that precious commodity.

We joined an exodus of expeditions moving down the Baltoro. The mountains had an end of season feel. Yet, as we hiked out, many climbers remained at K2 Base Camp, hoping for a break in the weather. Most at K2 were familiar names from books and magazines. A few were 'famous'. Some were vague acquaintances met over the years in the mountains. Others, like Alan Rouse, I knew personally. When I heard he was staying behind when all his expedition had decided to quit the Northwest Ridge of K2, I was not at all surprised. It seemed in character with my memory of him. He wanted that summit, and wouldn't leave till he had it.

The fifth death on K2 happened in July.

Amid a burst of successful ascents of the Abruzzi, two Poles, Jerzy Kukuczka and Tadeusz Piotrowski, set off on 3 July up a spectacular new route splitting K2's unclimbed South Face. Climbing lightly to the summit they would, like us on G IV, underestimate the difficulties before them and run out of food and gas at 27,000 ft on 7 July. Desperate for water, they would resort to melting cupfuls of snow with a candle. The difficulties of their route were concentrated in a huge couloir splitting the summit pyramid. It was imperative that they escape this feature quickly. On 8 July, after being slowed down by rocks so steep that an entire day of climbing gained no more than 100 ft they abandoned their bivouac gear and struggled up a subsidiary gully leading to the Abruzzi Spur on their right. Joining the Abruzzi at 27,250 ft, they reached the summit that evening. They had cut

Six climbers freeze to death in K2 blizzard

ISLAMABAD, Pakistan (AP) — Six mountain climbers, including two women, froze to death on K2, the world's second-highest peak, after a blizzard trapped them for more than a week, a survivor said yesterday.

Kurt Diemberger, an Austrian mountaineer and filmmaker, told The Associated Press in a telephone interview from the northern town of Skardu that two Austri-... and two Poles

near each other and close to the summit when a fierce blizzard hit on Aug. 7. They took refuge in a makeshift camp to try to outlast the storm. But the blizzard lasted more than week and the mountaineers ran out of food, becoming weak and ill from the cold and the lack of oxygen at the high altitude.

Five people died in the camp — Britons Julie Tullis, 47, and Alan Rouse; Austrians Hannes

News of the 1986 K2 tragedy appeared in headlines around the world.

their margins very fine, but had pulled off one of the most difficult ascents ever made of K2.

The weather quickly turned foul. The pair descended the Abruzzi through the storm and deep, loose snow, making little downward progress for two days, sleeping in snow holes with only bivouac sacks as shelter. On 10 July, after two bitterly cold nights out in the open, Kukuzcka left their snow hole early to break trail, leaving Piotrowski strapping his crampons to his boots. After a few hundred feet Kukuzcka saw the first signs that they were on the right path—the tents of a Korean expedition, at 24,000 ft. Until then they'd been lost in the 'big emptiness' of misty slopes on K2's south shoulder.

Between the Poles and the Korean camp lay a steep slope—the same slope where the American Art Gilkey had died during an early attempt on K2 in 1953. The slope was too steep to safely down-climb in their condition, so Kukuzcka awaited Piotrowski, who was carrying the rappel rope. But Piotrowski had absent-mindedly left it back in the snow-hole. So they faced the slope and began reversing down steep, hard ice. Kukuzcka, descending first, looked up just as Piotrowski's crampon fell off one foot. Kukuzcka shouted a warning—'Taddy, your crampon!' Piotrowski kicked his other foot into the ice. That crampon flew off too. Piotrowski dangled from the picks of his ice axes for a second, his feet skating against the ice, then fell onto Kukuzcka, almost knocking him off the slope. Kukuzcka watched helplessly as Piotrowski bounced down the slope and disappeared into some clouds. And so it was that Jerzy Kukuzcka descended from his eleventh 8,000er, sadly alone.

In mid July, Casarotto made his third attempt on the South-southwest Pillar, reaching 27,250 ft in a couloir in the summit pyramid, left of the one that the Poles had climbed. Again Casarotto's instincts warned him off the final stretch of rock and snow to the summit, for storm was quickly building. He had planned this attempt to be his last. Aftewards, he and Goretta, his wife and sole companion on all his solo expeditions, would pack up and return to their home. As he descended the mountain on 16 July and walked across the de Filippi Glacier he was watched by climbers in K2 Base Camp, all mouthing words of admiration for the quietly spoken 38-year-old soloist. Through binoculars, they watched him pause in front of a crevasse and move to hop across it. In an instant he dropped out of sight. The edge of the crevasse, crossed dozens of times that season, had crumbled. Casarotto plummetted 120 ft into a dark slot.

Lying in a pool of ice water in the bottom of the crevasse, Casarotto was alive, but badly hurt. He twisted about till he could reach into his pack and pull out his walkie-talkie. In Base Camp, alerted to his accident, Goretta had already switched her walkie-talkie on. Over the radio came Casarotto's voice. He whispered, 'Goretta, I am dying in a crevasse near Base Camp.'

By nightfall a rescue party of climbers and doctors from British, Italian, and German expeditions arrived at the crevasse. They quickly lifted him to the surface. Casarotto stood up, took a few steps, then collapsed and died from internal injuries. He had died one hour away from Base Camp.

The death toll now stood at six.

Storm then blew around the Baltoro for two weeks. During that time a second wave of expeditions ensconced themselves on the mountain. As August turned around, Poles on the South-southwest Pillar, assisted by the ropes left from the Americans' and Casarotto's ill-fated attempts, sat poised for the summit on that route. Simultaneously several climbers of different nationalities—Austrian, Polish, British, and Korean—moved from camp to camp, at different paces, up the Abruzzi. Of all those on K2, only the Koreans used supplementary oxygen.

On 3 August the Poles Petr Bozik, Przemslaw Piaseck, and Wojciech Wroz climbed the final rocks and snow ridge of the South-southwest Pillar to K2's summit. The going had been hard. They'd spent two bivouacs above the end of their fixed ropes, one of those in only bivvy sacks. On the summit they met the Koreans Jang Bong-Wan, Kim Chang-Sun, and Jang Byong-ho. The Koreans dumped their depleted oxygen bottles on the summit and all began descending the Abruzzi route as dusk fell, the Poles taking that course because of the great difficulties of finding a descent down the South-southwest Pillar.

At 11.30 pm, at about 26,600 ft, the Poles and Koreans were rappeling the last fixed rope in the bottleneck. Bozik, Piaseck, and Wroz descended one after the other, followed by the Koreans. But at the foot of the ropes Bozik and Piaseck, who'd just heard a sound like something falling, turned to see not Wroz behind them, but the Koreans. They could only conclude the worst, that in the dark, with only one functioning headlamp between them, Wroz had rappeled off the end of a fixed rope, probably at a point where there was a 3 ft gap between two ropes. Late that night, and in the pre-dawn hours of 4 August, the Poles and Koreans staggered into Camp Four, at 26,300 ft, where they met the polyglot British/Polish/Austrian group, bivouacing in three tents.

Those climbing up the Abruzzi were less of a team than a loosely knit contingent of members from four expeditions suddenly thrown together as a consequence of chance. On the Abruzzi were Alan Rouse, the last remaining member of the British expedition to the Northwest Ridge of K2; the Polish woman Dobroslawa Miodowicz-Wolf, whose nickname was 'Mrufka', or, translated, 'Ant', originally a member of the Polish South-southwest Pillar expedition; the Austrians Alfred Imitzer, Willi Bauer, and Hannes Wieser, who'd been at work on the Abruzzi for several weeks; and, as film makers on an Italian expedition, the Austrian Kurt Diemberger and the Englishwoman Julie Tullis, both of whom had been as far as the bottleneck, three weeks earlier. Most of the group had little in common other than great individual experience, and a burning desire to climb K2. By the evening of 2 August, all were camped at Camp Four, at 26,650 ft.

As the Korean and Polish climbers descending from the summit neared Camp Four that night of 3/4 August, Bauer, hearing shouts, shone his headlamp on the wall of his tent to guide them. Only four arrived from the summit—Wroz was dead, and a Korean had also disappeared now; he was bivouacing in the snow above. Since the two Poles had no tent, Rouse and Mrufka took them into their tiny shelter. The result was a sleepless night for all four, particularly Rouse, who slept half in, half out of the tent, with his feet in a snow hole. Meanwhile the Koreans and Austrians crammed in together, getting no more rest than Rouse and the Poles.

Already the summit-bound climbers had spent the previous night, 2 August, in overcrowded tents. Only Rouse and Mrufka were 100 percent self-sufficient, carrying their own tent and supplies up the mountain with them. Diemberger and Tullis carried tent, food, and fuel too, but had hoped to locate a cache of food and gas, left from their summit attempt of a few weeks before. It was gone, either blown away, or taken by Korean high altitude porters, leaving the pair with less gas and food than they'd hoped to have, but still with enough to get them to the summit. The setback, though, that had precipitated the crowding at Camp Four, lay with the Austrians, who had been ahead of everyone else on the Abruzzi. Bauer, Wieser, and Imitzer had counted on picking up their tent at camp Three, but after the long storm they'd found the camp destroyed, save for a single Korean tent pitched near theirs. At this point they struck a deal, by radio, with the Korean climbers one day behind them. They would carry the Korean tent to Camp Four, set it up, sleep in it on the night of 1 August, go to the summit on 2 August, then proceed down to Camp Three the same day so that the Koreans could use their own tent at Camp Four. It was a plan that would quickly change.

2 August, the Austrians' intended summit day, dawned perfectly clear. The three Austrians climbed into the bottleneck and began fixing rope across a steep ice traverse, but, moving slowly, they turned back at 27,600 ft. Yet instead of descending to Camp Three, in accordance with the agreement between them and the Koreans, they remained in Camp Four, planning another attempt on the summit the following day. When the Koreans arrived that night, an angry argument

broke out. The Koreans wanted their tent, the Austrians needed shelter. Finally Bauer and Weiser squeezed into the two-man tent with the three Koreans, Imitzer crowded in with Rouse and Mrufka. Only Diemberger and Tullis slept at all comfortably, refusing to crowd their tent. The problem was not theirs, and they well knew that a sleepless night could ruin their summit chances.

So sleepless was the night that only the Koreans climbed to the summit on the perfect day of 3 August. Everyone else remained at Camp Four that day, 'recovering'—an anomaly at such an altitude. Despite their more favourable sleeping arrangements, Diemberger and Tullis were among those 'resting' at Camp Four. The long climb, and the late-night argument, had drained them. Had the group been able to go to the summit that day, instead of sleeping and brewing drinks, subsequent events may have turned out differently.

On the morning of 4 August the missing Korean climber turned up and the two successful summit teams descended from Camp Four. Meanwhile, near Camp One on the Abruzzi, the Koreans' Pakistani sirdar, Mohammed Ali, became K2's eighth fatality that year when a rock bouncing down the mountain struck and killed him.

The morning had the first hint of storm about it but hopes for the summit were high. Rouse and Mrufka left Camp Four at 5.30 am. Following in their tracks came Imitzer, Tullis and Diemberger, then Bauer and Wieser. After 300 ft Wieser returned to Camp Four, fearing frostbite from his wet mittens. Mrufka soon tired and dropped behind, but Rouse persevered, breaking trail, till Bauer caught up with him and took over the lead 300 ft from the top. Bauer and Imitzer reached the summit at 3.30 pm; Rouse at 4.00 pm. Rouse draped the Union Jack over the empty Korean oxygen cylinders. His motivating ambition for the past three years was finally fulfilled: he had become the first Briton to climb K2.

On the descent Rouse and the Austrians met the exhausted Mrufka at about 28,000 ft. She lay half asleep in the snow, but was still crawling up. After a heated exchange Rouse shouted her down. Further down they met Tullis and Diemberger climbing up. By now the first cloud streamers over Chogolisa—K2's storm warning beacon—were blowing in thick and fast. Rouse advised them of the late hour and the conditions, but Diemberger and Tullis pressed on, to reach the summit at 5.30 pm. Theirs was an emotional moment. Together, Diemberger and Tullis had shared many climbs. Tullis was the first British woman to climb K2. For Diemberger, at 54, it was the crowning moment to a long Himalayan career that began with his ascent of Broad Peak in 1957. They spent a few minutes on top, then descended, with Diemberger leading down on their rope.

At about 27,900 ft Tullis slipped on hard snow. Alerted by her shout, Diemberger tried to hold the fall with his ice axe, but both were dragged toward the ice cliffs beside the bottleneck. Diemberger had seen Liliane Barrard's broken body a few days before. Now, he thought, the same thing was happening to them. But they came to a stop after 300 ft. Uninjured but shaken, it was dark by the time they gathered themselves together. Rather than risk another fall, they decided to spend the night in a shallow crevasse at 27,500 ft. Maddeningly, the emergency bivouac gear they'd carried from Camp Four was a only few hundred feet below them, but as inaccessible as if it were 10,000 ft away. During the night Tullis begins to wane. Frostbite attacked her nose and fingers. Her eyesight deteriorated. They clung to each other tightly, shivering all night while all the time a storm was building around the mountain. But they survived. On the morning of 5 August, crawling weak and in a whiteout, they reached Camp Four at 11.00 am, thinking the worst was over.

In Camp Four the seven climbers occupy three tents. They had intended to descend that day, but knowing the ease with which a climber can get lost on the shoulder of the Abruzzi during a whiteout—Parmentier's case was a recent example—and wary of powder avalanches, the climbers decide to wait for the storm to pass, hoping it will blow itself out during the night. But it rages at hurricane force for five days.

Diemberger's and Tullis's tent drifts in with snow and collapses. Diemberger moves in with Rouse and Mrufka, Tullis in with the Austrians. Tullis is weak, her vision faltering, from too long at altitude. On the night of 6 August, she dies in her sleep after drifting in and out of consciousness all day. When Diemberger is told this the next morning, he is utterly shattered, distressed that no one had called him earlier. The Austrians move Tullis's body back into the collapsed tent. The storm blows on.

On 8 August the last food and fuel runs out: dehydration sets in. Those in Camp Four slip further and further into a dream world of apathy and lethargy.

On 10 August the snow stops falling, but the wind still howls. The temperature is -20 degrees Fahrenheit. Those who can think clearly realize that they must descend now, or also die. Diemberger and Mrufka try to stir Rouse, but he is delirious, mumbling about a secret supply of water. The lean greyhound-like physique that had enabled Rouse to power his way to the summit was now depleted of moisture, of all energy. No one can get him to his feet. Diemberger places some snow on his lips and lets him rest. As they leave his tent they are under no illusions that they will ever see Rouse again.

Bauer, with Diemberger and Mrufka, then tries to rouse Imitzer and Wieser. They get them out of their tent but they collapse almost immediately. Try as they may, Bauer and Mrufka are too weak to support them. They leave them and start down through deep snow. Before starting down, Diemberger had remained behind for a final personal moment with Tullis. A short distance from the tents Diemberger finds the Austrians. Wieser lays face down in the snow, Imitzer on his back. Only Imitzer reacts at all to Diemberger's coaxing to get up, by waving his arms weakly, and murmuring he could no longer see. They are beyond help and Diemberger continues down.

The three survivors reach Camp Three, at about 24,300 ft, but find it buried by the storm. They continue to Camp Two, at 22,600 ft. Bauer and Diemberger reach it an hour apart, Bauer arriving first, at 9.00 pm. As they await Mrufka, they shelter in a tent and have their first drink and food in over 48 hours. But Mrufka never arrives. At a point at about 23,600 ft, where the fixed ropes drop over steep rocks, she weakens and slumps into her harness. Held to the rope by a sticht plate clipped to her waist, and by several loops of rope wrapped around her wrist, she dies.

Jet stream winds raking K2's summit.

Diemberger and Bauer wait for her until noon of 11 August before staggering down. Those in Base Camp had given up all hope for anyone above. All are astounded when Bauer, frostbitten and tattered, appears on the glacier with the news that he and Diemberger are the sole survivors. A search team reaches Diemberger at midnight. He too is frostbitten, and moves so slowly that he appears more dead than alive. The rescuers press on to about 23,300 ft, the last place Diemberger and Bauer could remember seeing Mrufka but they find nothing. A year later, during the summer of 1987, Mrufka's body would be discovered on the ropes by Japanese climbers attempting the Abruzzi Spur. The climbers will lower her body, by then the consistency of wood, and bury her with a respectful ceremony at the foot of the ridge.

And so it was that we learned these things after our climb and our return home. The news from K2 left me troubled. The weight of mortality bore upon my thoughts.

My encounter with Alan's life, and his with mine, had been no more than a vignette. Yet his death struck me with as much force as the death of a blood relative.

Blood is thick, but perhaps experience runs thicker. Simply, he, like Georges, like Peter, like Roger, like Don, had brushed by my life, leaving me hungry to know more about them all. That chance had gone now. Memories, stories, a few photographs to lend fire to those brief, powerful times would have to suffice.

As summer fell into autumn in Seattle I found myself trying to put these experiences in the high mountains into some perspective. But how to tie such disparate ends together? How best merge the good with the bad? And how, in light of the carnage on K2, could a pursuit that exacted such a toll be worth the risk? 1986 had been an ambitious year, a year like no other. Yet those thirteen deaths humbled all achievements. Newspapers, magazines, climbers, and laypeople would wonder how such a tragedy could happen? The mirror of hindsight would offer tempting reflections, perhaps even a few lessons. The simple fact was that in the Karakoram that year, among a heady, ambitious, inspiring setting, luck had swung fickle, letting some climbers escape with incredible follies, giving others no quarter at all. With the slim opportunities in the arctic-like weather, timing had been everything, yet timing, in the end, is nothing more than luck.

My mental effort to give an element of order to this circle of life, death and mountains, came to nothing. There really is no meaning to it. I could only remember the voice of that bar stool sage, Don Whillans, who in 1985, had died peacefully in his home, in his sleep, from heart failure. 'The mountains', Don had advised me, judiciously wagging a finger, 'will always be there. The trick is for you to be there as well.'

That's something to keep in mind.

About the Author

Greg Child, born in Sydney, Australia, and a resident of the United States since 1980, is a freelance writer, photographer, and lecturer about mountaineering and climbing in the great ranges of the world. He has published articles and photographs in *Climbing, Outside, Backpacker, Adventure Travel, Rock and Ice, Life,* and *National Geographic.* He is the author of *Mixed Emotions* and *Postcards from the Ledge.* In thirteen expeditions to the Himalaya, Child has climbed Everest, K2, Gasherbrum IV, and Trango Tower, and made a first ascent of Shipton Spire. He lives in Seattle.

THE MOUNTAINEERS, founded in 1906, is a nonprofit outdoor activity and conservation club, whose mission is "to explore, study, preserve, and enjoy the natural beauty of the outdoors. . . ." Based in Seattle, Washington, the club is now the third-largest such organization in the United States, with 15,000 members and five branches throughout Washington State.

The Mountaineers sponsors both classes and year-round outdoor activities in the Pacific Northwest, which include hiking, mountain climbing, ski-touring, snowshoeing, bicycling, camping, kayaking and canoeing, nature study, sailing, and adventure travel. The club's conservation division supports environmental causes through educational activities, sponsoring legislation, and presenting informational programs. All club activities are led by skilled, experienced volunteers, who are dedicated to promoting safe and responsible enjoyment and preservation of the outdoors.

If you would like to participate in these organized outdoor activities or the club's programs, consider a membership in The Mountaineers. For information and an application, write or call The Mountaineers, Club Headquarters, 300 Third Avenue West, Seattle, Washington 98119; (206) 284-6310.

The Mountaineers Books, an active, nonprofit publishing program of the club, produces guidebooks, instructional texts, historical works, natural history guides, and works on environmental conservation. All books produced by The Mountaineers are aimed at fulfilling the club's mission.

Send or call for our catalog of more than 300 outdoor titles:

The Mountaineers Books
1001 SW Klickitat Way, Suite 201
Seattle, WA 98134
1-800-553-4453
e-mail: mbooks@mountaineers.org
website: www.mountaineers.org

Other titles you may enjoy from The Mountaineers:

POSTCARDS FROM THE LEDGE: Collected Mountaineering Writings of Greg Child, *Greg Child*
Selections of the best writing of elite mountaineer Greg Child, from humorous observations of the sport to insightful reflections on controversial climbs, plus revealing portraits of some of the big names in the climbing world.

MIXED EMOTIONS: Mountaineering Writings of Greg Child, *Greg Child*
A collection of stories and essays recalling the people and events that shaped Greg Child's climbing career.

CAMP 4: Recollections of a Yosemite Rockclimber, *Steve Roper*
An anecdotal chronicle of the most significant climbs and most riveting controversies of the golden age of big-wall Yosemite climbing, including stories of such greats as Royal Robbins, Yvon Chouinard, Allen Steck, and Warren Harding, and discussions of the advances in equipment and style that revolutionized the sport.

ERIC SHIPTON: Everest and Beyond, *Peter Steele*
The first biography of adventurer, explorer, and mountaineer Eric Shipton, developer of the Alpine-siege style and the single biggest name in Himalayan exploration before Hillary.

KURT DIEMBERGER OMNIBUS: Summits & Secrets, The Endless Knot, Spirits of the Air, *Kurt Diemberger*
Three mountaineering classics, in one volume, by renowned climber, writer, photographer and filmmaker Kurt Diemberger, including a personal account of the "black summer" of 1986, during which thirteen climbers died on K2.

STORIES OFF THE WALL, *John Roskelley*
The candid, acerbic autobiography of world-famous climber John Roskelley, recounting the successes and failures of twenty years of climbing throughout the world by a man who relies on his own exacting standards, never luck.

ESCAPE ROUTES: Further Adventure Writings of David Roberts, *David Roberts*
A fascinating collection by writer, climber, and adventurer David Roberts that merges exploration with the writing life. Featured are tales of adventure throughout the world and stories about mountaineering legends like Jeff Lowe, Ed Viesturs, and Jon Krakauer.

Outdoor Books by the Experts

Whatever the season, whatever your sport, The Mountaineers Books has the resources for you. Our FREE CATALOG includes over 350 titles on climbing, hiking, mountain biking, paddling, backcountry skiing, snowshoeing, adventure travel, natural history, mountaineering history, and conservation, plus dozens of how-to books to sharpen your outdoor skills.

All of our titles can be found at or ordered through your local bookstore or outdoor store. Just mail in this card or call us at 800·553·4453 for your free catalog. Or send us an e-mail at mbooks@mountaineers.org.

Name_____

Address_____

City_____ State _____ Zip+4_____-____

E-mail_____

588-3

Outdoor Books by the Experts

Whatever the season, whatever your sport, The Mountaineers Books has the resources for you. Our FREE CATALOG includes over 350 titles on climbing, hiking, mountain biking, paddling, backcountry skiing, snowshoeing, adventure travel, natural history, mountaineering history, and conservation, plus dozens of how-to books to sharpen your outdoor skills.

All of our titles can be found at or ordered through your local bookstore or outdoor store. Just mail in this card or call us at 800·553·4453 for your free catalog. Or send us an e-mail at mbooks@mountaineers.org.

Please send a catalog to my friend at:

Name_____

Address_____

City_____ State _____ Zip+4_____-____

E-mail_____

588-3

BUSINESS REPLY MAIL
FIRST-CLASS MAIL   PERMIT NO. 85063   SEATTLE, WA

POSTAGE WILL BE PAID BY ADDRESSEE

**THE MOUNTAINEERS BOOKS
1001 SW KLICKITAT WAY STE 201
SEATTLE WA 98134-9937**

BUSINESS REPLY MAIL
FIRST-CLASS MAIL   PERMIT NO. 85063   SEATTLE, WA

POSTAGE WILL BE PAID BY ADDRESSEE

**THE MOUNTAINEERS BOOKS
1001 SW KLICKITAT WAY STE 201
SEATTLE WA 98134-9937**